Kenya Democracy
Tribal Power in Organization and Management

Author
Antony Kamau

SONITTEC PUBLISHING. All rights reserved. No part of this publication may be reproduced, distributed, or transmitted in any form or by any means, including photocopying, recording, or other electronic or mechanical methods, without the prior written permission of the publisher, except in the case of brief quotations embodied in critical reviews and certain other noncommercial uses permitted by copyright law. For permission requests, write to the publisher, addressed "Attention: Permissions Coordinator," at the address below.

Copyright © 2019 Sonittec Publishing
All Rights Reserved

First Printed: 2019.

Publisher:
SONITTEC LTD
College House, 2nd Floor
17 King Edwards Road,
Ruislip
London
HA4 7AE.

Table of Content

TABLE OF CONTENT 4

KENYA DEMOCRACY 1

PART ONE 1
KENYA: DEMOCRACY 1
Summary 1
Introduction 5
Kenya's transition to democracy 10
Ethnicity and democratic participation 16
Overcoming ethnicity 19
Citizenship, identity and the politics of belonging 21
The electoral system and political parties 27
Concentration of power and abuse of the rule of law 31
Local self-governance and the devolution of power 36
Devolved system of government 38
Conclusion and recommendations 40

PART TWO 44
KENYA: DEMOCRACY 44
Executive summary 44
Introduction 44
The socio-political context 45
The constitutional framework and citizenship rights 49
Public participation 51
Electoral reforms 52
Political parties 53
The legislature 54
General conclusion 55
Socio-political and historical background 56
The constitutional framework and international law 64
International instruments 65
Domestication of international instruments 73
The Independence Constitution 76
Agenda I–IV of the KNDR Process 86
Conclusion and recommendations 103
Citizenship and inequalities 106
Citizenship and international law 107
The constitution and citizenship laws 108

Non-discrimination and affection Action 119
Effort to introduce Affection Action 124
Protection of persons living with disabilities 134
Protection of minorities and marginalised groups 138
Immigrants and refugees 143
Conclusion and recommendations 144
Participation in the policy process 146
Freedom of expression and the media 148
Violation of media freedom 149
Access to information 161
Kenyans for Peace with Truth and Justice 166
Elections 171
Legal and institutional framework 173
Election administration 175
Constituency delimitation 178
Voter registration and participation 179
Voter education 185
The electoral system 187
The gentleman's agreement 'in lieu' of constitutional reforms 190
Electoral malpractices 193
Code of conduct 193
Abuse of state resources 197
Violence 199
Peace committees in the 2002 elections 201
2007 general elections 202
Election observation 205
Validity of results 208
The electoral system under the Constitution of Kenya (2010) 211
Conclusion and recommendations 213
Political parties 215
Legal framework 218
Principal parties contesting for office 224
Internal party democracy 235
Direct nominations 245
Party financing 249
Anglo-Leasing scandal 252
Ethnicity and political parties 257
Women's representation in political parties 267
Party competition and the role of the opposition 269
Conclusion and recommendations 274

Thelegislature	275
The legislature in pre-independent Kenya	275
Remuneration and support	285
Peoples' representation, pre-election promises and the failure to deliver	289
Law-making and debate	289
Oversight role	293
Rejecting presidential appointments	295
Public Investments Committee report on the accounts of state corporations (1)	298
Parliamentary reform	299
The role of parliamentary committees	300
Brief history of the Parliamentary Budget Committee	303
Public participation in the legislature	306
Control and audit of National Assembly fi	312
Conclusion and recommendations	314
Provincial and local governments	315
The Provincial Administration	317
Local government institutions	318
Relationship between central and local governments	320
Local government elections	323
Financing of provincial and local governments	324
Access to information	325
Local government and participatory democracy	326
Reducing debts through participatory budgeting	327
LASDAP in Korogocho	330
Oversight of provincial and local executives	332
The constitution and devolved government	332
Conclusion and recommendations	337
Taditionalauthorities	339
Pre-colonization	339
The colonial era	340
The post-colonial era	340
Development of traditional authority	342
Traditional authorities and the constitution	344
The role of traditional leaders in public life	346
Traditional governance and competitive politics	350
Conclusion and recommendations	353
Development assistance and democratisation	354
Access to information on development assistance	357

Trends in development assistance 358
Conditions for development assistance 362
International aid for democratic development 366

Kenya Democracy

Part One

Kenya: Democracy.

Summary

Violence engulfed Kenya following a dispute over presidential election results in December 2007. The violence spread fast and split the country along two main ethno-regional blocs. Not many expected Kenya to go up in flames that fast. The country had a history of political transition from one-party rule since the early 1990s and a tradition of regular elections. Although violence accompanied both the 1992 and the 1997 elections that were held after the return of multi-party democracy in 1991, the violence following the December 2007 election was unprecedented. It pushed the country towards the brink of civil war. The violence ended in February 2008 after mediation by the African Union Panel of Eminent African Personalities. The panel persuaded the two parties in the dispute, the Party of National Unity (PNU) of the incumbent President Mwai Kibaki and the main opposition, the Orange Democratic Movement (ODM) of Raila Odinga, to sign a National Accord committing to end violence and to share power in a coalition government. But the signs of this violence had shown early. The African Peer Review Mechanism (APRM) had warned in 2006 that Kenya was so deeply divided along ethnic lines that if the government did not address some of the reasons causing divisions, conflict would occur. The violence indeed occurred as a result of the failure to respond to long-standing governance issues. It continued to threaten the consolidation of democracy and it constrained political participation. Among these issues were: the manipulation of ethnic identity by politicians, the lack of comprehensive constitutional reforms, centralization of power in the executive, and the problems around the majoritarian electoral system.

Kenya normalized fast and held a peaceful referendum for a new constitution in August 2010 and, following this achievement, promulgated the constitution and later held a peaceful election in March 2013. Attempts to make a new constitution had failed to deliver one for about two decades, but the National Accord signed in February 2008 to end the violence, developed a framework and timelines for constitutional review and institutional reforms. The negotiations on the National Accord revealed that constitutional review, among other reforms, was urgently required to prevent a recurrence of violence. What is interesting in the evolving political economy dynamics, is that the two main ethnic communities that fought one another in the post-2007 election violence, the Kikuyu and Kalenjin, grouped together into a political alliance, the Jubilee alliance, which fi won the March 2013 elections. The alliance had both the presidential (Kikuyu) and deputy presidential (Kalenjin) candidates who were indicted by the International Criminal Court (ICC) for the post-2007 election violence. They mobilized the numeric strength of their hitherto communities and won the election. They were elected as

president and deputy president in spite of indictment for crimes committed during the post- election violence.

These are the abnormalities that characterize Kenya's politics of transition to democracy. This discussion paper unravels the challenges to Kenya's participatory democracy. The discussion seeks to fi out what went wrong with the project to bring 'democracy and participation' to Kenya. The paper is based on the fi of a detailed assessment of Kenya's compliance with standards adopted by African states regarding democracy, elections and popular participation in government. The paper discusses the key issues raised in the main report, and identify the key challenges to popular participation in the governance of the Kenyan society.

The discussion paper notes that the 2010 constitution has addressed some of the obstacles that prevent consolidation of democratic gains. It has established two levels of government: national and county government. It requires that appointments to public office reflect the face of Kenya. County governments are given resources to undertake development in their areas. The powers of the president have also been reduced; the president cannot make appointments without the approval of Parliament. The constitution has secured the independence of the judiciary and Parliament and, therefore, the executive cannot compel them to tend to its interests. To ensure that these gains are not reversed, the paper recommends strong oversight by civil society groups and the Commission for the Implementation of the Constitution (CIC), among others.

The discussion concludes that Kenya's fi (FPTP) electoral system undermines institutionalization of political parties, because it provides incentives for perpetual formation and reformation of ethnic alliances for the purpose of electoral contest. This system has embedded patronage politics and corruption in the political arena, thereby resulting in poor accountability of political leaders to the society. It is recommended that the electoral system be revisited with a view to establishing a system that would promote inclusivity, build stronger and institutionalized parties, and eliminate the zero-sum aspects of the current system. It is also recommended that the position of Registrar of Political Parties be adequately resourced to implement the relevant laws on political parties. It should be staff with competent individuals and be given adequate institutional, political and fi independence to carry out its mandate.

The constitutional promise to deliver democracy will not be realized if the values and principles of the new constitution are not translated into concrete actions. To realize these principles and anchor a democratic order, Kenya must nurture the rule of law by committing to enforce all laws and embracing constitutionalism. In this regard, the government should pass enabling legislation to realize these values and align other laws with the new constitution. In particular, the government must pass a strong leadership and integrity law to bring the new constitution to life and which should provide for the vetting of persons seeking public office through elections or appointment, to ensure they are persons of integrity as required under chapter 6 of the constitution. Such a law should allow for public input in the vetting of persons seeking public office It should also set a minimum threshold of standards for elections and appointment of persons to public office by paying attention to the person's integrity, competence, and suitability. This on its own will erode the fi foundation on which impunity in Kenya is founded. Related to this is the need to ratify key international and regional instruments, including the African Charter on Democracy, Elections and Governance. Tracking Kenya's performance in terms of improving the conditions for people's democratic participation at all levels of government and society in general, should be a central concern of all people and the various public oversight groups.

Introduction

Public participation requires that people be at the center of decision-making processes. This is an important element of democracy because 'rule by the people' is the underlying and founding principle of democracy. Thus, involving people in making decisions that concern their lives is a distinguishing feature of democratic societies. Participatory democracy, therefore, requires active and meaningful engagement of citizens in public affair It is a principle universally accepted as requisite for a just society. The Universal Declaration of Human Rights (UDHR), 1948, provides that 'everyone has the right to take part in the government of his/her country, directly or through freely chosen representatives'. The International Covenant on Civil and Political Rights (ICCPR) also provides that:

> Every citizen shall have the right and opportunity... (a) To take part in the conduct of public affair directly or through freely chosen representatives;
>
> (b) To vote and be elected at genuine periodic elections which shall be by universal and equal suffrage and shall be held by secret ballot, guaranteeing the free expression of the will of the electors; (c) To have access, on general terms of equality, to public service in his [or her] country.

Participation in public affairs is important in another respect. It builds people's abilities to hold authorities to account for the implementation of decisions and actions agreed upon. It is in this respect that the African Union's African Charter on Human and Peoples' Rights recognizes the importance of participation in public affair as an essential element of democracy. The African Charter on Democracy, Elections and Governance also requires the African Union member states to recognize people's participation as an inalienable right of the people of the continent.

The quest to promote participatory democracy and to make participation an important principle in the governance of public affair has been an important theme in debates on governance in Kenya. Because of this, and in recognition of protracted struggles for democratic reforms, article 10 in Kenya's new constitution has included democracy and participation of the people among the values and principles of governance, which bind all state organs and institutions as well as state office In assessing the quality of democracy in Kenya, there are questions whether successive governments have consistently upheld the rule of law, allowed citizens to freely elect their leaders, and whether or not people have been making political

choices without hindrance. Thus, transition to democracy implies progress in both opening up decision-making processes to active participation of the people, as well as enhancing the accountability of governments to their citizens. This transition involves developing a culture of constitutionalism and accountability to citizens.

Giving people freedom to make political choices, especially in elections, plays an important role in consolidating democracy. This freedom of choice enables them to put in place an accountable and responsive government whose mandate is renewed periodically – depending on the extent to which it has governed in line with the aspirations of the people. Thus, if the elected government applies the law without discrimination, citizens obey the law conscientiously. When the government however applies the law in an inconsistent manner, citizens tend to disconnect from the government. The distance between government and society widens in tandem with the failure of government to account to society and abide by the founding principle of democracy, rule by the people.

How to secure and consolidate participatory democracy has dominated discourses on governance in Kenya for a long time. The struggle for political liberalization from the late 1980s was particularly informed by the need to open the political space to competitive politics after several decades of domination by the one-party regime. These struggles placed primacy on people's participation in decision-making, because the government and the ruling party often imposed decisions that promoted parochial and individual political interests rather than the public good. But the protracted struggles for reforms have not translated into concrete participatory democratic practices. Some gains have been made in this respect but the same gains are constantly facing the spectre of reversal as a result of the competition for political power. Kenya was at a point of consolidating its democratic gains when a government with a reform agenda, the National Rainbow Coalition (NARC), came to power after winning the December 2002 general election. NARC had campaigned on a reform platform, promising to promote economic recovery and good governance reforms. The new government did then implement some good governance reforms, such as initiating the fight against corruption and setting up a semi-autonomous human rights agency. But the government abandoned the reform path halfway after the coalition collapsed due to internal disagreements over power and the distribution of spoils in particular. After the collapse, NARC, like the previous governments, began to secure power for those in leadership positions. A small group of ethnic elites close to President Mwai Kibaki pulled the government out of the reform agenda. They started to consolidate political power by manipulating the political environment and reneging on some of the promises made before coming to power. They manipulated the constitutional review process to come up with a draft that reflect their political interests. They preferred a constitution that favored their desire to secure a hold on power.

This contradiction, in which gains are made through struggles for democracy, but are then reversed through state actions and the practice of politics, has considerably undermined the concrete realization of participatory democracy. The continued reversal of these gains and political actions to promote the interests of a cabal of ethnic elites in leadership, laid a foundation for Kenya's post-2007 election violence. The dispute over the presidential election resulted in unprecedented violence, which divided the country into two major ethno-regional blocs that were fi opposed to each other. The post-2007 election violence reversed many of the democratic and economic gains made since the return of multi-party democracy in 1991. The space for the enjoyment of fundamental rights and freedoms contracted. Society became more polarized.

Ironically, the post-2007 election crisis paved the way for a greater gain: the promulgation of a new constitution. The crisis revealed a number of fundamental weaknesses in Kenya's political system that required addressing to prevent future conflict over contestation for political power. The international mediation resolved that constitutional and institutional reforms were a requisite in this respect. The parties signed a National Accord that outlined the steps towards a new constitution and institutional reforms. A new constitution was promulgated in August 2010. The new constitution entrenches a culture of accountability and includes democracy and people's participation, the rule of law, inclusiveness, social justice, human rights, and non- discrimination among the national values and principles of governance that the state and its office must abide by and respect when applying and interpreting the constitution. The new constitution promises a clear path to democracy. It recognizes the sovereignty of the people as the anchor of the nation and provides for participation of the people in decision-making at all levels. It fosters accountability and checks the powers of all organs of the government and state institutions.

The 2010 constitution provides for a break from the past; it charts the path for a new beginning in many ways. It reduces presidential powers, creates a new structure of governance and provides specifically for a devolved system of government where people effectively participate in the governance of their devolved units. In spite of this promise for a new beginning, it did not take long for old habits to creep back. Political parties and alliances continued to form along the old lines of ethnicity and regions. Parliament itself introduced weak laws to govern the transition to the new beginning. Because of this, leaders whose integrity had been questioned by the public, were nevertheless elected to office Additionally, the president and his deputy were elected to office when they were still facing criminal proceedings at the ICC over the crimes committed during the post-2007 election period. What promised to be a new beginning turned into 'business as usual'.

This discussion paper examines the challenges of democracy and participation in Kenya; it explores the general promise and failure of Kenya's hesitant transition to democracy. The paper seeks to fi out what went wrong with the project to bring 'democracy and participation' to Kenya. It identifies ethnicity, Kenya's electoral system, the dominance of the executive and its abuse of the rule of law as some of the obstacles to democracy and participation in Kenya. The paper is based on the fi of a detailed assessment of Kenya's compliance with standards adopted by other African states regarding democracy, elections and popular participation in government.

The discussion shows that the interplay of ethnicity and struggles over executive power has constrained people's participation and democratic transition in general. The paper notes that this interplay revolves around the capture and retention of the over-centralized executive or the presidency. The new constitution has addressed some of these challenges by establishing strong checks on the powers of the executive and by establishing two levels of government: national and county governments. However, the electoral system remains largely unaltered. The devolved system of government is likely to inherit the very challenges that the constitution is seeking to address, if implementation does not effectively reflect the spirit and letter of the constitution.

Kenya's transition to democracy

Since Kenya's independence in 1963, the development of democracy and public participation has had mixed results. Kenya adopted a Westminster style of democracy with multi-party institutions and a federal system of government. There was a devolution structure of government, popularly known as *majimbo*, under which the country had seven autonomous regions, some of whose boundaries were coterminous with ethnic settlement patterns. Some of the numerically large groups have a region to themselves and therefore some regions are identifiable with ethnic groups. Each regional government was responsible for setting and implementing a broad range of policies.

There were several political parties, the main ones being the Kenya African National Union (KANU) and the Kenya African Democratic Union (KADU). KANU's membership included some of the large ethnic groups, the Kikuyu and the Luo, while KADU coalesced the numerically smaller ethnic communities, many of which feared domination by large groups after independence.

The first government dismantled this set-up after independence. The ruling party, KANU, made it difficult for the regional governments to operate. The main opposition, KADU, joined KANU to form one party and govern with them. The government also introduced a series of constitutional amendments that centralized power in the presidency.

These changes significant constrained democratic participation. The government became increasingly intolerant of dissent. In 1966, some critics within government resigned their positions to form a new political party – the Kenya People's Union (KPU). Keen to consolidate power without rivalry, the government banned the opposition in 1969. This gave the then ruling party, KANU, unchecked dominance. More amendments to the constitution to centralize power in the executive followed. In 1982, Parliament changed the constitution to make Kenya a one- party state. The country remained as such until 1991 when pressure, through people's struggles for democratic change, compelled the government to repeal this constitutional provision and provide for a return of multi-party democracy.

Despite these political setbacks during the 1960s and 1970s, international commentators on Kenya cited the country as a successful development model of growth, with useful lessons for the rest of the developing world. With an average annual economic growth rate of more than 5% and relatively high per capita income compared to many developing countries, the West generally praised Kenya as 'one of the few economic and political ornaments to be held up, admired and analyzed to detect what might be transferable in its exceptional performance'. Explanations for the 'exceptional ornament' varied. Some argued that Kenya had followed a relatively free market economy compared to its neighbours. Others attributed this success to a generally stable political system. The 'Kenya debate' occasioned robust discussion on relations between development, indigenous capital, and state-society relations in developing countries. The return of multi-party democracy in 1991 led to the expansion of space for the enjoyment of civil and political freedoms. It generally enhanced the space for participatory democracy. The state loosened its grip on political space and allowed for the proliferation of political groups, including opposition political parties and human rights organisation. But these gains were not eff consolidated. The state paralyzed the opposition political parties by preventing them from operating in certain areas the government considered to be the strongholds of the ruling party. In other instances, the government would deny the opposition the license to hold political meetings. Thus, in spite of multi-party democracy, the ruling party (KANU) and its leader, President Daniel arap Moi, continued to constrain the new space through repressive measures. The 1992 and 1997 elections, in particular, were marred by serious political violence at the hands of militia organized by the ruling party. Through legal and extra-legal means, the government weakened the opposition political parties and obstructed the making of a new constitution. This enabled Moi and KANU to win both the 1992 and the 1997 general elections.

In 2002, the opposition parties formed an alliance, the National Alliance Rainbow Coalition (NARC), to compete against KANU in the December 2002 elections. They were aware that in the absence of comprehensive constitutional reforms, the ruling party would have advantages over the opposition and thus retain power. The alliance campaigned on a platform of comprehensive reforms and a promise to deepen democracy and they won the December 2002 general election. In line with the campaign promise to implement governance reforms, the new government enhanced the space for participatory democracy and general enjoyment of rights. From the outset, the government undertook to protect and promote fundamental rights and freedoms, and thus established the Kenya National Commission on Human Rights (KNCHR) for this purpose. The government introduced legislation to facilitate the fight against corruption and developed a sector-wide reform programme – the Governance, Justice, Law and Order Sector (GJLOS) – to guide governance and justice reforms. The government re-started the constitution-making process, established institutions to address corruption, and purged the judiciary of judges accused of corruption.

The NARC government also implemented a series of policies that resulted in the recovery of the economy and somehow restored the conflict of the people in government and its institutions. Kenya's economic growth had been below zero, but implementing the government's policy, the Economic Recovery Strategy for Wealth and Employment Creation (ERSWEC), increased growth to about 7.0% in 2007. Real per capita incomes increased by 3% and poverty declined from 56% in 2000 to 46% in 2007.

The coalition did not hold together for long. It disintegrated after the ethnic elites disagreed on how to share power. This created two factions.

One faction comprised the president and elites from his ethnic region, the former Gikuyu, Embu and Meru Association (GEMA) members or the Mt. Kenya cabal. The second comprised elites from other communities, notably, the Luo, Luhya, Kalenjin, and the Kamba, whom the president's faction had marginalized from the center of political power. Both factions had agreed on how to share power if they won the 2002 election but the president reneged on this agreement upon assuming office

The fi in the power structure undermined key reforms. In particular, factionalism spilled over to the constitution-making process. The president's faction preferred a presidential system of government with centralized powers while the opposing faction preferred a parliamentary system. Amidst these divisions, the government and the elites around the president fi their own version of the constitution that was presented to the country at a referendum in November 2005. The draft did not pass muster with the voters and did not receive sufficient support. People voted along the same ethnic divisions that divided the coalition. The draft got support from the president's Mt. Kenya region and a few other votes were brought in by promising future inclusion in government. Other regions of the country voted against the draft.

This polarization and deep ethnic divide shaped the violence after the disputed December 2007 presidential election results. The division gave rise to two political parties, the ODM, which drew members from communities whose leaders were excluded from power; and the PNU, which was hurriedly formed to enable President Kibaki to run for a second term in office By this time, national office of NARC had joined the ODM and refused to let the president use the party to run for the 2007 elections.

The government failed to recognize that the politics of exclusion had sharpened ethnic divisions in the society. The APRM report of 2006 had identify the politics of exclusion and marginalization of ethnic groups as critical fault lines and advised the government to attend to these concerns before the 2007 general election. The report also warned that the absence of accountability and impunity in general had weakened the relations between the state and citizens. The APRM warned that these would lead to a crisis if not addressed.

The divisions laid a fi foundation on which the post-2007 election crisis developed and spread. But the crisis had another important outcome. The violence brought to the fore the key weaknesses in Kenya's political system that required addressing to prevent a recurrence of violence. International mediation, under the auspices of the African Union's (AU) African Panel of Eminent African Personalities led by Kofi Annan, identify a lack of political inclusion, perceptions of marginalization and a culture of impunity as some of the factors that undermined democracy in Kenya and which required fundamental reforms. Similarly, a number of reforms were identified under what constituted Agenda Item 4 of the mediation. These included undertaking constitutional review and institutional reforms, addressing regional imbalances in development, implementing land reforms, promoting national unity and cohesion, addressing youth unemployment, promoting transparency and accountability and tackling impunity. As already noted, these were considered as the long-standing issues that had remained unaddressed. They were responsible for the cycle of violence that Kenya continued to witness during elections. To provide a framework for these complex reforms, the coalition government was formed and a roadmap for completing the constitutional reforms was developed within a year.

The results have been mixed. The most important achievement was the promulgation of the new constitution in 2010. A new constitution had remained elusive until a National Accord provided a framework and timelines for the review, under a bipartisan leadership, of the parties in the coalition government. The new constitution became the basis for institutional reforms. Some of the institutions began to undertake reforms and new institutions were established. Programmes to address youth unemployment were introduced as short-term measures immediately after the signing of the National Accord. A Ministry for the Development of Northern Kenya and other arid regions was established and the government later evolved plans to develop diff regions. But little progress was made in the fi against impunity; there were no major initiatives or political commitment against corruption or eff to reconcile the country.

Kenya's transition is characterized by a lot of back-and-forth. Democratic gains are yet to be consolidated. Citizens' effort to promote change are visible and well rooted in all spheres. Also, the political sphere is highly pluralized. There are many registered political parties and many people participate in periodic elections. There is a relatively free media and general respect for freedom of expression. In spite of this pluralized space, there is a weak culture of political accountability in that leaders rarely account for their actions. The political system is one in which ethnicity comingles with the electoral system to form a strong obstacle to democratic transition. The new constitution seeks to address some of the challenges to development and democracy.

The new constitution seeks to address some of the challenges to development and democracy. The new constitution is comprised of provisions to address some of the long-standing issues. A devolved system of government, for instance, is expected to promote development in all regions. An equalisation fund will provide resources to the marginalised areas so that they can catch up with other regions. The constitution also emphasises the establishment of a government that reflects the Kenya's diversity. All the same, there has been no coherent approach to addressing ethnic divisions. Formation and reformation of parties along ethno-regional lines remains a major challenge in this respect.

The new constitution identifies democracy and people's participation as essential to the national values and principles of governance on which the government is based. It also seeks to foster the accountability of leaders by privileging integrity and leadership as the key pillars of governance; it requires public officers to adhere to the principles of public service. It also seeks to punish self-service and to promote social justice; including making guilty parties take responsibility for past abuses. Important also is that the new constitution promotes rights and freedoms in an unprecedented manner. The Bill of Rights is fundamental and radical in many ways: the state is required to promote rights and freedoms while the courts are required to interpret the new law in a manner that seeks to promote these rights. Accountability to the people and participation of the people are key aspects of the framework of the new law.

Will the new constitution foster democratic accountability? The politics of ethnicity have presented an important challenge to democratic governance and the rule of law in Kenya. Ethnicity is appropriated for both good and bad. In some instances, it is appropriated to prevent enforcement of the law and is, therefore, responsible for a deepening culture of impunity. As noted above, the mobilisation of ethnic numbers in the communities where those indicted by the ICC come from, enabled the president and his deputy to win the election after forming an alliance (the Jubilee Alliance), in spite of their indictment over crimes committed during the post-election violence. On the whole, ethnicity comingles with other factors, including Kenya's electoral system, to establish formidable obstacles to the transition to democracy..

Ethnicity and democratic participation

Ethnicity, when viewed as the mobilisation of groups sharing a language, culture and ancestry, is the main fulcrum around which national and local politics in Kenya revolves. The ethnic structure and the quest to control the centralised executive powers accounts for this. Notably, Kenya comprises many ethnic groups but none of the groups are large enough to dominate another. Estimates show that the country has about 42 groups. On the basis of the 2009 population census, the major groups whose individual share of the national population exceeds 10% are the Kikuyu (17. 15%), Luhya (13. 82%), Kalenjin (12. 86%), Luo (10. 47%), and Kamba (10. 07%). Their total share of the population is 64. 4%. 10 The second largest cluster constitutes 15. 07%

of the population. 11 . These figures show that over 35 groups comprise only 8% of the population. They include Kenyan Europeans and Asians, as well as minority and marginalised indigenous Kenyan groups. They are all poorly represented in elective bodies and in public service..

The absence of a single numerically large group, the relative equality of the five main groups, as well as the presence of many smaller entities whose combined share of the population is still in the minority, have increased politicisation of ethnicity in Kenya. Political elites tend to mobilise support on an ethnic basis. An incentive for coalition-building in this regard is the first-past-the-post electoral system, which makes it possible for the presidency (and parliamentary as well as civic seats) to be won by a small proportion of votes cast. Both the electoral rule and the relative equality of the five ethnic groups have meant that the competing elites form coalitions or obtain substantial support from small but significant groups.

Several factors account for the dominance of ethnicity in the practice of politics in Kenya. First is the significance of centralised executive powers. This issue is discussed later. It suffices to say, that over the years the constitution was amended to provide for a powerful executive. The amendments removed inbuilt checks and balances and weakened other organs of the government. The presidency evolved as the most important institution because without checks on accountability, the president could use public resources to reward followers and to punish dissenters. The use of public resources for patronage purposes has, therefore, been widespread. Ethnicity is also central to politics because of inequalities in ethno-regional development which stems from the colonial policy of developing areas occupied by the colonial settlers, namely the White Highlands. The settlers favoured central Kenya and the highlands in the Rift Valley. These regional disparities in development also coincide with ethnic inequalities because the regional boundaries correspond to ethnic settlement patterns or territories. Groups in marginal and poorly developed regions blame successive governments for the failure to invest resources in their regions. This intensifies conflicts because they view access to and control of political power as synonymous with access to development resources. There is the view that a region from which the president comes is favoured in terms of development resources allocation. 'It is our turn to eat' becomes a mobilising slogan among groups during elections. Ethnic coalitions are formed on the promise of sharing power.

The actions by elites from the president's community, once in power, do not assuage fears of groups whose leaders fail to capture power. Appointments to public service favours the regions of those in power. Thus, the areas from which influential elites and the president originate tend to have a relatively higher share of senior public sector positions than those of other groups. The state is, therefore, not viewed favourably from an accountability point view. This perception has been entrenched by the actions of the Kikuyu elites in power under President Jomo Kenyatta and President Mwai Kibaki and by the actions of the Kalenjin elites under Daniel arap Moi. An ethnic audit of the civil service by the National Cohesion and Integration Commission has shown that members of the president's communities have been dominant in all senior and strategic positions in government ministries and departments. 12 The government that formed after the March 2013 general election has followed this familiar path. 13 Distribution of cabinet posts was skewed in favour of the president and deputy president's community. Their alliance, comprising their two communities, won the election and subsequently shared the spoils.

The skewed and imbalanced regional development has its origins in this tendency of distributing senior public posts along ethnic lines. This is followed by a skewed distribution of development resources in favour of the regions where these elites come from. Political elites consciously mobilise support on an ethnic basis to counterbalance each other and sometimes uses this model of skewed development to garner votes. Furthermore, to solidify their constituencies and numbers, politicians sometimes make derogatory statements against members of other communities. This often deepens divisions between groups.

Ethnicity has undermined efforts to hold the state accountable. There has been active citizen engagement in public affairs, but with very little consequence for state accountability because the competition for power takes place on an adversarial ethnic platform. This, on its own, makes the state and its institutions fragile. Ethnic leaders tend to identify with parochial community interests rather than the national good. And even when they do so, their own communities are not able to hold them to account, because the electoral system makes it difficult for ethnic leaders to be held accountable by voters outside their constituency.

Overcoming ethnicity

Despite the negative impact of ethnicity on Kenya's transition to democracy, people rarely discuss it publicly. In particular, the media do not mention names of communities when reporting. They are content to make innocuous references to a community. Nonetheless, the government has made some attempts to address the challenge of ethnicity in the public sphere. Some of these efforts were made after the post-2007 election violence.

The government introduced the National Cohesion and Integration Act (NCI Act) (2008) which directly addresses the problem of ethnic discrimination. The law established an independent National Cohesion and Integration Commission (NCIC) to facilitate and promote equality of opportunity, good relations, harmony and peaceful coexistence among different communities. The law mandates the commission to eliminate discrimination on the basis of ethnicity and to promote tolerance among Kenyans.

The NCI act outlaws discrimination on the basis of ethnicity, race, colour and religion. The law prohibits victimisation and even harassment on the basis of ethnicity. It prohibits discrimination in access to and distribution of public resources, in employment, in membership of organisations, property ownership and management and in a wide range of other fields. The law emphasises that discrimination against and harassment of any person on the basis of ethnicity is a violation of that person's dignity.

In recognition that the use of hate speech has played an important role in promoting ethnic divisions, this law prohibits the use of threatening and abusive language intended to arouse ethnic hatred and animosity. It also seeks to promote access to services by all, irrespective of their ethnic background, race, colour or religion. The new law directly upholds equality for all and seeks to promote access to opportunities by all people, especially in employment and other sectors. This law directly prohibits discrimination.

The 2010 constitution also outlaws discrimination on the basis of ethnicity. It specifically identifies non-discrimination towards and the protection of marginalised groups as part of Kenya's national values and principles of governance. The constitution also provides for equality and freedom from discrimination. It is emphatic that neither the state nor any person can discriminate against another person on the grounds of ethnicity, among a comprehensive range of other grounds.

Despite the enactment of NCI Act in December 2008 and efforts to punish hate speech, ethnicity remains an impediment to the efforts to consolidate democracy. The composition of public sector institutions remains skewed in favour of the president's Kikuyu, community. The Kikuyu comprise more than 30% of staff in some government ministries and departments. This has led to growing perceptions that the government is not inclusive enough. Transforming the state and making it more accountable to all will certainly impact on the challenge of ethnicity.

There is a challenge in enforcing and applying the new law and the constitution, especially now that there are two levels of government. To eliminate using ethnicity in a negative manner will require a range of other laws, because the practice is deeply embedded in Kenyan politics. It will require a culture of inclusive politics and merit-based appointments to public offices. Affirmative action measures should also be put in place to address inequalities in the public service. The constitution requires that appointments to public institutions reflect Kenya's diversity. There is a need to regularly monitor how the government ministries and departments are staffing various positions. This should be a task for the NCIC, among other agencies. Importantly, there is a need to establish a framework for monitoring and making recommendations regarding appointments to public posts.

Citizenship, identity and the politics of belonging

The challenge of fostering citizenship is tied to that of ethnicity as an impediment to Kenya's transition to democracy. The way ethnicity is utilised to advance or undermine socio-political interests has significant implications for the consolidation of citizenship rights. Indeed, the politics of belonging, or being 'insiders' or 'outsiders' of a particular group in power, has been central in defining exclusion and inclusion in Kenya's politics. .

Generally, the twin issues of citizenship and rights have come to occupy a central place in Kenya. The question of who is a member and who is not a member of an ethnic group plays perhaps the most important role in deciding how people vote and the type of rights they should enjoy at local level. The status of 'outsiders', or those who are not indigenous to an area, and that of 'insiders', remains central to conflicts in different parts of the country. Hostilities between these identities manifest during elections. Also, competing ethnic elites mobilise political support by demarcating these identities, thereby creating a basis for political discrimination against groups that are seen as 'outsiders'. Identity then becomes the basis for accessing opportunities in the public sector. In the end, this undermines the democratic principle of equality for all citizens. This use of identity results in a vertical form of inequality; it becomes the basis for inclusion or exclusion on ethnic grounds.

Erosion of citizenship has continued to occur even though the constitution, the old and the new, provides for equal rights for all citizens. The old Kenya constitution provided for the 'Protection of Fundamental Rights and Freedoms of the Individual'. Application and conferment of these rights was devoid of race, tribe, place of origin or other considerations, but subject to respect for the rights and freedoms of others, and for public interest. The constitution defined citizenship not in terms of belonging to groups but in terms of belonging to the Kenyan nation-state. The law then provides protection to citizens on the basis of belonging to Kenya, not a particular part of Kenya. In light of conflicts over land ownership, the law provides for individuals to own property anywhere in the country. While the legal framework for the enjoyment of rights is clear, the politics of belonging have eroded the basis for the enjoyment of such rights, and enforcement has been problematic. The new constitution has provided a radical Bill of Rights binding all state organs, private individuals and institutions. The 2010 constitution recognises human rights and freedoms to preserve the dignity of individuals and communities. These rights and fundamental freedoms belong to individuals and are not granted by the state. The discrimination on ethnic grounds that permeates politics in Kenya is reflected, and perhaps finds endorsement in discriminatory practices at national level with regards to granting Kenyan citizenship. The previous constitution discriminated on the basis of gender, thereby excluding women from the enjoyment of rights. A foreign woman married to a Kenyan man would obtain citizenship by registration, while the same right was not accorded to men who married Kenyan women. Kenyan men were the dominant bearers of identity. If only the mother of a child was Kenyan, she would not pass her nationality to her children born outside the country's borders.

Though the law does not provide for citizenship to be granted or withheld on the basis of ethnicity, in practice, discrimination in Kenya on ethnic grounds has been widespread. Individuals of Nubian and Somali origin have been systematically excluded from recognition as citizens, even when they are third and fourth generation Kenya residents. Members of border communities, descendants of migrants, and others living in geographically isolated areas, experience relatively more difficulties than other Kenyans in processing their registration as citizens. They undergo multiple vetting processes to ascertain their citizenship. Interestingly, corruption is increasingly blamed for the failure to give citizenship documents to some Kenyans in border communities. Among the Somali in Kenya, elders in vetting committees that recommend the awarding of citizenship documents, such as identification cards, are often blamed for passing off Somali citizens as Kenyans. The Kenyan Somali fail to get the documents if the elders do not recommend them. Thus, the problems of citizenship are expressed in multiple ways. Those in border communities have the challenge of proving their identity during the formal process of registering as citizens. They also have difficulties in consolidating their rights of belonging at local level, especially if their group is seen as comprising of 'outsiders'.

The discrimination in issuing citizenship documents disadvantages individuals in these communities in several ways. Without an identity card or passport, a person will be denied the right to vote and participate in public affairs. This official discrimination at national level is essentially reproduced in popular and official behaviour at local level, deepening the fragmentation of the communities. With the introduction of county governments, this is likely to be reinforced at county level, especially in multi-ethnic counties.

It is also worth noting that the population census often raises tension partly because it reproduces this fragmentation, and partly because it fails to list the identities of some groups. The census thus denies citizenship to some groups by failing to list them as distinct groups. Some of the smaller groups are listed as 'others' or lumped together, thereby negating or denying their identity and citizenship altogether. The last census was carried out in August 2009. Several groups complained that they were omitted from the list. Failure to recognise their identity leads to future challenges regarding citizenship rights. Significant also is that the census fragments some of the large groups into various sub-groups. This raises tension within the group because such fragmentation reduces their overall numeric strength and numbers are an important element in the voting patterns and the negotiations when forming ethno-political alliances that would compete to control power.

In an attempt to address the erosion of citizenship rights, the new constitution provides for a comprehensive Bill of Rights that applies to all, and binds state organs and all persons. It provides for the courts to make interpretations that favour the enforcement of rights and freedoms. The new constitution also provides for citizenship by birth and by registration. It also provides for dual citizenship, thus preventing a Kenyan citizen from losing their citizenship, because of acquiring the citizenship of another country. Furthermore, the constitution eliminates gender-based discrimination in the granting of citizenship rights. It now allows for both men and women to confer Kenyan citizenship to their foreign spouses and their children.

The various forms of discrimination against women impacted on their ability to participate in political processes. This is in addition to cultural attitudes, general lack of adherence to electoral laws during elections, lack of enabling legislation, threats of and actual use of violence, and the use of abusive language against women participating in competitive politics. This has resulted in very few women participating in elective politics. At independence, the Kenyan Parliament was all male. About five decades later, women in Parliament comprise 9.5% of the National Assembly. The number of women in other public sector posts is similarly low.

Efforts to pass the Affirmative Action Bill (2007) which sought to have over 50 women specially elected as members of Parliament, failed, but the new constitution has developed innovative approaches to increase the number of women in all public positions. The constitution requires that no more than two-thirds of the members of all elective and appointive positions in public bodies shall be of the same gender. This is aimed at guaranteeing representation of women at all levels and in all institutions. An important achievement is the requirement that membership in the new bi-cameral legislature comprise special seats for women.

The constitution makes provisions for gender quotas. The National Assembly reserves 47 (about 13%) out of the 349 seats for women. The Senate reserves 18 out of 67 seats for women nominated by political parties according to their proportion of elected members. However, the gender quotas for the National Assembly and the Senate lack precise formulation on how to meet the constitutional requirement that no more than two-thirds of the members in any elective or appointive posts shall be of the same gender. This lack of precise formulation does not provide adequate safeguards for women's representation in the

National Assembly and the Senate, especially if the women elected are less than one third in each of the houses. The Constitution of Kenya (Amendment) Bill (2011) (as further amended on 18 October 2011) sought to remedy this problem by re-writing the formula for the special seats relating to the National Assembly and the Senate, but Parliament did not pass the Bill. The Attorney-General referred the matter to the Supreme Court for an advisory opinion. The court did not resolve the matter; it did not compel Parliament to make a new law. The Court advised that gender quotas should be achieved progressively after the March 2013 general election, but not later than August 2015.

The principle of guaranteeing representation for women and other special groups such as those with disability and marginalised groups, is reflected in the devolved governments too. The constitution requires that no more than two-thirds of the members of representative bodies in each county shall be of the same gender. This guarantees relatively unconstricted women's participation at local level. Similarly, the law now requires political parties to fill positions by providing a list of qualified male and female candidates. The constitution requires that the parties alternate between male and female candidates when listing them in order or priority.

Will these new provisions guarantee quality representation and participation of women in the democratisation process? One important outcome of the new constitution is the guaranteed number of women representatives in elected bodies. The constitution guarantees a certain minimum number of women to be elected at different levels. It also creates opportunities for women to seek election alongside other candidates. This implies a possibility of having more women than the minimum provided for by law. The absence of clarity on how the gender quota for the Senate and the National Assembly will be achieved if less than one third of those elected are women, raises a major challenge for the new constitution.

These provisions are good on their own, but they will require new legislation and enforcement mechanisms. Kenya, however, has a poor track record in enforcing laws. This then calls for a strong mechanism to monitor the extent to which the government is implementing these new provisions. There are other challenges too. The constitution has not addressed the socio-cultural challenges that hinder women's participation in the electoral process. Again, this demands that new legislation be introduced to eliminate these and other obstacles.

These provisions will be enforced in the public sector. Yet, the private sector has similar inequalities in terms of representation of women and other marginalised groups. Thus, lobbying the private sector to take similar measures is essential. There is a need to lobby for the re-introduction of the law on affirmative action to address the rights and needs of marginalised groups in the private sector.

To address the problems of citizenship, Kenya should thoroughly revise its citizenship law, providing for a right to nationality on clear, objective and non-discriminatory grounds. In addition, it should formulate policies to ensure that officials responsible for issuing citizenship documents do not have discretionary powers regarding who qualifies and who does not. The government should also eliminate mass vetting of communities because this usually opens the door for arbitrary discrimination, which in turn leads to corruption in the procurement of registration documents.

The electoral system and political parties

By at least some standards, Kenya has consolidated an election culture. Since independence, Kenya has held regular and periodic elections roughly every five years. The principle of free and fair elections is legally enshrined in Kenya's constitution and provided for in the Elections Act and the Political Parties Act. In addition, Kenya has Ratified many international and regional treaties that contain standards on the conduct of democratic elections. It has signed, but not yet Ratified, the African Union's Charter on Democracy, Elections and Governance.

Although Kenya has consolidated a culture of elections, the electoral system of first-past-the-post has prevented the institutionalisation of democracy and political parties. This echoes the findings of the Independent Review Commission (IREC), later referred to as the Kriegler Commission after its chairman Justice Johann Kriegler, on the general election of 2007, which found that Kenya's electoral system was not founded on the principle of the equality of votes. The system had been distorted for a long while through gerrymandering. The Kriegler Commission pointed out that the system contained gaps and weaknesses that warranted radical review in order to provide free and fair elections. 1.

Elections are won or lost by a simple majority, regardless of the number of registered voters in a constituency that cast their ballots. This system reinforces ethnicity by privileging the mobilisation of communities through discourses that emphasise the need to access and control state power for the benefit of those elites that win the presidency. For these reasons, parties are formed and reformed along ethno-regional lines as vehicles for electoral competition only, causing people to associate any new government with the community of the president. The majoritarian electoral system thus makes rivalry for power a constant element in Kenya's political life. Because winning an election using the first-past-the-post system requires mobilising sufficient numbers, elites enter into ethnic coalitions using the numeric strength of their respective communities as a bargaining chip. This leads to a cycle of formation and break up of ethnic coalitions every election period. Many of these alliances break up after the election and few live beyond one election.

The new constitution has not radically altered the electoral system. Although there were discussions about introducing Proportional Representation (PR) or Mixed Member Proportional Representation (MMPR), the constitution generally retained the first-past-the-post system, because MPs did not want to give up representing their constituencies. PR and the MMPR electoral systems in particular, would have strengthened democracy in several ways. It would have assisted in laying a foundation for stronger political parties as institutions, because people would be voting for political parties rather than their ethnic leaders. MMPR would have weakened ethnicity as a basis for political organising and representation by ensuring that membership of parties is national and that the parties have a membership that represents the diverse interests and groups that make up Kenya. By allocating seats in Parliament to political parties on the basis of their share of the national vote, the contentions around representation that arise with the delimitation of boundaries for single member districts in a first-past-the-post system, would have been addressed. The system would have provided incentives for parties to organise nationally rather than regionally. It would have reduced disparities in the representation of different groups and interests in society.

The team drafting the constitution nonetheless sought to give Kenya a fairer electoral system through the establishment of a two-round system (TRS) in the presidential elections and a first-past-the-post system with gender quotas for the National Assembly, the Senate and county assemblies. The constitution requires the winning presidential candidate to receive more than half of the votes cast in an election and garner at least 25% of the votes cast in more than half of the 47 counties.

The electoral system has not radically changed. It nonetheless requires that a winning president enjoys broad support from at least half of the counties. This failure to radically alter the electoral system might lead to the continuation of conflict because it still promotes a winner-take-all culture. Furthermore, the new constitution provides for the delineation of boundaries on the basis of population size, among other factors. The electoral system will require further reforms for it to sufficiently contribute to democratic governance.

The electoral system has prevented the institutionalisation of political parties. It motivates parties to form along ethno-regional lines since what is required is to win by a simple majority. Mobilising ethnic numbers then becomes a priority for leaders as they compete against one another. The parties are at best institutionally weak and are formed as vehicles for electoral politics. Very few, if any, live beyond one election period in their current form in terms of size of membership and support. A party's membership is ethno-regional and revolves around ethnic leaders. Thus, if a party leader moves on to form a new alliance, the party ceases to exist or exists as an empty shell. The parties generally revolve around wealthy ethnic elites, as they heavily rely on ethnic coalitions or singular ethnic groups as their primary bases of support.

Many parties do not espouse a coherent ideology or doctrine on which to articulate interest, mobilise supporters and shape public opinion. To address these weaknesses, the Political Parties Act (2011) creates an institution specifically responsible for the regulation of political parties, the Registrar of Political Parties. However, enforcing the law remains problematic because the main parties are under the leadership of senior politicians in government who have failed to make their parties accountable. Furthermore, the parties are themselves formed for election purposes. Their leaders pay little attention to them until election time when the parties are dissolved to form new alliances. Although the new constitution provides for improved governance of political parties, enforcing the law will remain a challenge as long as political leaders retain positions in both the parties and government.

nstitutionalising political parties requires commitment to the rule of law. It requires effective enforcement of the laws governing the operations of political parties. The constitution has established a new elections management body, the Independent Electoral and Boundaries Commission (IEBC), with a broad mandate, including the supervision of party nominations of candidates. The Political Parties Act also provides for how political parties should be regulated and governed. Thus, the laws are very much in place, what is lacking is effective enforcement. This failure to enforce the law is a running theme in Kenya's political life. It is informed generally by the dominance of the executive and the attendant tendency to interfere with the running of independent institutions.

The law established the post of Registrar of Political Parties, but the post remained vacant for long. The Registrar operates from within the IEBC, which does not guarantee the institutional autonomy required to transform political parties into agencies for consolidating democracy. As already mentioned, there is a need to fill the post through a competitive process. The office should also be provided with adequate resources and be given, by law, the independence required to carry out its mandate. The capacity of the office should be improved to enable it to commit parties to the rule of law.

Concentration of power and abuse of the rule of law

Successive governments have manipulated the constitution to concentrate more powers in the presidency. Amendments to the constitution began at independence in 1963 in order to create a powerful 'imperial presidency' by combining the powers of the queen (head of state) and those of the Prime Minister (head of government). The amendments sought to create a powerful president, who was both the head of state and head of government. These powers were centralised and concentrated in the presidency but with minimal checks. With absolute powers, the first president, Jomo Kenyatta, and the cabal of ethnic elites around him, began to amend other provisions of the constitution. Amendments were made to dismantle the semi-federal system of government and later on the bi-cameral legislature was abolished. In other instances the government would use administrative fiat to cause changes in the practice of politics. For instance, from 1969 the government did not allow opposition political parties to operate. This practice of politics and increased appetite to concentrate power in the executive was passed on to the regime of President Moi who assumed office after Kenyatta's death in 1978. Constitutional amendments were made to constrain dissent and suppress viewpoints that differed from those of the government and the ruling elites in KANU.

The amendments to concentrate power in the executive watered down the foundational principles and values of the Independence Constitution and undermined participatory democracy. In the end, the amendments resulted in a dominant executive. The amendments also eroded the independence of other organs, the legislature and the judiciary. They also evolved the executive into the dominant player in the policy-making arena. Furthermore, influential politicians had an overwhelming impact in the policy arena. Their informal power was so overwhelming that they would subjugate the government ministries/departments in policy-making. Political influence took primacy over everything else and undermined the capacity of state institutions to make policies. Even within the executive, it became increasingly

difficult to independently formulate policies, because everything had to be referred to the president or be sanctioned by him. Civil servants, who delayed implementing the different directives or questioned them, were punished.

The first few years of President Kibaki's rule saw a radical departure from these approaches. During this time, before the fragmentation of the ruling coalition, the government expanded the space for policy-making to include civil society and non-state actors in general. The government would use an inclusive and participatory approach to policy-making. Thus, civil society organisations (CSOs) participated in the drafting of the Economic Recovery Strategy (ERS), the policy framework that NARC used to guide planning and national development. CSOs also contributed to the development of a framework for governance and justice reforms immediately after the new government came to power. So much so that the new government's policies borrowed the language and thinking of civil society and other pro-reform groups. But the collapse of the alliance saw a return to the tendency by government to consult minimally with civil society.

The collapse of the alliance meant the government could not without effort deliver on its legislative agenda in Parliament. The government had to look for new allies, which included political parties that were initially part of the opposition and individual politicians who had limited or no interest in pursuing the radical reforms that NARC had promised to undertake. With these new allies, NARC reduced its interest in governance reforms. This had immediate consequences. The momentum for reforms dissipated as the government had no interest in any reform that could hurt its quest to maintain adequate numbers in Parliament.

Although the NARC government did not amend the constitution to concentrate powers in the executive the same way the previous governments had done, the government's actions to ensure a tight grip on political power halted the pace of implementing governance reforms. Furthermore, as argued above, the government watered down the draft constitution in 2005 to come up with one that concentrated powers in the presidency. This was not NARC's position when their new allies were still part of the opposition. The president's party, the Democratic Party (DP), favoured a parliamentary democracy with reduced executive powers. The new government was moving fast to take actions that would lead to a strong executive.

The absence of strong checks against the executive made it easy to concentrate power in one institution. Centralisation of power in the executive led perhaps, most damagingly, to the subjugation of the powers of the legislature and erosion of the independence of the judiciary. Thus, Kenya's Parliament has in the past acted as a rubber stamp for executive fiat while the judiciary tended to make judgements that favoured the executive. Without respect for the principle of separation of powers, Parliament and the judiciary lost their independence. This considerably weakened the accountability of the executive.

The resolution of the post-2007 election violence inadvertently resulted in another problem. The sharing of power by a coalition government comprising of the two parties initially involved in the dispute, eliminated opposition within Parliament. It is usually the opposition that holds the government to account. This absence of opposition was heightened by smaller parties joining either of the two main parties so as to benefit from the power sharing arrangements and it led to the absence of structured criticism in the legislative processes. It meant the absence of effective vigilance over the activities of the government. This also reduced opportunities through which people could impact on decision-making. The two partners in the coalition lacked unity of purpose and therefore at times failed to pass important policies. Party interests increasingly undermined the spirit of bipartisanship.

The March 2013 election resulted in the formation of two main alliances. Leaders of communities that hitherto remained protagonists cobbled together alliances to unify their communities for the purpose of the 2013 election. The two main alliances, the Jubilee alliance and the Coalition for Reform and Democracy (CORD), were formed for the purpose of capturing state power rather than to promote national good. Because of this, the alliances are not institutionalised and any disagreements will result in fragmentation.

Kenya's new constitution has addressed some of the factors that made it easy for the executive to amend the constitution. The new constitution provides for the independence of the judiciary and the legislature. It has provided for the establishment of an independent Judicial Service Commission (JSC) to promote the independence and accountability of the judiciary. It also strengthens the powers of the Parliamentary Service Commission (PSC) which plays a similar role in Parliament. Article 255 requires amendments relating to the functions of the president, Parliament, and the independence of the judiciary, to be the subject of a referendum. To pass, the amendment must be supported by at least 25% of voters in at least half of the 47 counties, and must win by a simple majority at the referendum. This certainly implies that future governments will not easily amend the constitution to concentrate powers in the hands of a few individuals. After the promulgation of the new constitution, the executive attempted to make nominations for judicial appointments without following the provisions of the constitution. This provoked unprecedented protests from the public. The judiciary also ruled that the president had no powers to make these appointments. He withdrew the nominations.

The new constitution has also imposed a radical change to the structure of government and governance. Firstly, it has identified values and principles of governance by which all state institutions and citizens must abide. Among others, democracy and participation of the people are identified as key principles to guide the conduct of public officials. The constitution also underlines that public office is entrusted to the nominated officials and they must, therefore, bring dignity to the office they hold. The importance of these provisions is that public participation in decision-making is now a constitutional obligation. Key decisions must have public support and must be developed through public participation. For this purpose, the government should develop and implement a policy to guide how people will participate in the making of key decisions at different levels of the government. The government should also introduce a strong freedom of information Bill to enable people to gain access to the information they require to effectively participate in public affairs and to the information they require to hold the executive accountable.

Local self-governance and the devolution of power

Kenya's local government system has operated under the authority of the central government and the Minister for Local Government. The mandate, management and operations of the local government authorities were set out in the Local Government Act. Their core mandate was to provide public services with the support of the central government, collect revenue, promote good governance and stimulate economic growth in their territories. The country had 175 local authorities, which were further clustered into city municipalities, as well as town and county councils. Each of the local authorities was governed by its own set of by-laws. Membership of councils consisted of elected and nominated members. The nominated councillors articulated the interests of the central government in all important issues under consideration by the local authority. The Minister for Local Government therefore had considerable influence in the management of local authorities and was consulted on virtually every activity. Local governments also lacked the independence to make and implement critical decisions.

A mayor (or chairman) elected by councillors during the first full council meeting after a general election headed the council. In most local councils, mayoral elections had been acrimonious and often violent. The reasons for this included the desire to access and be in control of patronage resources under the control of the local authorities. The local authorities would give these to elected leaders and senior government officials without any form of accountability. For instance, local authorities held land in a trust on behalf of the local communities, where the land has not been privatised and individuals given title deeds. Also, urban local authorities had the power to award licences for trading within their jurisdictions. Conflicts arose between elected leaders and administrative officials in local authorities. Administrative officials, who were employees of the central government, implemented policy decisions at local level in line with instructions from their superiors. However, elected officials usually sought to control implementation of such decisions. This resulted in conflicts between the two. Further, the gaps in the law were usually exploited to create opportunities for corruption and patronage. There were demands to democratise governance of local authorities but these have not yet been met.

Although Kenya had a local government structure, its effectiveness was limited by the central government. Moreover, local government was a structure of administrative decentralisation; it lacked financial and political independence to make decisions. This limited the extent to which local authorities could promote governance at grassroots level and the extent to which citizens could effectively participate in decision-making. There was little participation in local government affairs and even elections, because the units at this level were seen as low-value and providing inadequate services.

Devolved system of government

This arrangement of local government, however ended after the March 2013 elections when

the devolved system of government began to operate. The country now has two levels of government, national and county level. There are 47 counties. The devolved governments, under the new structure, are required to reflect three basic principles: democratic principles and the separation of powers; reliable sources of revenue and autonomy to govern and deliver services effectively; and inclusion of not more than two-thirds of the members of representative organs from the same gender. These also relate to the national values and principles of government espoused under article 10, which underlines, among other principals, participation of people in decision-making and adherence to transparency and accountability.

A county government comprises of a county assembly and a county executive committee. The executive authority of a county is exercised by the county executive committee, comprising of an elected governor and deputy county governor, together with an executive committee appointed by the governor from non-county assembly people. Voters directly elect the county governor, deputy governor and members of the assembly. The county governor serves only for two terms. The county assembly contains special seats for women and persons with disabilities, as well as the youth.

The constitution protects the devolved system of government from unlawful national government interference. The national government is required to share revenue with the county governments. The constitution requires that the government sets aside at least 15% of revenue for them as unconditional grants. A grant system supports operations, but counties are also allowed to raise their own revenue by collecting levies. Most important is that the number of counties and their roles cannot be altered without a constitutional amendment through a referendum. An Equalisation Fund is available to provide basic services for marginalised counties. These provisions prevent the political mischief that frustrated operations of the devolved system of government after independence. It also prevents interference in counties by the national government as it happened with local authorities above.

The governments at the national and county levels are distinct and interdependent; none is subordinate to the other. The constitution provides that they interact through consultations and cooperation. This implies independence to make decisions in functional areas without interfering with each other. However, the constitution requires the national government to ensure access to its services in all parts of the country 'as far as it is appropriate to do so'. This need to be done with mutual respect, because article 189(1) requires both levels of government to perform 'functions, and exercise its powers, in a manner that respects the functional and institutional integrity of governments at the other level, and respect the constitutional status and institutions of government at the other level and, in the case of county government, within the county government'. To promote interdependence and cooperation between the two levels of government and even among the county governments, the Inter-governmental Relations Act (2012) established several organs. These include the National and County Government Coordinating Summit. This is the apex body and comprises the president and the 47 county governors. It is established with the aim of promoting national cohesion, unity and national interest. It also has the responsibility of facilitating and co-ordinating the transfer of functions, power and competencies to either level of government but in line with the constitution. The Inter-government Technical Committee serves as the secretariat of this body.

The second body is the Council of County Governors. This was established for the consultation among county governors on matters of common interest. The council also facilitates the sharing of information, dispute resolution and builds the capacity of governors. It receives reports and monitors implementation of inter-county agreements, especially those concerning inter-county projects. The council has the mandate to establish other inter-governmental forums and sectoral working groups.

Although the structure to support devolution is very much in place, there has been tensions between those who want a centralised government and supporters of devolution. What took place in the formative years of Kenya's independence is being repeated. The national government and the executive would prefer to have total control rather than let local institutions operate as independent units. Although the government has introduced legislation to support county government, there must be vigilance against those who want the centre to maintain control over the devolved units. Although the Senate will play this role, it is possible that the centre will begin clawing back some of these gains. The Transitional Authority, the institution that is helping the transition to county government, should be provided with sufficient resources to secure the process of establishing county governments.

Conclusion and recommendations

This discussion has identified several problems that impact on the efforts to bring 'democracy and public participation' to Kenya. Ethnicity and identity politics, centralisation of power in the executive and a majoritarian electoral system are some of the issues underlying the failure to consolidate democracy and participation.

Ethnicity is the problem around which major political events in the country revolve. The centralised power of the executive and the winner-take-all electoral system reinforce ethnic cleavages. Ethnicity is not the problem, per se. It is a symptom of the structure of political power and how that power is abused to provide resources to unaccountable elites. Its mobilisation for political use has exacerbated the fragility of state institutions.

Despite the centrality of ethnicity in Kenyan politics, the country has no policy on how to address its impact on governance and politics. There is a reluctance to confront ethnicity as a problem in policy and politics, yet it is the central pillar in Kenya's politics and development and, therefore, critical to democracy and participation. There is a need to confront ethnicity by developing relevant policies and laws, as well as taking appropriate political actions. In this respect, Kenya may consider passing laws that demand that the composition of public office holders reflect ethnic diversity. There is a need to formulate policies to guide composition of public and private sector positions and ensure transparent and equitable distribution of public positions.

The first-past-the-post electoral system polarises the society along ethnic and other lines.

The system has de-institutionalised political parties and transformed them into vehicles for transporting voters and their leaders from one election to another. The new constitution has not radically altered the electoral system. The winner-take-all system was largely adopted, except for special seats in the National Assembly, the Senate and the county assemblies. It will not be easy to comprehensively review the system, given that members of Parliament prefer to retain their single member districts. Moreover, Mixed Member Proportional Representation and Proportional Representation in general did not rise to the pile of important discussions during the constitutional review process. In mitigation, there is a need to establish citizen-led oversight bodies in the constituencies and in every county to promote discussions on the quality of representation. There is also a need to establish public interest litigation centres in every county to ensure that those elected are first vetted to establish their qualities with regard to integrity and leadership as laid out in the constitution. Thirdly, civil society should develop qualifications indicators and lobby for their adoption by the Ethics and Anti-Corruption Commission. This new body should then use these indicators to vet those vying for public positions.

The new constitution promises to alter the structure of governance in fundamental ways. It creates a new Kenya, complete with new institutions and values. It also shields these new institutions from political patronage. But the challenges facing the creation of a new Kenya are many. First, implementation of the new constitution is dependent on the old political and bureaucratic elites. The transitional provisions did not allow for a new election immediately after the new constitution was promulgated. Its implementation will depend on the old elites, including those who were opposed to it. The new constitution has nonetheless raised public expectations on the possibilities of a new culture of governance in Kenya. The new constitution fosters accountability in the conducting of public affairs, but impunity is still widespread. It is this culture of impunity that is likely to frustrate efforts to promote democracy and participation of the people in remaking Kenya.

The road ahead is challenging. How Kenya addresses these numerous challenges will, in many ways, have a bearing not only on its stability but also on the wider legitimacy of the ruling elite, as well as on citizens' confidence in participating in the reconstruction of the state.

Part Two
Kenya: Democracy.

Executive summary

Introduction

It is widely recognised that participatory democracy or the active and meaningful participation of citizens in public affairs is the distinguishing feature of democratic societies. The extent to which governments open up public affairs to active citizen engagement, as well as the level of accountability are the hallmarks of democracy. Thus, the question of how to enhance participatory democracy is one that has continued to dominate discourses on governance and political development in Africa as many countries make efforts to expand democratic space.

The political liberalisation process that began on the continent in the early 1990s, and the subsequent opening of African states to multi-party democracy, is a major milestone in the enhancement of participation of citizens in public affairs. But the practice of politics across Africa, and the continuing domination of the executive arm of government over other institutions, has constrained the efforts to achieve democracy. Consequently, there are challenges in electing leaders in many countries on the continent as citizens do not entirely make free choices. In fact, there are instances where leaders choose voters by manipulating voter registration process.

This report is about the challenges of participatory democracy in Kenya. It is a reflection on the status of citizens' participation in public affairs and democratic endeavours in general. It examines the institutional, and legislative process that would contribute to participatory democracy in Kenya. The report explores the available instruments, such as the Constitution of Kenya 2010, and draws insights on how to improve citizens' engagement in public affairs

The socio-political context

At independence in 1963, Kenya adopted a Westminster-style democracy with multi-party institutions. There was a semi-federal system of government, popularly known as Majimbo, comprising eight autonomous regions whose boundaries were largely coterminous with ethnic territories and settlement patterns. Each regional government was responsible for setting and implementing a broad range of policies. There were several political parties, the main ones being the Kenya African National Union (KANU) – endowed with the numerically rich Kikuyu and Luo ethnic groups – and the Kenya African Democratic Union (KADU) with membership from

smaller groups brought together by the fear of possible domination by larger groups.

KANU won the independence elections and formed the government. Thereafter, KADU dissolved itself and its members joined KANU in 1964. Without opposition, the KANU government dismantled the federal system of government. That marked the beginning of both the contraction of the democratic space and restriction of political participation. In 1969, the government banned the operations of opposition political parties. From then on, Kenya remained a one-party state until 1991 when the government acquiesced to pressure to allow for the return of multi-party democracy.

In the first two general elections after the re-introduction of multi-party democracy (1992 and 1997) KANU retained power. However, the elections were marred by serious malpractices, including politically instigated violence fomented by the police and the militia organised by the ruling party. The government further obstructed reforms by weakening the opposition political parties through intimidation and co-option.

In 2001, the main opposition parties hurriedly put together an alliance, the National Rainbow Coalition (NARC), for the purpose of uniting against KANU ahead of the December 2002 general election. Daniel arap Moi willingly handed over power to the winner, Mwai Kibaki, following a landslide win.

Between 2003 and 2004, the new government introduced several laws in line with its promise to promote good governance and revive the economy. A law establishing the Kenya National Commission on Human Rights (KNCHR) was enacted and so was the Public Officer Ethics Act (POEA), as well as a law establishing the Kenya Anti-Corruption Commission (KACC). The government also formulated the Economic Recovery Strategy for Wealth and Employment Creation (ERSWEC). Implementing this policy and some of the laws saw an economic growth increase from a negative growth in 2002 to about 7% in 2007. The policy also saw real per capita income rise by 3% per annum and the prevalence of poverty reduced from around 56% in the early 2000s to 46% in 2007. Primary school enrolment figures also rose by about 2 million (from 6.1 million in 2002 to 8.1 million in 2003) after re-introduction of the Universal Free Primary Education programme. NARC did not hold together for long. No sooner had the party won the elections and formed a new government than members began competing for posts in line with a pre-election agreement reached before the December 2002 elections. The president reneged on some of the key principles of the agreement thus splitting the coalition into two main factions: one allied to the president, and the other to the Liberal Democratic Party (LDP) leader, Raila Odinga.

A splintered government meant little opportunities for effective people's participation in public affairs. Each faction would mobilise its respective ethnic constituencies to outcompete the other. The new political space became increasingly ethnicised. The government initiated the constitution review process, but the differences within the two factions of government stood in the way of an affirmative referendum. The president's faction and many delegates from his region withdrew from the constitutional conference leaving behind delegates from other parts

of the country, which deepened the political divisions. The government, through the Attorney General, developed a new draft constitution that was presented to the electorate at a referendum held in November 2005. Over half of the voters rejected the draft.

The divisions from the referendum gave rise to two main political parties – the Orange Democratic Movement (ODM), which led the rejection of the draft constitution and whose support came especially from the ethnic leaders marginalised by the president's faction, and the Party of National Unity (PNU) with support from the president's Kikuyu and allied communities. By this time, there were very few, if any, leaders loyal to the NARC alliance. They remained in Parliament only because they had not formally renounced the coalition after the fall out. The president and his close associates hurriedly formed the PNU when it was difficult to gain control of NARC from the registered officials, whom the president's faction had marginalised from power.

The referendum created a hostile political climate leading to the December 2007 general election. Indeed the African Peer Review Mechanism (APRM) report of 2006 identified politics of exclusion, ethnic divisions and animosity as well as Kenya's electoral system as constituting the major fault lines that required addressing before the 2007 elections. The government paid little attention to these issues. During the elections, the ODM and PNU dispute over the final result of the presidential election led to unprecedented violent conflict in which over 1 200 people were killed and another 650 000 displaced. The country was on the brink of civil war. International mediation under the chairmanship of the former United Nations Secretary General, Kofi Annan, resulted in the two main parties to the conflict agreeing to end violence and committing to share power in a coalition government. Parliament enacted the National Accord and Reconciliation Act (2008) to give effect to the agreement. The National Accord also required the two parties to undertake far-reaching reforms on long-standing issues that had contributed to the crisis.

In line with the requirements of the National Accord, the constitution review process was re-initiated and a draft constitution developed from the various drafts that existed from the previous process along with fresh input from Kenyans. The proposed constitution was approved in a referendum vote on 4 August 2010, and was promulgated on 27 August 2010.

The Constitution of Kenya 2010 is a major improvement over the former. It alters the structure of power and governance in many ways. It creates national and devolved levels of government and establishes new institutions to promote governance, as well as introducing the principle of separation of powers. It also introduces values and principles of governance, which all state officers must embrace. Importantly, requirements for involving and consulting the public are well articulated in almost all chapters. The constitution enhances the role of the public in the governance process and provides for increased public participation in public affairs.

Equally important is that Kenya held a peaceful election in March 2013. A peaceful transition

followed this election with the coalition government ending its term of office and handing over to a new administration comprising leaders of communities that fought against one another in the post-2007 electoral violence. The International Criminal Court (ICC) indicted the two leaders for crimes committed during the violence. Prosecution by the court notwithstanding, the two mobilised their numerically large constituencies and support from smaller groups and won the 2013 general elections. They began the process of leading the country under a new constitution and in the face of changing international and diplomatic dynamics around Kenya.

The constitutional framework and citizenship rights

The twin issues of citizenship and rights have come to occupy a central place in Kenya. The status of 'outsiders', or those who are not indigenous to an area, and that of 'insiders', remains central to conflicts in different parts of the country. Border communities, descendants of immigrants, religious and racial minorities experience difficulties in registering as citizens. This has led to continuous exclusion from political processes and slower economic growth.

The law does not provide for citizenship to be granted or withheld on the basis of ethnicity. However, in practice, discrimination on ethnic grounds is widespread. Individuals of Nubian and Somali origin have been systematically excluded from recognition as citizens, even when they are third and fourth generation Kenyan residents. They undergo several stages of vetting in order to get citizenship documents.

The new constitution has addressed these challenges in many respects. First, every citizen is entitled to rights and privileges of citizenship: a Kenyan passport and any other identity document required for citizens within the limitations the law can impose. Citizenship may be acquired by birth or registration but cannot be lost through marriage or dissolution of marriage. Article 14 further provides that a person is a citizen by birth if on the day of the person's birth, whether or not in Kenya, either parent is a citizen. Any child of less than eight years found in Kenya, and whose nationality and parentage is unknown, is presumed to be a citizen by birth.

The new constitution has established a relatively better framework for citizenship than Kenya's previous laws. It perceives citizenship in two interrelated ways – citizenship by birth, and by registration.

The constitution provides for improved status of women and requires the government to initiate affirmative action programmes and other policies that would address historical disadvantages. It requires that not more than two thirds of members of elective or appointive bodies shall be of the same gender. There are protective measures entrenched in the constitution to ensure that these actions are clearly effected. The constitution has also addressed the plight of marginalised groups and minorities in several ways. The preamble recognises ethnic and cultural diversity and the determination to live in peace and unity within the context of this diversity. Protection of the marginalised is also identified as an essential national value and a principle of governance. Additionally, the Bill of Rights contains provisions for affirmative action for groups discriminated against in the past. Although the 2010 constitution is comparatively better in terms of promoting and protecting citizenship rights, it contains gaps that can be exploited through arbitrary administrative actions to undermine these rights. Indeed, the previous constitution and laws provided for non-discrimination against people but this did not protect women, border communities and other minorities from being denied certain citizenship rights. It is recommended here that, among other things, the government should pass legislation to make it possible to confirm one's nationality from birth. The government should also, by law, provide for the elimination of the problem of statelessness and should provide citizenship documents to groups denied this right under the previous laws.

Public participation

For many years, the executive dominated the space for participation in policy-making. The government was generally responsible for making and implementing key decisions and would do so without accommodating dissent or criticism. The space for public participation opened up with the re-introduction of multi-party politics in the early 1990s but remained constrained through bureaucratic control of the processes for making policies. The coming to power of a new government in 2003 enhanced this space; the government began inviting the public to contribute to the making of policies, including the budget-making process. Civil society groups also became increasingly active in influencing government policy-making.

The new constitution has identified democracy and public participation as some of the values and principles of governance. Public involvement is a theme that runs through all the chapters of the constitution; it is a requirement of not only the electoral process but also an ethos of the entire structure of governance under the constitution. The Parliament and county assemblies are required to open their proceedings to the public. State agencies and public officials are also required to involve the public in making key decisions including having a say in financial management. Although this is an important achievement, Kenya has not developed a framework on how citizens can engage meaningfully in the policy-making processes. In many instances, their participation is through elected and appointed officials.

It is recommended that a policy framework be developed to guide how citizens and civil society engage in the policy-making processes. International development partners should provide support to civil society organisations to improve their capacity to play this role, as well as to enable them to educate the citizens to be more effective in their responsibilities in respect of participating in public affairs. Civic education to improve the capacity of citizens to take up an active role in governance should be prioritised. There is also a need to introduce a strong freedom of information law to promote access to information, media freedom and freedom of information. In addition, the law should be forward-looking to address emergent issues such as social media, hate language and speech, and the abuse of information communication technology.

Electoral reforms

Kenya has held regular and periodic elections since independence in 1963. The elections have been competitive but results for presidential elections have tended to reflect national ethno- regional settlement patterns. The electoral system, first-past-the-post (FPTP), has undermined the potential of elections to enhance democracy. The FPTP system leads to intense conflicts over access to state power because it focuses on capitalising on the numeric strength of various

communities.

The constitution has not radically altered the electoral system and, therefore, violent conflicts are bound to occur around elections (primarily because of the pitfalls of the system). The ICC intervention may reduce the potential of violence in the short term but there must be established complementarity mechanisms to prosecute other perpetrators in order to demonstrate a commitment to address impunity and electoral violence. The masterminds of electoral violence and crimes remain at large.

The government has shown limited commitment to enforce existing laws on elections and political practice. There are several laws in place to regulate political behaviour but these are poorly enforced. The Independent Electoral and Boundaries Commission (IEBC) and the office of the Registrar of Political Parties have shown limited commitment to the implementation of the new laws. The political parties, the executive and the legislature are also not interested in effective implementation of these laws because it would hurt political interests. Impunity is itself deeply embedded in the society and those in leadership prefer to control the implementation of the law as long as it does not disadvantage them.

To address these problems, it is recommended that civil society closely monitors the electoral process and implementation of existing legislation, and engages in public interest litigation when they find breach of electoral laws. The IEBC should on its part seek support from the Attorney General, the Director of Public Prosecutions, the judiciary and the police to implement the electoral laws.

Political parties

Political parties in Kenya are institutionally weak. The main parties have revolved around wealthy individuals and have relied on ethnic coalitions or singular ethnic groups as their bases of support. They are characterised by poor internal governance, lack of effective programmes and weak societal linkages. Parties are often formed to act as vehicles for transporting political leaders during an election period, thus many of them do not live beyond a particular election period. Furthermore, many parties do not espouse coherent ideologies or doctrines upon which to base their articulation of interests, mobilise supporters and structure public opinion. For those that have manifestoes, they have been strikingly similar in form and content, the discernible differences being only in the details. As a result, many political parties have been functionally ineffective in the political process.

Although laws to strengthen political parties are in place, they are poorly enforced, resulting in indiscipline within the parties: politicians breach the rules of their own parties without any injurious consequences. The failure to substantively fill the post of Registrar of Political Parties is partly responsible for this. It is recommended that the IEBC should present to Parliament an amendment to the law that would facilitate recruitment of a Registrar of Political Parties. The Office of the Attorney General should support the IEBC to present the amended legislation to the National Assembly.

The legislature

The executive dominated Kenya's Parliament for a long while. The return of multi-party democracy saw Parliament begin to re-assert itself as an independent institution. From then on, there has been a good attempt to regain independence and to effectively play an oversight role, especially through different parliamentary committees.

The 2010 constitution requires Parliament to conduct its business in an open manner. It also makes the National Assembly and the Senate more accessible and accountable to the people. The constitution further provides for the right to recall a non-performing member of Parliament (MP). Although this is only to be initiated twenty-four months after the election of the MP and not later than twelve months immediately preceding the next general election.

To enable Parliament to play the oversight role in an effective manner, it is recommended that the capacity of the various House committees be improved. It is important that MPs and the various House committees are well oriented towards their duties and equipped with the essential skills and competencies necessary for the execution of their tasks. The Speaker should also develop a framework for the improvement of the capacity of senators and the county assembly representative.

General conclusion

This discussion has identified several problems that impinge on 'democracy and public participation' in Kenya. It has identified ethnicity as one issue affecting the democratisation process in the country. The discussion has also noted the fault in Kenya's electoral system: the FPTP electoral system results in violence and the general polarisation of the nation along ethnic lines. The system has de-institutionalised political parties to the extent that few, if any, live beyond one election year.

The 2010 constitution has not radically altered the electoral system. The winner-take-all system is largely intact, except for special seats provided. Unfortunately, it will not be easy to comprehensively review the system given the nature of vested interests around it. This raises the need to establish citizen-led oversight bodies to promote discussions on the quality of representation at all levels.

The constitution promises to alter the structure of governance in fundamental ways. It creates a new Kenya, complete with new institutions and values. Most importantly, the constitution provides for broad principles that guarantee openness and public access to government institutions. It entrenches firm requirements for participation and the involvement of people in decision-making processes.

However, the challenges facing the creation of a new Kenya are many. First, implementation of the new constitution is dependent on the old political and bureaucratic elites who prefer the status quo. Secondly, many of the provisions are not self-executing; they require not only the making of new laws but also enforcement. Unfortunately, Kenya has a poor record of political commitment to laws that threaten the interests of leaders. This has contributed to a culture of impunity that continues to undermine efforts to promote democracy and the political participation of the people.

Socio-political and historical background

Pre-colonial Kenya was made up of present-day ethnic groups, settled in various regions and engaging in different activities according to their ecological environments. Except the Wanga of Western Kenya, all the other groupings were acephalous – they were egalitarian and did not have centralised political leadership. They were governed by councils of elders who also represented them in council meeting. Further, they were involved in trade and intermarriages, and intermittent warfare characterised inter-ethnic relations. At the coast, there was vibrant trade especially with the Arabs, who had established lasting contact with the region for centuries.

The pre-colonial societal structure changed from 1895 when the British established formal administrative presence by making Kenya part of the British Empire, which they maintained as a protectorate. The British government took over the running of the region from a private company – the Imperial British East

Africa Company, which had taken control of the region beginning 1887 – to expand the company's commercial interests into the interior. The protectorate continued to pursue strategic and economic interests and built a railway line into the interior for that purpose, opening up the interior and bringing many communities into contact and conflict with the British. Nonetheless, the British established a strong presence through a settler economy and strong administrative control of the society. In 1920, Kenya became a British colony governed by the Crown laws. The first governor took office and established administrative structures to entrench colonial rule.

Modern-day Kenya attained independence from Britain on 12 December 1963, at which time the country adopted a Westminster-style democracy with multi-party institutions and a Majimbo,the country had eight autonomous regions, mostly carved along the boundaries of the former eight administrative provinces of Kenya. These boundaries are coterminous with ethnic settlement patterns. Some of the numerically large groups (see below) had a region to themselves. Each regional government had policy-making and implementation powers for a broad range of issues. Independent Kenya was characterised by several political parties, the main ones being the Kenya African National Union (KANU) and the Kenya African Democratic Union (KADU). KANU's membership comprised some of the large ethnic groups, the Kikuyu and the Luo, while KADU fused together the numerically smaller ethnic communities, many of which feared domination by large groups after independence. Those parties formed by the white settlers, and which received support from the British colonial government, joined the latter grouping.

Kenya has over 42 ethnic groups, although their exact number is difficult to obtain given the fluid nature of their identities.

Further, some of these groups can still be broken down into more sub-ethnic groups, with distinct dialects – the Kalenjin and the Luhya are examples. What is more, some ethnic groups only developed a common name and identity in the last few decades. According to the 2009 National Housing and Population Census, five ethnic groups constitute 64. 4% of the national population: the Kikuyu (17. 15%); Luhya (13. 82); Kalenjin (12. 86%); Luo 10. 47%); and Kamba (10. 07%). Other numerically significant groups include the Kenyan Somalis (6. 17%); Gusii (5. 71%); Mijikenda (5. 07%); and Meru (4. 29%). The rest of the groupings, over 37, are so small numerically that their combined share of the population is less than 12%. All these groups live in distinct territories or regions as discussed above – for example, the Kikuyu in Central Kenya, the Kalenjin in the Central Rift Valley, the Luhya in Western Kenya, the Kamba in the Lower Eastern region, the Luo in Nyanza, and the Somali in North Eastern Kenya. This structure, where no single ethnic group is large enough to dominate the others, has significantly affected political participation in the country since independence. The structure of political power, and how that power is accessed and controlled, have also reinforced ethnic cleavages and impacted on the democratisation processes in the country, as discussed in subsequent sections. KANU won the pre-independence elections and formed the first government, but from early 1964, the KANU government, under President Jomo Kenyatta, a Kikuyu, began to dismantle the Westminster-style of government by amending the constitution to provide for a strong and centralised executive – the presidency – as well as controlling party politics. For that reason, in 1964, the main opposition political party, KADU, wound up merging with KANU. The government frustrated the Majimbo system of government by denying regional authorities the financial muscle and independence to operate; eventually, the regional governments and the second chamber legislature were dismantled.

The tendency to constrain democracy and political participation intensified in the early years of independence, reaching its peak in 1966. In that year, some members of government, frustrated by official failure to institute land reforms as promised during the struggle for independence, broke away to form an opposition political party, the Kenya People's Party (KPU). Only three years later, the government had banned the operations of the KPU, to make Kenya a de facto one-party state. In 1982, Parliament amended the constitution to make Kenya a de jure one-party state by law. Despite such political setbacks, international commentators touted Kenya, during the 1960s and 1970s, as a successful development model of growth in the periphery, with useful lessons for the rest of the developing world. With an average annual economic growth rate of more than 5% and a relatively high per capita income when compared to other emerging and developing countries, the West generally praised Kenya as 'one of the few economic and political ornaments to be held up, admired and analysed mainly in order to detect what might be transferable in its exceptional performance'. By the 1980s, however, growth had slackened and the space for democracy and political participation had become severely constrained. State legitimacy was increasingly questioned, which, in turn, drew out authoritarianism. Protracted struggles for democratic change were born in that environment. In 1991, the government acquiesced to increasing demands to amend the constitution to allow a return to multi-party democracy.

Although real democratic gains were made in the early 1990s, they were soon eroded. President Daniel arap Moi – a Kalenjin – under the banner of KANU, was re-elected in the 1992 and 1997 general elections in polls marred by serious political violence fomented by party- funded militia. The government obstructed reforms that would have facilitated the consolidation of democracy, and weakened the opposition political parties through constraining their participation in public affairs.

Aware that only a united opposition would defeat KANU, the main opposition parties began to craft an alliance in 2001 for the purpose of the following year's general election. In October 2002, the National Alliance Rainbow Coalition (NARC) was formed, and later agreed on a single candidate to run against KANU. The coalition won the election in December that year. NARC's presidential candidate, Mwai Kibaki, formed a new government in January 2003, which came in with a plethora of promises about reforming fundamental institutions in the country.

Between 2003 and 2004, the new government, with the promise of promoting democratic governance, enacted legislation to promote freedoms, basic human rights and to strengthen the fight against corruption. The government also unbanned popular organisations that the previous regimes, including the colonial government, had proscribed. It introduced new policies to revive the economy that saw real per capita incomes rise by over 3% per annum and the prevalence of poverty reduce from around 57% in 1996 to 46% in 2007. Primary school enrolment figures also rose by about 2 million – from 6.1 million in 2002 to 8.1 million in 2003 following the launch of the Universal Free Primary Education programme. However, once in government, simmering differences over unequitable distribution of top jobs among alliance members split the coalition into two main factions. One was led by elites from President Kibaki's Kikuyu and allied groups, previously lumped together under the Gikuyu,

Embu and Meru Association (GEMA) constellation. The second faction was made up of elites from other main ethnic groups – the Luo, Kalenjin and the Kamba, among others excluded from the centre of power by the GEMA elites. Political factionalism spilled into the continuing constitution review process, which the new government had promised to complete within the first

100 days of assuming office. Failure to agree on devolution and the system of government resulted in a breakdown in the review process. A draft presented to the country in a November 2005 referendum was rejected.

The polarisation and deep ethnic divisions around power sharing and the referendum vote created the hostile political climate leading to the December 2007 general election. The divisions from the referendum gave rise to two main political parties: the Orange Democratic Movement (ODM), which drew support from members of ethnic communities whose leaders were excluded from the power axis, and the Party of National Unity (PNU) with a following mainly among the president's Kikuyu and allied communities.

Those events were a harbinger of the political violence that would sprout from the December 2007 general election. Although polling on 27 December 2007 and in the preceding period had been peaceful, a hot dispute arose between the ODM and PNU factions over flaws in vote counting and the final result of the presidential election. The Electoral Commission of Kenya (ECK) announced the incumbent, President Kibaki of the PNU, as winner, despite complaints of vote tallying irregularities and allegations of rigging. That announcement sparked violent conflict in at least six of the country's eight regions, many of which were also the ODM's strong support bases. Retaliatory attacks against ODM supporters in the PNU's strongholds followed. Consequently, over 1 000 people were killed and at least another 650 000 displaced. The country was on the brink of civil war. An international mediation process, under the chairmanship of the former United Nations Secretary General, Kofi Annan, resulted in the two main parties to the conflict agreeing to end violence. The government side, composed of the PNU, ODM-Kenya (ODM-K) and the ODM committed to share power in a coalition government. The constitution was amended to provide for power sharing. Parliament enacted the National Accord and Reconciliation Act (2008) to give effect to the agreement, creating the post of prime minister and two deputy prime ministers. The National Accord also required the two parties to undertake far reaching reforms to prevent a recurrence of violence. The two parties committed to undertake constitutional and institutional reforms. They identified many other long-standing issues that had contributed to the crisis, including constitutional, legal and institutional issues, lack of land reforms, regional imbalances in development, youth unemployment, weak national cohesion and unity mechanisms, as well as transparency, accountability and impunity.

The coalition implemented some of these reforms but lacked the internal coherence to address some of the critical problems that had contributed to the violence. Lack of common policy positions in the coalition on a broad range of issues generally delayed the undertaking of some of the most important reforms.

The conclusion of the review and the adoption of a new constitution, however, is easily one of the coalition government's greatest achievements. The National Accord required the government to put in place constitutional reforms within a year. The government established the mechanisms to facilitate that process by constituting a Committee of Experts in early 2009 to harmonise different drafts and identify contentious issues that required consensus-building. The committee finalised the draft constitution, which was presented to the country in a referendum vote on 4 August 2010. Voters approved the Constitution of Kenya 2010 and it was promulgated on 27 August of the same year.

The passing of the constitution through a peaceful referendum marked a major positive milestone in Kenya's political history. It was the culmination of years of protracted struggles that had defined the second phase of democratic consolidation after the reintroduction of multi-party democracy in November 1991. Kenya's constitution enjoys popular support and legitimacy, seen in the large number of people who turned up to vote (72% of all registered voters) and those that approved it (67% of all the votes cast). What distinguishes the August 2010 referendum from past major political events is its popularity, the legitimacy of the constitution and, of course, the newfound level of the people's confidence in the electoral process and the new Electoral Management Body (EBM), the Interim Independent Electoral Commission (IIEC), which preceded the Independent Electoral and Boundaries Commission (IEBC), established in 2011 under the Constitution of Kenya 2010.

The Constitution of Kenya 2010 signalled a take-off for important reforms that have been pending for a long time. It also fundamentally restructures governance in several ways. First, the constitution has re-introduced a bi-cameral legislature. However, the powers of the Senate are drastically reduced compared to the powers of the Senate in the bi-cameral legislature that was abolished in the 1960s as the presidency sought to concentrate power in the executive. Secondly, there are two levels of government – national and county. Although the powers of the county governments are not comparable to those of the regional governments abolished in the 1960s, they are based on the principle of devolution of power and resources. Thirdly, the constitution places people's participation at the centre of decision-making, requiring that their voices be heard in all affairs of government. Democracy and people's participation are underlined as essential principles on which the government is to be run. Finally, the constitution creates an open government, where transparency and accountability are core principles in the management of the state. What is more, the constitution has introduced some changes in the electoral system, bringing in, for example, a two-round system (TRS) in the presidential election, and the first-past-the-post system (FPTP) with quotas for the National Assembly, Senate and county assemblies.

The first general election under the Constitution of Kenya 2010 was held in March 2013. That election was unprecedented in scale and complexity – it required voters to vote for six candidates: the president, county governors, Senate representatives, members of the National Assembly, county assembly representatives, as well as women's representatives in the National Assembly.

In spite of those changes, the implementation of the constitution faces a number of challenges. Primary among these is that the old order has been fighting back to maintain the status quo. Furthermore, some of those who opposed the constitution during the referendum in 2010 won elective posts in the 2013 general election and, ironically, now drive the process of constitutional implementation. This explains the challenge of breaking with the past. Vested interests continue to constrain implementation mainly through the introduction of weak laws to operationalise various provisions of the constitution. There is also an element of institutional weakening to entrench status quo interests. Weakening some of the institutions has had significant outcomes. For instance, it led to the courts permitting the president and the deputy president to run for office in the 2013 election even though they are being prosecuted at the International Criminal Court (ICC) for crimes committed during the post-2007 election violence

The constitutional framework and international law

Kenya has Ratified virtually all major international treaties relating to democracy, political participation and non-discrimination, with just four exceptions: the Convention on the Political Rights of Women (CPRW), the 1954 Convention

Relating to the Status of Stateless Persons, the 1961 Convention on the Reduction of Statelessness (CRS) and the 1990 International Convention on the Protection of the Rights of All Migrant Workers and Members of their Families.

Kenya has also signed the relevant African Union (AU) treaties and shown commitment to implementing AU protocols. It was one of the first four countries to go through the African Peer Review Mechanism (APRM) in 2006, which gave it a favourable governance rating. Unfortunately, Kenya's remarkable achievement in terms of governance reforms was watered down by the post-election crisis of late 2007 and early 2008. Consequently, the APRM Summit of January 2009 decided that Kenya should undergo a partial second review focusing on its political and democratic governance pillar, but the government conceded to a full review, which took place in July 2011. However, the report was not presented for review at the APRM Summit in either January or July 2012.

International instruments

Kenya is party to most of the international treaties on democracy and participation, and has Ratified most of them. In 1966, the country signed the 1951 Convention Relating to the Status of Refugees (CRSR) and later, in 1981, acceded to the Protocol on the convention. In 1972, Kenya signed two significant conventions: the International Covenant on Civil and Political Rights (ICCPR) and the International Covenant on Economic, Cultural and Social Rights (ICESCR), both of 1966. It is, however, not a party to the Optional Protocol to the ICCPR. This protocol enables the Human Rights Committee set up under the ICCPR to receive and consider communications from individuals claiming to be victims of violations of any of the rights set out in it. Five years after the passage of the 1979 Convention on the

Elimination of All Forms of Discrimination against Women (CEDAW), Kenya signed on as a party. It is, however, yet to ratify the 1966 Optional Protocol to this convention. In the Optional Protocol, state parties recognise the competence of the Committee on the Elimination of Discrimination against Women to receive and consider communications from persons who claim their rights as set out in the convention have been violated. In 2001, Kenya acceded to the 1966 International Convention on the Elimination of All Forms of Racial Discrimination (ICERD) but has yet to accept the amendment to article 8 of the convention. The country is also a party to the 2006 Convention on the Rights of Persons with Disabilities (ICRPD). It Ratified the convention in May 2008 but the Optional Protocol to the convention is yet to be signed.

As mentioned earlier, Kenya is not a party to three important treaties relating to democracy and political participation, which are the Convention on the Political Rights of Women (CPRW), the 1954 Convention Relating to the Status of Stateless Persons, and the 1961 Convention on the Reduction of Statelessness (CRS). It has, however, acceded to the 1990 International Convention on the Protection of the Rights of All Migrant Workers and Members of their Families, for which article 2(5–6) of the Constitution of Kenya 2010 introduces some binding obligations.

Table 1: Kenya's status on international treaties, covenants and charters (relating to political participation, democracy and non-discrimination)

International instrument	Date of Ratification
united Nations Charter	16 December 1963
Convention on the Status of Refugees (CSR)	Accession 16 May 1966
International Covenant on Economic, Social, and Cultural Rights (ICESCR)	Accession 1 July 1972
International Covenant on Civil and Political Rights (ICCPR)	Accession 23 March 1976
Optional Protocol to CSR on the Status of Refugees	Accession 13 November 1981
Convention on Discrimination Against women (CEDAW)	Accession 9 March 1984

International instrument	Date of Ratification
Convention of the Rights of the Child (CRC)	Ratification 30 July 1990
universal Declaration of Human Rights (UDHR)	Accession 31 July 1990
Convention against Torture	Accession 21 February 1997
African Charter on Peoples and Human Rights (ACPHR)	Accession 25 July 2000
Convention on the Elimination of Racial discrimination (ICERD)	Accession 13 September 2001
International Convention on the Elimination of All Forms of Racial Discrimination (ICERD)	Accession 13 July 2001
The International Convention on the Protection of the Rights of All Migrant Workers and Members of their Families, New York, 18 December, 1990	July 2003
UN Convention Against Corruption	Signed and Ratified 9 December 2003
Protocol against the Smuggling of Migrants by Land, Sea and Air, supplementing the united Nations Convention against Transnational Organised Crime, New York, 15 November 2000 (Palermo Protocol)	Accession 5 January 2005
Rome Statute of the International Criminal Court	Ratified 5 March 2005
Convention on the Rights of Persons with Disabilities (ICRPD), 2006	Ratified 18 May 2008
Optional Protocol to CEDAW	No action
The Convention on the Political Rights of Women	No action
united Nations Charter	16 December 1963
Convention on the Status of Refugees (CSR)	Accession 16 May 1966
International Covenant on Economic, Social, and Cultural Rights (ICESCR).	Accession 1 July 1972
International Covenant on Civil and Political Rights (ICCPR)	Accession 23 March 1976
Optional Protocol to CSR on the Status of Refugees	Accession 13th Nov 1981
Convention on Discrimination Against women (CEDAW)	Accession 9 March 1984
Optional Protocol to CEDAW	No action
The Convention on the Political Rights of Women	No action
Convention of the Rights of the Child (CRC)	Ratified – 30 July 1990
universal Declaration of Human Rights (UDHR)	Accession 31 July 1990

Convention against Torture	Accession 21 February 1997
African Charter on Peoples' and Human Rights (ACPHR).	Accession 25 July 2000
International Convention on the Elimination of All Forms of Racial Discrimination; (ICERD)	Accession 13 July 2001
Convention on the Elimination of Racial discrimination (ICERD)	Accession 13 September 2001
The International Convention on the Protection of the Rights of All Migrant Workers and Members of their Families, New York, 18 December, 1990	July 2003

International instrument	Date of Ratified
UN Convention Against Corruption	Signed and Ratified 9 December 2003
Protocol against the Smuggling of Migrants by Land, Sea and Air, supplementing the united Nations Convention against Transnational Organised Crime New York, 15 November 2000 (Palermo Protocol)	Accession 5 January 2005
Rome Statute of the International Criminal Court.	Ratified 5 March 2005
Convention on the Rights of Persons with Disabilities (ICRPD), 2006	Ratified 18 May 2008

Ratification and domestication of these conventions has not prevented the government from considering withdrawing those inimical to the political interests of the elites in political power. For instance, upon winning the March 2013 election, the new government began a mobilisation process against the Rome Statute of the International Criminal Court (ICC) because the president and the deputy president are facing charges at the ICC for crimes committed during the post-2007 election violence. Before the March 2013 general election, the previous government had unsuccessfully lobbied the United Nations Security Council (UNSC) to defer the Kenyan cases. After election, the new government continued to lobby for deferral and withdrawal from the ICC altogether.

Kenya has also committed itself to most instruments that have a bearing on democracy and political participation agreed to and adopted under the auspices of the AU. It signed the 2001 Constitutive Act of the AU in 2001 and has also Ratified the Protocol on Amendments to the Constitutive Act. Kenya is also a party to the AU Convention Governing the Specific Aspects of Refugee Problems in Africa, which it Ratified in 1992. In the same year, Kenya also Ratified the African Charter on Human and Peoples' Rights as well as its Protocol on the Establishment of an African Court on Human and Peoples' Rights.

Kenya also, after many years, Ratified the Protocol to the African Charter on Human and Peoples' Rights on the Rights of Women in Africa, which it had signed it in 2003. The protocol provides for women's rights to participate in political and decision-making processes and requires states to take action to promote participative governance and the equal participation of women in the political lives of their countries through affirmative action and enabling national legislation.

In 2008, Kenya signed the 2006 African Charter on Democracy, Elections and Governance (ACEDG) but is yet to ratify it. The government hopes to deposit the instruments of Ratification of the charter once the relevant legislation is in place because the passing of the Constitution of Kenya 2010 required a new legislative framework to guide Ratification of international and

regional instruments. The ACEDG seeks, among other things, to:

- Promote the values and principles of democracy; Enhance adherence to the rule of law;
- Promote the holding of regular, free and fair elections; Promote and protect the independence of the judiciary; and
- Promote the establishment of the necessary conditions to foster citizen participation, transparency, access to information, freedom of the press and accountability in the

- management of public affairs

Table 2: Kenya's status on African Union treaties, conventions, protocols and charters (relating to political participation, democracy and non-discrimination)

Title of treaty	Date of Ratification
The African Charter on Human and Peoples' Rights, Nairobi	Signed June 1981 Ratified 23 January 1992
Treaty Establishing the African Economic Community. Abuja, 3 June 1991	Signed 3 June 1991 Ratified 18 June 1993
OAU Convention Governing the Specific Aspects of Refugee Problems in Africa, 10 September 1969	Acceded to 4 February 1993
Protocol to the African Charter on Human and Peoples' Rights on the Establishment of an African Court on Human and People's Rights	Signed 7 July 2003 Acceded to 4 February 2004 Deposited 18 February 2005
Protocol to the Treaty Establishing the African Economic Community relating to the Pan-African Parliament, Sirte, 2 March 2001	Signed 7 July 2003 Ratified 19 December 2003
Constitutive Act of the African union, Lome, 11 July 2000	Signed 2 March 2001 Ratified 4 July 2001
OAU Convention on Preventing and Combating Corruption	Signed 17 December 2003 Acceded to 3 February 2007
Protocol on the Amendment to the Constitutive Act of the African union, Maputo, 11 July 2003	Signed 17 December 2003 Ratified 22 May 2007
Protocol Relating to the Establishment of the Peace and Security Council of the African union, Durban, 9 October 2002	Signed 17 December 2003 Ratified 29 December 2006
Protocol to the Court of Justice of the African union, Maputo	Signed 17 December 2003 Ratified 11 July 2003
The Protocol to the African Charter on Human and Peoples' Rights of Women in Africa	Signed 17 December 2003 Ratified 8 October 2010
The African Youth Charter, Banjul	Signed 2 July 2006
Title of treaty	**Date of Ratification**

The African Charter on Democracy, Elections and Good Governance, Addis Ababa	Signed 30 January 2007
Constitutive Act of the African union. Lome 11 July 2000.	Signed 17 December 2003 Ratified 4 July 2001
Protocol on the Amendment to the Constitutive Act of the African union. Maputo, 11 July 2003	Signed 17 December 2003 Ratified 2 May 2007
Protocol to the Court of Justice of the African union. Maputo,	Signed 17 December 2003 Ratified 11 July 2003.
Protocol Relating to the Establishment of the Peace and Security Council of the African union. Durban, 9 October 2002.	Signed 17 December 2003 Ratified 29 December 2006
OAU Convention Governing the Specifi Aspects of Refugee Problems in Africa. 10 September 1969	Acceded to 4 February 1993
Treaty Establishing the African Economic Community. Abuja, 3 June 1991.	Signed 3 June 1991 Ratified 8 June 1993
Protocol to the Treaty Establishing the African Economic Community relating to the Pan-African Parliament. Sirte, 2 March 2001.	Signed 7 July 2003 Ratified 19 December 2003
The African Charter on Human and Peoples' Rights, Nairobi	Signed June 1981 Ratified 23 January 1992
Protocol to the African Charter on Human and Peoples' Rights on the Establishment of an African Court on Human and People's Rights	Signed 7 July, 2003 Acceded to 4 February 2004 Deposited 18 February 2005
The Protocol to the African Charter on Human and Peoples' Rights of Women in Africa	Signed 17 December 2003 Ratified 8 October 2010
The African Youth Charter, Banjul	Signed 2 July 2006
The African Charter on Democracy, Elections and Good Governance, Addis Ababa	Signed 30 January 2007
OAU Convention on Preventing and Combating Corruption	Signed 17 December 2003 Acceded to 3 February 2007

Kenya has been an active and key player within the AU, particularly in the adoption and implementation of the APRM.

Kenya was among the first four states, along with Ghana, Rwanda and Mauritius, to accede to the memorandum of understanding establishing the APRM in March 2004 in Abuja, Nigeria. Subsequently, Kenya volunteered itself for review under the process and was one of the first three countries (including Ghana and Rwanda) to complete it. Kenya also pioneered identifying and establishing a focal point for the implementation of the APRM in the Ministry of Planning and National Development. As already mentioned, a second review was undertaken in July 2011, but the government declined to present the report for review in the two APRM Summits convened in January and July 2012, citing lack of preparedness. The government cited what it considered erroneous and non-factual findings by the Country Review Team, and wanted the panel to review the report before the government could agree to be reviewed. The team did not revise the report, and Kenya's second review is yet to take place.

The APRM has a tremendous potential to promote, entrench and advance democratic governance; it is also an opportunity for governments in Africa to demonstrate commitment and political will to build mutual trust and reinforce citizens' confidence in the effectiveness and fairness of their governance systems and the integrity and honesty of political leadership. The APRM provides citizens with the opportunity to participate effectively and meaningfully in the decision-making processes that affect them. For both governments and citizens, implementation of the APRM presents opportunities to strengthen institutions of governance and reinforce structures and mechanism of democracy and good governance. The APRM process provides opportunities for Africans to explore the possibilities of forging and promoting democracy and good governance appropriate to their situations. Kenya has also lent support to other African standards related to democracy and political participation, including the Memorandum of Understanding on Security, Stability, Development and Cooperation in Africa of 2002, The

New Partnership for Africa's Development's (NEPAD) Democracy and Political Governance Initiative, the 1990 African Charter for Popular Participation in Development and Transformation, the 2000 Declaration on the Framework for an Organisation of African Unity (OAU) Response to Unconstitutional Changes of Government, and the 2002 Declaration on the Principles Governing Democratic Elections in Africa.

Domestication of international instruments

Owing to the fact that Kenya has been a dualist state, both executive and legislative actions are required before international treaties can take effect. The negotiation, signing of and final assenting to international instruments has been an executive function vested in the president. Although the old constitution was silent on this matter, it was presumed that the presidential power to commit the country to international obligations was covered within the executive powers vested in the president under section 23 of the constitution. In practice, this power was exercised through the Ministry of Foreign Affairs and the Department of Treaties in the Attorney General's office. The two offices were primarily involved in the process of negotiating the treaties. The president then would sign the final documents, thereby committing the country to the obligations set out in the instruments.

While outlining the sources of law, Kenya's Judicature Act did not mention international

treaties and, therefore, provisions of international instruments required to be domesticated by Parliament before they could take effect. Domestication occurred through the normal law-making processes in which Parliament either amended or repealed existing legislation to cater for the new treaty provisions, or enacted a new law. However, that changed with the Constitution of Kenya 2010, which made it explicit that the general rules of international law shall form part of the Kenyan law, and that any treaty or convention Ratified by Kenya shall form part of Kenyan law. This implies faster domestication of international treaties and conventions. Specifically, the constitution has provided for how international law becomes part of the law of Kenya. Article 2(5) provides that the general rules of international law shall form part of the law of Kenya. At the same time, the constitution provides that 'any treaty or convention Ratified by Kenya shall form part of the law of Kenya'under the constitution.

Notwithstanding the above, in practice, Kenya has domesticated few of the international treaties relating to democracy, political participation and non-discrimination. The Refugees Actdomesticates the provisions of the international instruments on refugees. The provisions of the 2006 Convention, for example, on the Rights of Persons with Disabilities have largely been incorporated into the Persons with Disabilities Act of 2003, including the establishment of the National Council for Persons with Disabilities and the progressive implementation of the constitutional provision that at least 5% of all appointive and elective seats be reserved for people living with disabilities (PLWD). Failure to domesticate international treaties continues to be an issue, and so is enforcement. The APRM Country Review Report noted that 'though Kenya had signed and Ratified several international, regional and continental codes that have a bearing on democracy and human rights, it has, thus far, neglected to entrench them through legislation'. The report further noted that international provisions relating to the rights of women, children, refugees and migrant workers are yet to be translated into domestic laws. In its recommendations, the report urged Parliament to pass all laws that have a bearing on Kenya's commitments in international law. The administrative details regarding international instruments are of some concern. First, there is no central registry that details Kenya's commitments to international treaties both at the wider international level and that of the AU. Such details are scattered across ministries and departments. The Council for Law Reporting, working with the Ministry of Foreign Affairs and the Attorney General's office, plans to establish a central registry of Kenya's international law commitments. Secondly, follow-up on treaties to which Kenya is a party has also been less than average. There are no clear records showing the level to which Kenya's laws comply with the treaties it has so far Ratified. Again, such details can only be gleaned from the relevant ministries and departments, the country reports to treaty bodies, civil society organisations (CSOs) shadow reports, and also the concluding observations made by respective treaty bodies, which have expressed concern with Kenya's delays in treaty reporting.

Third, Kenya's reporting record has not been impressive. The government is late in submitting some reports on core human rights treaties. These include reports on: the ICESR due in 2000; the ICRC due in 1997, and which required tabling in 2012; the Committee against Torture (CAT) due in 1998, but was reported in 2008. Under CERD, no report has ever been made. The reports submitted also tend to lack critical details and illustration of the exact situation on each right. Core challenges to reporting include lack of political will, lack of records and availability of information from government departments. Lack of clarity of the office on which reporting responsibility lies, was a noticeable problem until 2003 when the Ministry of Justice and Constitutional Affairs was established. In some cases, where Kenyan law has complied with international standards, it often appears to be more out of coincidence than deliberate effort to fulfil treaty obligations. There also appears to be a weak link between the legislature and the executive in domesticating international treaties. However, with the Constitution of Kenya

2010, the president has obligations (solely in the executive after the first general election) to 'ensure that the international obligations of the Republic are fulfilled through the actions of the relevant Cabinet Secretaries'. In the president's annual speech to Parliament, 'he/she shall submit a report for debate to the National Assembly on the progress made in fulfilling the international obligations of the Republic'.

The Independence Constitution

Kenya's Independence Constitution (1963) resulted from intense negotiations between various political parties on the one hand, and the white settler community and the British government on the other. Each group sought to safeguard and secure its interests. Although Kenyans were fairly united during the struggle for independence, discussions on the Independence Constitution began to create divisions and differences between various groups because of divergent ethnic and gender interests. In the end, the final document aggregated the interests of the different negotiating parties and the manner in which these interests had been balanced and harmonised. The 1963 constitution provided for a multi-party, parliamentary democracy and a federal structure of government, known as Majimbo. While the constitution provided for a democratic system of government and the separation of powers, minimal provision was made for public participation in state affairs. The provisions crafted for implementing the Majimbo system were Following independence, the new government introduced a series of amendments that extensively altered the constitution and centralised power in the executive. Notably, the amendments abolished the Majimbo system of government and created a strong central government. The bi-cameral legislature was also abolished. The amendments also gradually weakened the Bill of Rights and whittled down the powers of Parliament, while strengthening those of the executive, particularly the president's. The abolition of regional governments also led to the strengthening of the Provincial Administration, the tool the presidency used to control the country. Further amendments introduced in the 1980slegalised the one-party state and decreed that the Kenya African National Union (KANU) was the country's only political party.

The erosion of democratic space and violation of human rights following these amendments fuelled demands for constitutional reforms. Most of the constitutional amendments between 1963 and 1991 ended up bolstering powers of the executive arm of the government at the expense of both the judiciary and the legislature, thereby stifling checks and balances. The constitution ceased to be a social contract between the governed and the governors, instead becoming a tool for the advancement of the interests of political and business elites. An overhaul of the constitution was overdue because it had failed to deliver on the promises of independence. Moreover, the Independence Constitution was the result of negotiations between elites, with little participation by ordinary people.

The constitution review process
As alluded to above, concentrating power in the presidency occurred in tandem with the consolidation of authoritarianism. These developments resulted in protracted struggles and demands for democratic change, and constitutional reforms in particular. Ordinary citizens organised themselves differently. Civil society, donors and individuals as well as those opposed to the mode of governance, put enormous pressure on the KANU government, through public demonstrations, advocacy and lobbying, to undertake constitutional reforms. As a concession, KANU agreed to amend the constitution in November 1991 to allow for a multi- party democracy. But that concession alone was not sufficient to deepen democracy. It did not further

citizens' participation in the democratisation process, which the ruling party and the government continued to constrain. Even though KANU won in the 1992 and 1997 general elections, it was clear that the president had been returned to power through use of the state institutions and resources.

Between the 1992 and 1997 elections, more pressure was piled on the government to allow for and effect reforms, win piecemeal legal and constitutional amendments to reduce presidential powers and restore elements of democracy and political participation. Though valuable, these amendments made it clear that a full review of the constitution was still necessary.

It was anticipated that such a review would ensure full democracy, people's participation and better protection of rights. Still the KANU government remained reluctant to allow radical reforms that would enhance people's participation in public affairs. Demands for democratic accountability were received with increased repression.

Pressure for reforms continued to build as the 1997 general election approached. The opposition parties, together with civil society, threatened to boycott the elections if no fundamental constitutional changes were undertaken. Reacting to this, the government convened the Inter- Parties Parliamentary Group (IPPG), a forum to negotiate the form of reforms required before the election. The forum agreed on a wide range of reforms, which were enacted before that year's elections. Among other issues considered by the IPPG was to amend legislation inhibiting freedom of expression and assembly in Kenya. The IPPG tabled and obtained key amendments to the principal legislation through the enactment of the Statute Law (Repeals and Miscellaneous Amendments) Act (1997). The Act amended the Public Order Act (chapter 56 of the Laws of Kenya), section 5. The Act substituted the legal requirement that a licence must be obtained before a rally can be held with a simple notification requirement. This opened up the space somewhat for political parties to hold rallies without interference. Notably, with regard to constitutional review, the IPPG package provided for the establishment of a commission to review the constitution that would be answerable to the Parliament. It was entrenched in law when the Parliament passed the Constitution Review Commission Act. Disagreements over some of the provisions in the review law necessitated negotiations with a large number of stakeholders between June and October 1998. A stalemate pitting two sides against each other held off progress. One side, comprised of religious and civil society organisations that used to meet at Ufungamano House (they formed what came to be known as the Ufungamano Initiative) was led by the official opposition party and its allies and set up a People's Commission of Kenya. The other, consisting mainly of KANU and allied political parties, amended the review law to pave way for the establishment of the Constitution of Kenya Review Commission (CKRC). Each side commenced its own review work. The existence of the two commissions was evidence of severe disagreement in the process. When the chairperson of the CKRC was appointed, he undertook to merge the two processes and secured an agreement to do so in December 2000.

The constitution review process was clearly delayed and constrained by political interests, especially politicians allied to the ruling party, the government and the incumbent president. They desired a review process that they could exclusively control in order to secure a constitution

that served or accommodated their political interests. The desire to influence the constitution

continued to give shape to the review process and, as argued later, finally resulted in the rejection of the proposed new constitution (PNC) at a referendum held in November 2005.

After the merger of the two initiatives, the review Act was amended once more to provide for a 'people-driven' or a participatory and inclusive process. This was evident in its preamble, which stated that review of the constitution was to be 'by the people of Kenya'. The law further required that the people of Kenya be actively involved in each stage of the review process. It required the organs of the review to be accountable to the people of Kenya, to accommodate the diversity of the Kenyan people, and to provide the people with an opportunity to actively engage in the process. Constituency constitutional forums, a national constitutional conference, the referendum and the National Assembly were identified as the key organs of the review process. Only then did a participatory and inclusive journey towards a new constitution start in earnest. The commission embarked on a massive countrywide civic education exercise at constituency level before collecting public views which it would use to prepare a report of its findings and a draft bill. The first National Constitutional Conference (NCC) was convened from April and sat until June 2003 at the Bomas of Kenya, a cultural centre in Nairobi. Its successor, Bomas II, sat in August and September 2003, and the final, Bomas III, was held between January and April 2004. The NCC comprised members of the National Assembly, the commissioners, and three representatives from each district, at least one of whom was a woman and only one of whom could be a councillor sent on behalf of his or her county council in accordance to the commission's rules. Civil society and political parties, too, sent representatives. The three conferences discussed the draft in its various stages. Bomas II, in particular, discussed the commission's report and draft bill through several technical working committees.

The review process was, however, politicised on the basis of the interests of leading elites, and that began to affect proceedings. The composition of the various technical committees to discuss the draft was the first flashpoint. Some of the committees were perceived to be more important than others. Accordingly, delegates began to caucus along provincial and ethnic lines to secure their interests in specific committees. The conference's steering committee thus decided to organise the delegates along provincial lines before assigning them evenly to all the committees.

A number of contentious issues emerged. The structure of the executive and the legislature, the mechanisms for holding legislators accountable to the electorate, the inclusion of Kadhi's courts in the constitution and the corpus of Kenyan law, as well as the framework for devolution of power, became sticking points.

The Rapporteur General, noted that 'what made these issues contentious was not so much the propriety or constitutional value of proposals made in the draft bill, but rather their implications and consequences in contemporary Kenyan politics'. Some delegates were apprehensive about the overall system of government since this had profound implications for the existing power arrangements. Some preferred a presidential system while others were for a parliamentary democracy. Each had consequences, though different in magnitude, on existing power arrangements, and tended to threaten the political interests of the elites in power. Other delegates were unable to extricate themselves from deep-seated cultural, religious and ethnic biases. Preferences for a system of government and various other provisions happened to be viewed from these prisms. Debate on proposals to restructure the legislature, and the role of legislators and their accountability to the people was hampered more by the fear of loss of status and privilege for the sitting MPs than by strict constitutional principles. The Rapporteur concluded that 'attention to these concerns was inevitable and not in the least surprising. After all, constitution-making ... is the continuation of politics by other means'. Bomas II was adjourned on 26 September 2003 to resume on 17 November 2003. As the resumption date approached, however, it became clear that powerful political forces did not want the conference to reconvene and preferred to scuttle the process entirely. This was evident in the tactics employed in some of the twelve committees. In addition, Parliament extended its sittings to the end of the year, well past the expected date of reconvening the conference. Since nearly one third of the delegates were MPs, the reconvening had to be postponed.

The conference reconvened for the third round of talks on 12 January 2004. There was a dramatic change in the tempo of work. Delegates appeared to have resolved to complete their mandate within the shortest time possible without unnecessary interruptions or sideshows. The issues that were regarded as particularly contentious were isolated in order to build consensus around them both outside and within the conference. One initiative, the Coalition of National Unity (CNU) comprising several political parties, facilitated the building of consensus on these issues but it was not supported at the conference. Its recommendations were rejected.

The collapse of this initiative led the steering committee to form a conference consensus- building group. After its numerous meetings, it produced a report on a number of issues identified as contentious. Again, the conference rejected the recommendations of the consensus group, bringing to the fore the longstanding issues that informed debates at the conference. Among these were new political divisions that were emerging within the ruling coalition, the National Rainbow Coalition (NARC). The tensions within the coalition followed ethnic fault lines and they found their way into the conference deliberations. After the rejection of the second initiative to build consensus, a section of delegates allied to the president, walked out of the conference, led by the Minister for Justice, thus creating the perception that the government was not keen to proceed with the review because it could not influence the contents of the draft constitution. That is, the president's faction of the coalition felt that it would be difficult to develop a constitution that would serve their interests. Despite the walkout, the conference continued until 23 March 2004 when the Draft Constitution of Kenya 2004, commonly referred to as the Bomas Draft,

Just before the conference adjourned, a number of delegates and observers went to court challenging the validity and legitimacy of the entire constitutional review process as well as its outcome. The cases had the effect of throwing the review process into disarray. The partisan interests that spilled into the conference and coloured deliberations continued to affect decisions on how to ratify the draft the delegates had adopted. Some argued that a referendum was necessary to operationalise the Bomas Draft while others said passing it as an act of Parliament was sufficient. Again, discussion on the referendum did not take place in order to legitimise the draft. Some preferred the referendum to assist in gauging the amount of political support they would have if an election were to be held. Thus, it was not the constitution that was at stake – personal political interests were. These interests gave impetus to a new set of intricate negotiations on the draft constitution. In turn, these negotiations resulted in additional revisions of what the delegates had adopted at the Bomas conference. Sometimes, the delegates' deliberations were overlooked as politicians sought to accommodate each other's proposals for a constitution that would serve their individual and group interests.

The Parliamentary Select Committee (PSC) on the constitution sought to provide direction, but members were also divided along party lines. Eventually, the government-friendly members of the PSC prepared a new draft constitution thereby amending the draft adopted at the conference. Again, through compromises, Parliament passed that draft. The Attorney General subsequently published the PNC (also referred to as the 'Wako Draft') in the official Kenya Gazette and a referendum on it was held on 21 November 2005. The draft was rejected by about 57% of voters against 43% who were in favour. The referendum results were not only about the 'Wako Draft' per se, but a political contest between two factions in the government with one faction aligning

with the opposition. These factions had ethno-regional bases of political support. The referendum portrayed a deeply divided Kenya, with divisions essentially following ethno-regional lines. These divisions were also reflected in the patterns of voting during the referendum. Significantly, the referendum pitted the incumbent president and members of his Kikuyu and related communities against other major ethnic groups. Eventually, the two ethno-regional alliances consolidated into political alliances, largely ethnic in character, which registered as distinct political parties to compete in the December 2007 election. Those who voted 'No' registered the Orange Democratic Movement (ODM) as a political party. They argued that the government had manipulated the constitution review process and that those around the president had marginalised other ethnic communities. Those around the president, on the other hand, had voted 'Yes' and formed the Party of National Unity (PNU), arguing that the president had revived the economy and that the other faction was making it difficult to improve on growth because they were perpetually engaged in politics. The narrow political considerations that undermined the NCC and considerably altered the Bomas Draft deepened divisions along ethno-regional lines. This is the context in which the 2007 general election was held.

The December 2007 election, ensuing violence and the making of a new constitution

As the results of the general election started trickling in, the parliamentary and civic results announced by the Electoral Commission of Kenya (ECK) did not bring cause to worry until the presidential results were announced. President Kibaki trailed most of the time and only started catching up well into the tallying exercise. He was ultimately announced the winner (by 231 728 votes) in the late afternoon of 30 December 2007, and then hurriedly sworn in that day. A violent conflict engulfed the country immediately after that announcement and the swearing-in ceremony late that evening at State House, Nairobi. While the electoral process itself was peaceful, a hot dispute immediately emerged between the ODM and PNU regarding the election results.

The ODM disputed the announced results and argued that there were several cases of flawed vote counting and tallying by the ECK. On its part the PNU dismissed those allegations and stated that the ODM was being dishonest by making such allegations. Regardless, widespread protests broke out in at least six of the country's eight provinces, mainly in ODM strongholds. The violence raged between 29 December 2007 and 28 February 2008. More than half a million people were displaced and 1 133 killed in respect of the period between 27 December 2007 and 29 February 2008. The violence took an ethnic dimension, dividing the country into two blocs. The intensity of the violence and the subsequent consolidation of these blocs threatened the existence of Kenya as a nation-state.

During international mediation under the auspices of the AU's Panel of Eminent African Personalities, the two parties committed to undertake actions to end violence. Under the leadership of the former United Nations Secretary General, Kofi Annan, the parties signed the Kenya National Dialogue and Reconciliation (KNDR) Accord, agreeing to undertake actions under four main agenda items. They, in particular, signed the National Accord and Reconciliation Act, establishing a grand coalition government comprising the president and the prime minister as the main principals in sharing executive power. While signing the National Accord, the mediation team noted that:

> [The] crisis triggered by the December 2007 disputed presidential elections has brought to the surface deep-seated and long-standing divisions within Kenyan society. If left un-addressed, these divisions threaten the very existence of Kenya as a unified country. The Kenyan people are now looking to their leaders to ensure that the country will
>
> not be lost. Given the current situation, neither side can realistically govern the country forward and begin the healing and reconciliation process without the other. There must be real power sharing to move the country forward and begin the healing and reconciliation process. With this agreement, we are stepping forward together as political leaders, to
>
> overcome the current crisis.

The parties agreed to actions on four agenda items, where some were short-term reform measures, others were to address long-term issues and solve root causes of the violence, as seen in the box below

Agenda I–IV of the KNDR Process

Agenda Item One of the KNDR mediation process was about ending violence and restoring fundamental rights and freedoms. This was important because the government had restricted freedom of assembly and expression as well as banned the media from making live broadcasts of events.

Agenda Item Two concerned ending the humanitarian crisis and promoting healing and reconciliation. The parties undertook to allow humanitarian agencies to reach displaced persons and also to allow the displaced people to move to areas where they felt safer after the ethnic-based attacks. The agreement also emphasised the need for the two parties to hold joint rallies in areas affected by the violence to promote reconciliation among communities. 55

Agenda Item Three concerned ending the political crisis by forming a coalition government. They agreed to amend the constitution to allow for the new positions of prime minister and two deputy prime ministers in the executive. Also, the parties agreed to share positions on a 50-50 basis. 56 The parties agreed that the president and the prime minister would be the two main principals driving these agenda items.

Agenda Item Four identified long-standing issues that had remained unaddressed and that had contributed to the crisis. They included constitutional and institutional reforms, land reforms, regional imbalances in development, youth unemployment, national cohesion and unity, and issues of transparency, accountability and impunity. This last agenda was developed, complete with a roadmap and dates by which the government would have completed the various reforms

On 4 March 2008, the negotiating committee agreed on this road-map towards completing the constitutional review process. In order to speed up the review process, there would be five stages and consultations with stakeholders at each stage

The Constitution of Kenya (2010)
Under the wider agreement, the parties agreed to complete constitutional reforms within a year from August 2008. The parties agreed to urgently pass the relevant laws to facilitate the process. By December 2008, Parliament had passed requisite laws and a Committee of Experts (CoE) on Constitutional Review to review the constitution put in place at the beginning of 2009, as required by the new legal framework. The CoE was required

to harmonise the existing drafts, including those developed by the CKRC at Bomas and earlier, as well as the one that was subjected to the referendum in 2005. The CoE also undertook wide stakeholder meetings across the country before drafting the harmonised draft and, thereafter, conducted civic education for the eventual proposed new constitution.

Indeed, the Constitution of Kenya Review Act (No. 9 of 2009) provided express provision that obligated the CoE to ensure public participation. For example, it stated that the review processes ought to provide 'the people of Kenya with an opportunity to actively, freely and meaningfully participate in generating and debating on proposals to review and replace the constitution'. Section 23 of the same Act also required the CoE to 'facilitate civic education in order to stimulate public discussion and awareness of constitutional issues'. The CoE comprised Kenyans and non-Kenyan nominees of the AU Panel of Eminent African Personalities to provide additional skills and cancel out any narrow political and ethnic tensions that would arise among the local experts. The CoE encouraged democracy and public participation by ensuring the public participated through oral and written submissions, especially on the issues they had isolated as contentious – transition, devolution, the executive and legislature. Further, the CoE held various stakeholder consultations around the country to ensure that all people were involved in the preparation of various drafts, up to the last draft – the PNC. That is, the CoE produced various drafts that were then discussed by the public and the Parliamentary Service Commission on Constitutional Review and MPs, where the latter began a series of negotiations on various issues, but hostility between the two main parties sometimes placed consensus beyond reach.

The ODM preferred a parliamentary system of government, a three-tier devolution structure, and a bi-cameral legislature comprising a Senate and a National Assembly. The PNU, on the other hand, preferred a presidential system without a devolved government. Furthermore, internal conflict within the ODM, arising from competing individual political interests, began to stifle the party. One faction began to support the PNU on some positions that the ODM leadership was opposed to. The lack of cohesion within the ODM resulted in the party softening its position on some issues. Through negotiations with the CoE, the parties reached consensus on some of the issues while others remained outstanding. They tried solving the latter by attempting to amend the draft constitution through over 15 proposals but the House could not garner the requisite two-thirds majority (145 MPs) to amend it.

Although the above failed, the two principals in the coalition government, the president and the prime minister, jointly mobilised support for the new constitution. They took a common position and argued that amendments could follow and that there was no need to delay the review process any further. They held joint campaign rallies, mobilising support for the document before the referendum on 4 August 2010.

The legitimacy of the new constitution is not in doubt. The large number of voters who approved it is high. Furthermore, it was democratically drawn up and borrowed from previous texts that had input from a broad consultative process. By all standards, the Kenyan constitutional review process has been very participatory. The CKRC consulted citizens up to the constituency level. The representative delegates' conference debated various proposals put forward. The 2005 referendum which followed this highly consultative process returned a negative verdict because the document presented did not reflect the same level of participation and consultation.

The constitution has considerably altered the structure of governance, particularly by: a) restructuring the executive to be independent from the legislature; b) establishing two Houses in the legislature; and c) establishing a very independent judiciary whose judges are hired by an equally independent Judicial Service Commission (JSC). Furthermore, all the three branches of government have mechanisms through which they account to the public; they have various avenues and levels of public participation. As well, the constitution has established new institutions to deepen democratic governance. Importantly, the new constitution identifies the people of Kenya as the sovereign authority. It states that all sovereign power belongs to the people of Kenya, who may exercise it directly or through elected representatives. Article 10 of the constitution specifically identifies democracy and people's participation as some of the key national values and principles of governance.

Referenda are enshrined in the constitution in the event that any amendments touching on the Bill of Rights, national values and principles of governance, the structure of devolution, functions of Parliament, and the term of Office of the President, among others, need to be revised. The public must approve such alterations through referenda. The new constitution thus embeds strong conditions for participatory democracy and ensures that neither the executive nor Parliament can amend the constitution without the people's approval. For example, in article 256, any amendment proposed by Parliament should be discussed in public at least for three months between the first and second readings. Further, if members of the public desire a constitutional amendment, they can initiate it through the popular avenue that requires among other things, one million signatures.

Institutions of democratic governance
Kenya severed links with Britain by declaring itself a sovereign Republic in 1964. It was a semi- presidential system of government, which comprised an elected president, who appointed the vice president and the Cabinet from among MPs.

Besides running a large supervisory administration department that represented the presidency to the lowest level of society, the executive also had overweening influence on the functioning of other arms of government. The president appointed judges in courts and controlled the calendar of the Parliament. To date, both the judiciary and the legislature have not had the independence required in some of their operations. The constitution secures the country as a multi-party democratic state founded on national values and principles of governance. The constitution establishes and guarantees the independence of both the judiciary and Parliament. It also provides for devolved government – where executive power is exercised at the national level and in the 47 counties. Devolution of power, including fiscal decentralisation, through county governments, is also entrenched as a national value and a principle of governance. Each county elects a governor and a legislative assembly directly. County governments, consisting of a governor, the executive he or she appoints, and the local legislature, make decisions on behalf of the people.

The executive

The former constitution vested executive authority in the president, who would be directly elected by the highest number of voters, besides enjoying at least 25% support from five of the country's eight provinces. The president would then exercise power either directly or through subordinate officers. It provided for a vice president and ministers, appointed by the president from among members of the National Assembly. The president appointed judges, controlled the calendar and agenda of Parliament and controlled the public service. Such was the power of the executive that it earned the moniker of 'the imperial presidency'.

The National Accord and Reconciliation Act (2008) altered the structure of the executive by providing for a prime minister and two deputy prime ministers in the Cabinet. The National Accord did not affect the status of the president as head of state and government. Further, the president retained powers to appoint the prime minister and the two deputies. The prime minister would be the elected member of National Assembly, who is the leader of the party with the largest number of MPs. The Accord also provided that:

> The persons to be appointed as ministers and assistant ministers from the political parties that are partners in the coalition, other than the president's party, shall be nominated by the parliamentary leader of the party in the coalition. Thereafter, there shall be full consultation with the president on the appointment of ministers.

The law further provides that the composition of the coalition government should at all times reflect 'the relative parliamentary strengths of the respective parties and shall take into account the principle of portfolio balance'.

The power sharing agreement was, therefore, a necessary short-term arrangement aimed at ending the crisis. It was not envisioned as a permanent feature of the constitution. The

amendment to the constitution clearly provided for termination of this arrangement:

the coalition government's term would end after a new election or after the coming into force of a new constitution or when one side withdrew from it.

Although the constitution establishes a presidential system of government, it has transitional provisions that allow the executive to function as it did under the old order and the National Accord and Reconciliation Act 2008 until the first general election is held under the constitution. In the new order, the national executive comprises the president and the deputy president, who are jointly elected by a majority of all the votes cast, and 22 Cabinet secretaries who do not hold any other state office.

As before, the president is the head of state and government as well as the commander-in-chief of the Kenya Defence Forces. The president is also the symbol of national unity.

The new constitution prevents the president from interfering with Parliament's autonomy or influencing its operations. Parliament controls its calendar and shall be involved in the budgetary process before the eventual national budget is presented before it. The president's presence in Parliament relates to addressing it during opening sessions and special sittings.

The constitution has improved checks on the president's powers by mandating Parliament to take the role of investigating, vetting and determining major decisions. Ideally, the president, for example, can only appoint and dismiss state officers – such as Cabinet secretaries, the Attorney General, principal secretaries and others – only with the approval of the National Assembly. These powers to make appointments are, however, not adequately checked since there are no specific qualifications for some of the jobs. Be that as it may, the chapter of the constitution that addresses leadership and the integrity of public office holders requires that state officers act in public trust and promote public confidence in the integrity of the offices they hold. They are required to be accountable to the people in exercising their powers.

The president and the Cabinet exercise executive authority on behalf of the people. The president is also required to ensure that international obligations are fulfilled through actions of relevant ministries, and can declare war with the approval of the Parliament. The president can only be elected to two terms of five years each, with the beginning and the end of each term spelt out. The president is to be elected on the same day that MPs, senators, governors, members of the county assembly and women county representatives to the National Assembly are elected – on the second Tuesday of August, every fifth year. Only citizens by birth qualify to be elected as president. Such a person must be nominated by at least 2 000 voters from at least half of the 47 counties. For a candidate to be elected as president, she or he must garner more than half of all the votes cast in the election, and at least 25% of the votes cast in more than half of the 47 counties. If no candidate is elected, there shall be a second round of elections within 30 days for only the two top candidates. These two requirements are crucial, especially in an ethnically divided society where large ethnic groups present their individual presidential candidates or form alliances to outcompete one another. The provisions are also better compared to the previous constitution because they require a winning

president to have broad regional and popular support. The two-round system or run off also

ensures the legitimisation of the president by the citizens, who must participate in the second round so that the winning president enjoys popular support. The president has to win over 50% plus one of the total votes cast, meaning the president has to enjoy support from over half of the electorate. Importantly, the president must get support from over one quarter of voters each in half of the 47 counties. Getting this support from half the counties implies a broad ethnic support, because counties are largely homogenous in ethnic composition. One glaring shortcoming of the coalition government was that its nature influenced ethnic and regional divisions. First, the coalition government lacked oneness, policy coherence, and projected an image of 'two-governments-in-one'. Members were often opposed to decisions that tended to negatively impact on their side of the coalition. Secondly, the Cabinet was bloated, with 44 ministers whose roles overlapped because of poorly distinguished responsibilities. Conflicts were common. Thirdly, the coalition did not have a dispute resolution mechanism. Their unity of purpose was driven by the relationship between the two principals (the president and the prime minister) only. And even then, the two had no overwhelming influence over their members because the main parties they represented, the ODM and PNU, were themselves alliances of regional interests or smaller parties, which made it difficult to enforce discipline within the coalition and in Parliament.

The legislature

Under the old constitution, Parliament was made up of members of the National Assembly, the president, and the Speaker and Attorney General as ex-officio members. Cabinet ministers would also continue to serve as MPs. Kenya's tenth Parliament was weakened by three main strands: first, about half of the MPs were recruited into the executive as ministers and assistant ministers. Because of this, they tended to vote in support of the executive on matters before the House. Many also tended to be absent themselves from voting, especially if the matter were likely to affect negatively the side of government. Secondly, the tenth Parliament, owing to the coalition government, had no clear demarcation between parties in government and those in opposition, meaning that the traditional checks did not exist. Where opposition occurred, it was because of disagreements particularly between the two principals or the two factions – the ODM and PNU allied parties. Flowing from the above two points, the third weakness was that Parliament was unable to pass a vote of no confidence in the government, or in the president, but had some modicum powers of sanctioning or censoring ministers.

The transitional arrangements vest enormous powers in the tenth Parliament, which was playing the dual roles of the future National Assembly and the Senate. The Parliament, constituted after the disputed 2007 election violence, was deeply divided along ethno-regional and other lines. Self-interest had increasingly shaped the direction of key reforms since the signing of the National Accord in 2008. MPs tend to reject or pass bills depending on how they advance or undermine their respective ethno-regional interests. They form alliances or break existing

ones to further partisan interests. For bills to become laws, they go through three stages in the

National Assembly – they are introduced, debated and amended, then put to the vote before being sent to receive the president's assent. Within 21 days of receiving a bill, the president must give his assent or refuse to do so, stating why in a memorandum to the Speaker and recommending amendments. In such an event, the National Assembly would reconsider the bill and approve the recommendations or resubmit it as it was by at least 65% of its members. In the latter case, the president would have to assent to the new law within 14 days. But that can also be delayed and the National Assembly can do nothing about the delay, or even refusal, by the president to assent to the law within those 14 days. The constitution has overturned this by providing that if the president does not assent to the bill within seven days upon its passage for the second time through the National Assembly, or does not refer it back to Parliament as per the provisions of referral, the bill shall be taken to have been assented to on tSection 68(1) of the former constitution. luence over a pliable Parliament to occasion many amendments to the Independence Constitution. The new constitution limits the powers of Parliament in this regard.

The 2010 constitution establishes a bi-cameral legislature consisting of the National Assembly and the Senate and gives it the authority to make laws. Kenya's legislative authority is vested in both Houses.

The National Assembly represents the people in electoral constituencies and special interests. Among other roles, the National Assembly deliberates and resolves issues of concern to the people and enacts laws. It also determines the allocation of national revenue between the national and the county governments. It reviews the conduct of the president and other state officers, and initiates the process of removing them from office.

The new National Assembly comprises 349 seats – 290 members each elected by the registered voters in 290 single-member constituencies, 47 women members elected by voters from each of the 47 counties and another 12 members nominated by parliamentary political parties according to their proportion of members in the National Assembly. The Speaker is a non-voting ex-officio member.

The Senate comprises 47 seats representing the 47 counties, 16 women members nominated by political parties on the strength of the proportion in the Senate, two members representing youth and another two representing persons with disabilities. The Senate represents the counties and protects their interests as well as those of their respective governments. Among other functions, the Senate considers bills concerning counties and determines the allocation of revenue among them. Senate also considers and determines any resolution to remove the president from office.

These functions of the National Assembly and Senate show that the two are seen as equal. They participate in the oversight of state officers by considering and determining any resolution to remove from office the president or deputy president. Apparently self-interests of the MPs shaped the structure of Kenya's legislature during the negotiations that preceded the August 2010 referendum. Many did not want the establishment of a Senate or a Second Chamber on argument that another chamber would supplant the powers of the National Assembly. Because of this, they were opposed to the use of the terms Upper House and Lower House. They were opposed to any inclination to introduce a hierarchy of chambers and were keen to have a weaker Senate. The full extent of the provisions on the legislature came into effect after the first general elections under the constitution (March 2013). Several laws are required to guide the relationship between the Senate and the National Assembly as well as between the Senate and the county governments. Sticking points in this transition will be determining which House, between the National Assembly and the Senate, should wield what influence and political power. This will certainly depend on the quality of representatives elected in the first general elections under the constitution. This quality of representation will be critical for creating a culture of democratic governance and leadership in the Senate and the National Assembly. Further still, various provisions in the constitution make both Houses more accessible to the public and hence create an avenue to participate in the revision, enactment or repealing of any law

The judiciary

The former constitution provided for a judiciary headed by the Chief Justice (CJ). Judges of the High Court and those of the Court of Appeal, as well as magistrates, served under the Chief Justice. The executive also had influence over the judiciary in a significant manner. The president would appoint the Chief Justice as well as the judges, on the advice of the JSC. The JSC comprised the Chief Justice as its chair, the Attorney General, two persons appointed by the president from among the High Court judges and the chairman of the Public Service Commission of Kenya (PSCK). The composition of the JSC has often raised issues. Lawyer Muciimi Mbaka captures the position thus:

Three of its members, the Chief Justice, the Attorney General and the chairman of the Public Service Commission are direct appointees of the president. Similarly, two other members, being judges, are appointees of the president (though, in theory, indirectly). The Attorney General and the chairman of the Public Service Commission are express members of the executive arm of government. In this regard, the executive actively participates in the management of the affairs of the judiciary.

Mbaka goes on to say that:

The existence and the functions of the JSC notwithstanding, in practice, this commission 'hardly ever initiates the appointment of judges' and that 'in practice, the president abides by informal political rules . [therefore] appointments tend to be overwhelmingly sensitive to political realities'.

in the judiciary. In 1998, the Committee on the Administration of Justice (headed by appellate judge Richard Kwach) proposed the inclusion of independent bodies in the JSC, in particular the Law Society of Kenya (LSK) and the Kenya Magistrates and Judges Association (KMJA), as well as elected representatives from the High Court and the Court of Appeal. In an apparent effort to address this issue, and given the fact that past appointments placed low quality individuals on the bench, some asked that qualifications for judges include 'intellectual ability as demonstrated by academic qualifications and eminence in legal practice or public service'. The Constitution of Kenya 2010 enhances the independence of the judiciary and promotes judicial accountability to the people. The Chief Justice is the head of the judiciary but is appointed through the JSC, whoseinted by the president. The appointment also must be approved by Parliament, a measure meant to secure autonomy from the executive. Three superior courts are established, in addition to the subordinate courts. There is now a S Supreme Court, while other courts will be presided over by a judge elected by his or her peers, a marked departure from the past practice under the old constitution where the Chief Justice administratively appointed judges to preside over the courts. The new requirement aims at improving the transparency in decision-making, and ensuring that those appointed command the respect of their peers and that they are loyal to the institution of the judiciary.

Judicial autonomy is further enhanced by the provision that requires the JSC to initiate the process of removing the Chief Justice and judges. It introduces a transparent process that respects the principle of due process. In doing so, the commission can act on its own or on petition 'by any person'. The president is required to establish a tribunal to inquire into any such matter that may require the removal of the Chief Justice or a judge. For purposes of transition, the members of the judiciary are to be vetted in accordance with principles and values of the new constitution, according to chapter six of the constitution on leadership and integrity.

For independence and public confidence to be restored in the judiciary, the CoE agreed to have the judges and magistrates, who served before the promulgation of the Constitution of Kenya 2010, to undergo a vetting process. The chairperson of the CoE noted that the judiciary, after considerable hesitation and misplaced suspicion, finally accepted that the vetting of judges and magistrates was meant to re-invent integrity in the system of the administration of justice and to inject public confidence in the work of judges and magistrates. Because of well-documented factual and historical reasons, Kenyans would have been sceptical of any new constitutional dispensation which did not include some realignment of the judiciary.

The Vetting of Judges and Magistrates Act does not guarantee that the vetting shall be done in public, unless the judge or magistrate wishes it to be so. The first public hearing was held in May 2012, after one women judge agreed to be vetted in the full glare of the media and public. Nonetheless, the process as led by the Vetting Board, encouraged and allowed for public participation through submission of written or oral memoranda, where civil society, the LSK and other stakeholders did submit information relevant to the vetting of the Court of Appeal judges, which saw the first four 'causalities' of the Court of Appeal fired from the judiciary. Opinions are varied as to the methodology and final results of the vetting of the Court of Appeal judges, where some have praised the Vetting Board, and some chastised itprovides for a central role for courts in the implementation of the constitution, particularly its values. If judges are not committed to these values (and some indeed are not), the values will be disregarded in the scales of justice, and nothing will change in public life and morality. Honest judges are central to justice. The drafters of the constitution realised that the executive and the legislature would have a vested interest in undermining constitutional reforms (a fear that has proved well justified). They, therefore, decided that the independence of the judiciary had to be strengthened and the quality of judges enhanced and courts given the ultimate responsibility for the protection of the constitution, placing them, in this respect, above the legislature and the executive. These responsibilities can only be fulfilled if the judges are both competent and honest and courageous.

Owing to these provisions, the JSC is more independent than before. Its composition gives it much needed credibility and accessibility, which has not been the case in the past. Currently, the JSC is constituted by:

- The Chief Justice, who is the chairperson;
- One Supreme Court judge elected by the judges of the Supreme Court;

- One Court of Appeal judge elected by the judges of the Court of Appeal;
- One High Court judge and one magistrate – one a woman and one a man – elected by the members of the Judges and Magistrates Association (JMA);
- The Attorney General;
- Two advocates – one a woman and one a man – each of whom has at least fi teen years' experience, elected by the members of Law Society of Kenya (LSK);
- One person nominated by the Public Service Commission;
- One woman and one man to represent the public, not being lawyers, appointed by the president with the approval of the National Assembly; and
- The Chief Registrar of the judiciary, who is also Secretary to the Commission.

The JSC under the 2010 constitution exudes much more credibility in its operations, particularly because of the concept of the nomination of judges before their formal appointment by the president, unlike under the former constitution. Members of the JSC are also accountable to the public unlike under the previous order. Indeed, the Chief Justice lauded the JSC for its thoroughness in recruiting for the bench. The appointment of the new Chief Justice has facilitated marked reforms in the operational, administrative and structural sectors of Kenya's judiciary. Among others, the digitisation of court records is underway; judges no longer wear robes, which is said to have reduced aloofness and inaccessibility by both advocates and the public; there is a leadership committee in place that gives direction to reforms in the judiciary; and an ombudsperson to receive and act on public complaints against the judiciary. Further, the CJ has given impetus to judges and magistrates to give independent, brave and firm rulings even in suits in which the state has vested interest, unlike previously. A celebrated ruling is one which gave directions to the executive (Ministry of Internal Security) to arrest Sudan's president, Omar Al-Bashir – a fugitive of international crimes and wanted by the ICC – if he visits Kenyan territory. The judiciary is a critical pillar in the transformation of societies, and the transformation of Kenya's own judiciary goes on to highlight some key areas where it could be said to be on the path of reform. Key areas include the creation of a new code of ethics and conduct for judicial officers, the digitising of cases to redress backlogs, performance contracting for the judiciary, and the enforcement of deadlines for making or writing of judgments, among others.

Conclusion and recommendations

The Constitution of Kenya 2010 has underlined democracy and people's participation as important national values and principles of governance. It has also provided for Ratified international treaties and conventions to form part of the law in Kenya. In the composition of the national executive, Parliament, as a representative of the people, has the mandate to vet and approve members of the Cabinet or any other constitutional office or commission before they are appointed. The legislature has been opened up for public scrutiny in the roles of approving budgets and making laws. The judiciary has opened up to an aggrieved public, especially in the vetting process, to re-establish credible, independent and accountable judges and magistrates. Finally, government ministries, departments and agencies (MDAs) have also been much more transparent, even as it is conceded that some still operate under the old order of secrecy and covertness in the execution of public affairs.

From a policy and legal perspective, the implementation of the constitution has been done openly. Where offices have been established, the public has been aware, mostly – either directly or through independent selection panels, or even through their representatives in

Parliament. Kenyan civil society has mobilised and organised public participation forums, especially in providing feedback on laws before their enactment. Unfortunately, bills are often rushed through Parliament, which has affected not only the quality of the bills themselves but also hampered public input into the process. A case in point is the hurried passing of eleven bills before the 27 August 2010 deadline, which defeated the value of public participation as enshrined in article 10 of the constitution.

Nonetheless, even as the above display important achievements, experience with implementation of any law in Kenya has often exhibited a general lack of commitment in the implementation of what is not in the interest of the executive. The constitution is cognisant of this and, therefore, provides for a Commission for the Implementation of the Constitution (CIC). Although somehow overwhelmed by its mandate, the CIC is spearheading constitutionalism to ensure all laws, policies and operations are done in accordance with the constitution. However, a major shortcoming of the change following the promulgation of the new constitution is the absence of a new class of political and bureaucratic elite to support its implementation. This would have been possible if an election had been held immediately after the promulgation of the constitution. Another shortcoming is the continued application of some sections of the former constitution and laws, especially regarding the powers of the presidency and the executive. This has been utilised to either delay policy, legal and institutional reforms in Kenya or abandon them altogether.

In light of this, the following recommendations are made. That:

- Kenya Ratifiedes the AU Charter on Democracy, Elections and Governance before the next general election scheduled for August 2017 and that civil society, international development partners, and APRM forums put pressure on the government to ratify the charter.

- The government and the international development partners increase the allocation of resources to civil society, specifically to strengthen their oversight role, for the purpose of putting pressure on the government to implement the constitution.

- Civil society prioritises the use of public interest litigation measures against state officers and institutions whose actions threaten effective implementation of the constitution. The media, Kenyan civil society and the private sector constitute an organised grouping for prevailing upon the government to ensure the effective implementation of the constitution.

- The government allocates more resources to the CIC to oversee the implementation of the constitution. Similarly, a greater allocation of funds should be given to the constitutional commissions and independent offices, established under chapter 15 of the constitution, to facilitate performance of their respective roles in promoting the

- values of the constitution and promoting people's participation in public affairs. This

- will assist in developing a culture of constitutionalism which is required at this early stage of a new dispensation in Kenya.

- Civil society, the media and the organised private sector combine efforts to 'make effective implementation of the constitution' the main platform for electoral politics in future elections. The organised forum should also ensure that Parliament has a significant number of elected leaders to champion for effective implementation of the constitution.

Citizenship and inequalities

Belonging to a community guarantees certain rights, as well as granting obligations and responsibilities. Citizenship is, therefore, the foundation to the right to political participation. It guarantees a space for citizens to engage in the affairs of their communities, which, in turn, grant rights to citizens as well as certain responsibilities. Citizenship has, however, assumed a restricted meaning in certain contexts. It is often defined in relation to the legal relationship or bond between a citizen and the state to which the citizen belongs. This relationship prescribes the rights that the citizen should enjoy and the obligations of the citizen to the state. In this regard, the state guarantees its citizens certain rights for the advancement of the dignity of the individual. These include the right to permanent residence within the state, the right to freedom of movement, and the right to vote and to be elected, among others. Kenya's laws and its constitution uphold the principle that all citizens are equal, and outlaws discrimination on a wide range of grounds. These laws and provisions notwithstanding, registration of citizenship is fraught with discriminatory practices. Under the former constitution, women would not confer citizenship to a foreign spouse or a child. To date, members of border communities are subjected to relatively more cumbersome procedures, in comparison to other citizens, to prove their citizenship before registration. Also ethnic minorities face multiple challenges. They have inadequate access to basic services and lack adequate mechanisms to participate in public affairs, particularly because they are poorly represented in elective and other public decision-making organs. This is one challenge of ethnicity, the fulcrum around which politics and decision-making revolves. This section discusses unequal citizenship and its consequences for participation in public affairs.

Citizenship and international law

Article 15 of the Universal Declaration of Human Rights (UDHR) provides that every person 'has the right to a nationality' and that no person 'shall be arbitrarily deprived of his nationality or denied the right to change his nationality'. Despite this bold assertion, international law remains relatively undeveloped in comparison to other areas of international law. The inclusion of citizenship in the UDHR obligates states that have Ratified the relevant treaties to respect citizenship as a human right. The granting of nationality has largely been regarded as being within the discretion of the state concerned. But with the era of democracy based on universal suffrage and acknowledgement that all those with the nationality of a state have the right to participate in its government, the distinction between nationality and citizenship has become increasingly less relevant. Globalisation and increased migration have made the determination of who is a citizen (with full citizenship rights) more important and complex. The recognition of dual citizenship in constitutions of many nations also has reduced the significance of nationality by birth as the main basis of citizenship rights.

A number of international treaties provide principles with regard to nationality and citizenship. The 1961 Convention on the Reduction of Statelessness (CRS), which entered into force in 1975, makes it a duty of states to prevent statelessness in nationality laws and practices. Several human rights treaties also give reference to citizenship. The International Convention on the Elimination of Racial Discrimination (CERD) requires that the right to nationality shall not be denied for discriminatory reasons. Although it does not discuss the citizenship of adults, the International Covenant on Civil and Political Rights (ICCPR) recognises the right of every child to acquire a nationality. The Convention on the Rights of the Child (CRC) places a duty on states to guarantee the right of every child to acquire a nationality.

The African Charter on Human and Peoples' Rights does not provide for the right to nationality. However, numerous articles of the charter apply to cases related to citizenship and have contributed to the citizenship jurisprudence of the African Commission on Human and Peoples' Rights (ACHPR). Such articles include the right to non-discrimination, to equal treatment before the law, to dignity and to due process and fair trial. The African Charter on the Rights and Welfare of the Child repeats the provision of the UN Convention on the Rights of the Child on the right of a child to acquire a nationality. While weak on citizenship rights, the Protocol to the African Charter on Human and Peoples' Rights on the Rights of Women in Africa places strong non-discrimination requirements on states. In most African countries two basic concepts apply to citizenship laws, that is, jus soli (right of the soil) and jus sanguinis (right of blood). Under the concept of jus soli, one obtains citizenship because he or she was born in a particular country while, under jus sanguinis, citizenship is based on descent from parents who themselves were citizens.

The constitution and citizenship laws

The twin issues of citizenship and rights have come to occupy a central place in the Kenyan national and political dialogue. The question of who is a member of an ethnic group and who is

not plays, perhaps, the most important role in deciding how people vote, and the type of rights they should enjoy at local level. The status of 'outsiders', or those who are not indigenous to an area, and that of 'insiders', remains central to conflicts in different parts of the country.

The question of citizenship is also raised in relation to members of border communities and, in particular, those that straddle the borders between Kenya and neighbouring countries. There are discourses of 'outsider' Kenyans and 'insider' Kenyans. In some regions, such as northern Kenya, citizens feel like 'outsiders' because their citizenship gets questioned constantly, and in particular, at the time of seeking citizenship documents. Thus, problems of citizenship are expressed in multiple ways. People experience discrimination in multiple forms. Those in border communities have the challenge of proving their identity during the formal process of registering as citizens. They also have the challenge of consolidating their rights of belonging at local level, especially if their group is seen as an 'outsider' outfit.

Though the law does not provide for citizenship to be granted or withheld on the basis of ethnicity, in practice, discrimination in Kenya on ethnic grounds is widespread. Individuals of Nubian and Somali origin, for instance, have been systematically excluded from recognition as citizens, even when they are third and fourth generation Kenya residents. Members of border communities generally experience difficulty in obtaining necessary paperwork to obtain identification documents such as passports. Interestingly, corruption is increasingly blamed for the failure to supply citizens in border communities with identification documents. Elders are required to vet citizens in border communities before they are given documents to facilitate the acquisition of citizenship documents. Apart from such vetting, the Somali, Nubians and Kenya Arabs undergo additional vetting by government officials, which causes delays in their being issued with citizenship documents, and creates opportunities for the bribing of officials. On the other hand, among the Somali in Kenya, elders in vetting committees that recommend the awarding of citizenship are often blamed for passing off Somali citizens as Kenyans. The Kenyan Somalis fail to get the documents if the elders fail to recommend them.

Without any identity document, a person is denied the right to vote, participate in public affairs or even obtain state services. This official discrimination at the national level is essentially reproduced at lower levels. The population census often raises tensions, partly because it reproduces this fragmentation, and partly because it fails to identify some groups. The census process thus denies citizenship to some groups by failing to list them as distinct entities. Some of the smaller groups are not officially recognised as distinct ethnic groups. They are not ascribed any official code in the national census or in the record of ethnic groups used for issuing citizenship documents such as identification cards. As such, they end up losing their identity and citizenship altogether. In the last census carried out in August 2009, several groups complained that they were omitted from the list and were not identified as being distinct entities. Failure to recognise their identity has implications in regard to accessing citizenship rights because registration is dependent on recognised places of birth, which invariably imply ethnic groups.

Erosion of citizenship rights has continued to occur even though the Independence

Constitution guaranteed equal rights to all citizens. This constitution defined citizenship not in terms of belonging to groups but in terms of belonging to the Kenyan nation-state. The law then provided protection to citizens on the basis of belonging to Kenya and not to particular parts of Kenya. Of critical importance here is that the law provided for individuals to have property anywhere in the country. While the legal framework for the enjoymSection 89 of the constitution. This provision restricts citizenship to persons who at the date of their birth, the fatheryment of such rights.

It has been argued that the national identity card and the Kenyan passport are today accepted as evidence of citizenship. The use of a national identify card as evidence of citizenship is, however, a practice that began in the late 1970s after the collapse of the East African Community (EAC). BefIbid, section 92. Ibid, section 93. Ibid. nly for labour market purposes and was issued at 16 years of age. After the collapse of the EAC, the government increasingly used the identify card to differentiate between Kenyans and non-Kenyans. The card was also used in the registration of voters for the first time in 1983. The government increased the age at which people should get the card to 18 years and from then it was made a requirement to have the card before one is registered as a voter. The issuance of identity cards has often been abused by public officials around election periods. There have been, for example, allegations of the government issuing the cards to those aged 18 years but only in areas likely to support the ruling party or the dominant faction of a coalition.

Nevertheless, persons who hold either of these documents are recognised as citizens of Kenya and are entitled to enjoy the rights, privileges and benefits of citizenship. They can vote or seek election for public office. Those who are denied these documents are, therefore, prevented from participating in political processes and democratic governance. Discrimination has been widespread since independence.

What follows then is a discussion on the comparison between the old and the new constitution in terms of rights associated with citizenship. The discussion pays particular attention to the improvements that the new constitution has made in this respect, as well as to gaps in citizenship.

The old constitution provided and upheld the principle that all citizens are equal. But although it outlawed discrimination on a wide range of grounds, there were many gaps with regard to the right to citizenship; there were discriminatory practices for various groups. As expounded upon elsewhere in this document, women would not confer citizenship to a foreign spouse or a child. Further, and as is still the case to date, members of border communities, and a select number of communities, such as the Nubians and the Somali, were subjected to more cumbersome procedures to prove their citizenship before registration. Ethnic minorities or marginalised groups faced comparatively more challenges than other groups. They were marginalised and had inadequate access to basic services. They had many limitations in participation in public affairs; they were also poorly represented in institutions of governance and decision-making organs at all levels of the society.

Kenya's Independance Constitution did not define who a Kenyan was but it catered for the acquisition of Kenyan citizenship by citizens of the United Kingdom and its colonies or British protected persons. It was assumed that members of all indigenous or native ethnic groups

were citizens of Kenya. The constitution also provided for the acquisition of citizenship by birth, registration and naturalisation. Specifically the following categories of people would qualify for citizenship upon application. Those:

- Born in Kenya after 11 December 1963 and one parent was a citizen;Born outside Kenya after 11 December but the father was a citizen;Women married to a citizen anwhich the provisions of section 92 applied, or those who had been living in Kenya for a prescribed period; and

- Who had reached the age of 21 years and had been lawfully living in Kenya for twelve months.

- Who had reached the age of 21 years and had been lawfully living in Kenya for twelve months.

Evidence of citizenship, to date, includes the national identity card and the Kenyan passport. Persons who hold either of these documents are recognised as citizens of Kenya and are entitled to the rights, privileges and benefits of citizenship. They can vote or seek election for public office. Those who do not have either of these documents because they have been denied or because they have not been issued with them have no right to participate in political processes.

The old constitution and the 1963 Citizenship Act discriminated against women, minorities and citizens in border communities, including Nubians, Swahili Muslims and Arabs. It restricted citizenship and the right of belonging by curtailing the citizenship rights of women, the border communities, and marginalised groups in general. In granting citizenship, the old constitution and its attendant laws, the documents for applying for a Kenyan passport required a woman to obtain the consent of her father (where single) or her husband (where married). Furthermore, section 90 of the old constitution provided for a person born outside Kenya to become a citizen, if the father was a citizen of Kenya. If the mother was a citizen of Kenya, that person could not automatically acquire Kenyan citizenship. Section 91 discriminated against women married to Kenyan citizens from becoming citizens, as they can only became citizens through registration. Further, only a woman who was married to a Kenyan man could apply to be registered as a citizen, but the same did not hold where a Kenyan woman married a foreign man. Section 91 also affected the status of children born of a Kenyan mother and non-Kenyan father. They would be foreigners and not entitled to citizenship if they were not born in Kenya.

To reiterate, the old constitution discriminated against minorities and those from border communities, subjecting them to extra scrutiny and screening procedures when they applied for Kenyan citizenship documents. Minorities such as Muslims underwent multiple identification

processes. Kenya's Somali citizens and Nubians were victims of this process as well. The government introduced additional identification cards in the late 1980s and early 1990s to differentiate Kenyan Somali citizens from Somali people born in the Republic of Somalia. However, Nubians have remained without identification documents yet they have lived in Kenya before Kenya became a colony in 1919. Some had settled in Eldama Ravine by 1883. By 1904, Nubians had settled in Kibra in Nairobi, which was an extension of the Lang'ata Barracks. Today they live in several parts of the country, including Kibra, without secure rights to property and citizenship. Article 78(2). ernments have failed to issue them with citizenship documents. Other groups such as the Somali and Arabs continue to experience certain challenges in respect of the enjoyment of citizenship rights. Kenyan Somali and Arab citizens have to produce their parents' national identity documents besides their own birth certificates to be issued with citizenship documents. The overall implication of this is that restrictions on citizenship rights for these groups have continued to constrain their participation in democratic processes and in public affairs. Without citizenship documents, they cannot vote or be voted into office, and cannot participate in political processes.

The old constitution also restricted citizenship in other respects. Anyone who attained the age of 21 years while holding Kenyan citizenship as well as the citizenship of another country ceased to be Kenyan if that person did not renounce the other citizenship – that is, the constitution prohibited dual citizenship. In other words, the former constitution restricted the right of belonging and discriminated against women, people from minority communities and religious backgrounds.

The struggle for democratic governance beginning in the early 1990s sought to address some of these challenges. The process of political liberalisation and subsequent widening of space for freedoms and rights in the 1990s did not address the core problem of citizenship. The constitutional provisions that undermined citizenship remained in place, with little efforts by Parliament to amend them. Demands for amendments of the provisions that made it difficult for Kenyan women to pass citizenship to foreign spouses and their children were reiterated at the 39th Session of the Committee on the Elimination of Discrimination against Women (CEDAW). The meeting noted that:

The [former] constitution does not provide equal citizenship rights for women. The Committee is particularly concerned that Kenyan men may confer citizenship to their wives and children while Kenyan women do not enjoy the same right. The Committee is also concerned that children born to Kenyan mothers abroad have to apply for citizenship and given entry permits of limited duration only, while no such restrictions apply to children of Kenyan fathers born to non-Kenyan mothers.

The new constitution and the Citizenship and Immigration Act (2011) have generally addressed these challenges. First, every citizen is entitled to rights and privileges of citizenship, a Kenyan passport and any other identity document required for citizens within the limitations that the law can impose. Citizenship may be acquired by birth or registration but cannot be lost through marriage or dissolution of marriage. Any person born outside the country but who has a Kenyan parent or parents is a citizen of Kenya. Article 14 further provides that a person is a citizen by birth if, on the day of the person's birth, whether or not in Kenya, either parent is a citizen. The constitution also ensures that children do not become stateless. Article 14(4) provides that any child of less than eight years found in Kenya, and whose nationality and parents are not known, is presumed to be a citizen by birth. The Citizenship and Immigration Act (2011) actualises some of these provisions in a restrictive manner. With regard to limitations of descent, section 7 of the Act provides that 'a person born outside Kenya shall be a citizen by birth if, on the date of birth, that person's mother or father was or is a citizen by birth'. This precludes those whose parents were or are citizens by registration.

The constitution addresses the discriminatory tendencies in the Independence Constitution and the 1963 Citizenship Act. For instance, the provisions for citizenship under the new constitution apply even to those persons born before its promulgation in August 2010. Thus, those who might have lost their citizenship because of becoming citizens of another country can reclaim Kenyan citizenship on application. Further, a person who is a citizen by birth does not lose citizenship by reason only of acquiring the citizenship of another country; one can hold dual citizenships.

Nevertheless, there are limitations on citizenship rights. Article 16 of the constitution provides that 'a citizen by birth does not lose citizenship by acquiring the citizenship of another country'. The import of this is that only citizens by birth are entitled to dual citizenship; those who are citizens by registration or naturalisation may not enjoy this right. Also a person who has been married to a citizen for at least seven years, or has lived in the country for a similar period, can apply for citizenship if he or she satisfies the conditions of the law to be enacted.

Although the new law recognises dual citizenship, it places several restrictions on those with dual citizenship. Section 8 of the Citizenship and Immigration Act (2011) spells out that 'a citizen of Kenya by birth who acquires citizenship of another country shall be entitled to retain citizenship of Kenya subject to the provisions of this act and the limitations relating to dual citizenship prescribed in the constitution'. There are other limitations on the rights of dual citizens. For example, 'a person is not qualified for nomination as a presidential candidate if the person ... owes allegiance to a foreign state'. State officers and also members of the defence forces 'shall not hold dual citizenship'. With a wide constitutional definition of 'state officers' to include most of the members of the national and county governments, this limitation is also wide.

The government can revoke citizenship acquired through registration if it has been acquired through fraud or false representation. If someone who registered as a citizen engages in or associates with an enemy of Kenya when Kenya is at war, he or she can lose that citizenship. Also, citizenship by registration can be revoked if the person commits an offence and is imprisoned for a term of more than three years, provided the person is not rendered stateless. Citizenship by birth can also be revoked if it was acquired by fraud, false representation or concealment of any material fact. Further, the state can revoke citizenship by birth if the nationality or parentage of a person becomes known, and it is revealed that the person was a citizen of another country.

These provisions seek to address the challenges of citizenship under the old constitution and the 1963 Citizenship Act. They are a substantial improvement on what existed under the old constitution and the law. The constitution enforces citizenship retroactively in an attempt to redress past shortcomings. It perceives citizenship in two interrelated ways – citizenship by birth, and citizenship by registration. The latter is based on the right of relationship either by blood of a spouse or parent arentage or nationality is unknown.

It is noteworthy that that the citizenship provision for children was contentious during the debates in the run-up to the referendum on the constitution. Those opposing these provisions argued that the automatic award of citizenship for children aged eight years or younger whose nationality and parents were not known would attract an exodus from unstable neighbouring countries that were experiencing conflicts, particularly from the state of neighbouring Somalia the Kenyan Somali people are border communities and it is difficult to know their country of origin. But article 17(2) clearly provides grounds upon which such citizenship could be revoked, as seen above.

Two laws have been enacted to facilitate the provisions of chapter 3 (on citizenship) of the constitution. The Kenyan Citizenship and Immigration Act (2011), mentioned above, and the Kenya Citizens and Foreign Nationals Management Service Act were passed by Parliament in 2011. The former regulates matters relating to citizenship, issuance of travel documents and immigration while the latter establishes the Kenya Citizens and Foreign Nationals Management Service, which provides for the creation and maintenance of a national population register and the administration of the laws relating to births and deaths, identification and registration of citizens, immigration and refugees, administration of laws relating to marriages and for such connected purposes. The new legal framework has addressed the citizenship problems that the previous constitution failed to solve. The new framework seeks to eliminate statelessness in Kenya and recognises citizenship rights of ethnic groups that were not recognised as citizens. It also seeks to give citizenship status to migrant communities that did not have citizenship rights. The problem, however, is that the law provides these groups citizenship status by registration, which would limit their right to political participation.

The provisions on citizenship in the new constitution are an improvement on the old constitution. The new constitution has laid a better framework for citizenship rights. However, the attendant laws still contain gaps that can lead to arbitrary administrative actions or be subject to the discretion of public officers responsible for enforcing citizenship provisions. Chief among these are the restrictions on the acquisition of citizenship by registration, especially for migrants. One is required to have sufficient knowledge of Kiswahili or another dialect. This may be subjected to arbitrary interpretation or be at the discretion of public officers. Moreover, there are individuals whose first language is English, yet this is not a Kenyan dialect. The law also requires adopted children to acquire citizenship by registration rather than by birth if they are adopted by a parent who is a Kenyan citizen.

Non-discrimination and affection Action

The Independance Constitution protected the fundamental rights and freedoms of individuals and appeared to have borrowed heavily from the European Convention for the Protection of Human Rights and Fundamental Freedoms, and the UDHR. Specifically, the old constitution provided that every person in Kenya was 'entitled to the fundamental rights and freedoms of the individual (irrespective of) one's race, tribe, place of origin or residence or other local connection, political opinions, colour, creed or sex', but subject to respect for the rights and freedoms of others and for the public interest. The old constitution also outlawed discrimination, which was defined as affording different treatment to different persons attributable wholly or mainly to their respective descriptions in terms of race, tribe, place of origin or residence, or any other relation.

The old constitution also provided that 'no person shall be treated in a discriminatory manner by a person acting by virtue of any written law or in the performance of the function of a public office or public authority'. However, these non-discrimination provisions could cease to have effect when Kenya is at war or if the president declared a state of emergency. Also, the former constitution did not expressly require the state and private bodies to respect the provisions on non-discrimination (and the Bill of Rights as a whole).

Kenya's Independence Constitution lacked enforcement procedures and institutions. Although there were provisions for going to court where rights relating to non-discrimination had been contravened, no special bodies were established to enforce these rights, particularly the provisions on non-discrimination. Instead, the constitution vested original jurisdiction in the High Court and appellate jurisdiction in the Court of Appeal.

Although there were laws prohibiting discrimination and abuse of rights, abuse of human rights and discrimination on the basis of ethnicity and gender were widespread. The space for the enjoyment of civil and political rights expanded after the re-introduction of multi- party politics in November 1991. This expansion of space for freedoms, nonetheless, did not prevent the abuse of rights and the curtailment of civil liberties. Authoritarianism deepened as did ethnic divisions in Kenyan society. Tribal and ethnic divisions widened as the ruling elites sought to consolidate political power by using ethnic groupings against one another. The government became increasingly identified with the president's ethnic community – the Kalenjin at the time, until 2002. This continues to manifest itself to date. They were numerically dominant in all senior and strategic positions in the public sector. Composition of public sector institutions was skewed to favour the president's ethnic community and allied groups. This practice deepened and widened inequalities, following a pattern established by the previous regime – that of President Jomo Kenyatta – which held power from independence in 1963 to his death in 1978. The NARC government came to power in 2003 and establishedNational Cohesion and Integration Act, No. 12 of 2008. MPs Fred Kapondi and Wilfred Machage who were arraigned in court alongside a businesswoman were later acquitted onints, providing redress for violations, and carrying out advocacy campaigns and research to inform policy and legislation on economic, social and cultural rights. It was also tasked with human rights education and building the capacity of institutions in its area of specialisation. These functions generally address issues of discrimination and the abuse of rights in general.

The KNCHR has investigated complaints relating to discrimination on the grounds of race, class and gender. It conducts preliminary inquiries by offering the subject of the complaint an opportunity to respond to allegations before carrying out further investigations. This may involve collecting and presenting evidence or summoning persons key to the complaint. The KNCHR then provides for redress of the violations. From its inception, the Commission has profiled human rights protection in an unprecedented manner. It has conducted high profile investigations and responded to many human rights complaints. But the high profile campaign to hold state officers and institutions accountable for human rights abuses, motivates officials to introduce administrative and bureaucratic constraints to the Commission's work, with some even demanding the Commission's dissolution.

The Constitution of Kenya 2010 established the Kenya National Human Rights and Equality Commission (KNHREC). The constitution provided that its membership be drawn from the KNCHR and the National Commission on Gender and Development. The functions include promoting the protection of human rights in all spheres and investigating and taking steps to secure appropriate redress where human rights violations occur. The Commission has the mandate of investigating complaints of denial of rights by any person. In addition to these two, the constitution has provided for the establishment of an ombudsperson, the Commission on Administrative Justice (CAJ) in 2011. The mandate includes receiving and acting on complaints that border on maladministration including discrimination of persons. On the whole, there are three constitutional bodies addressing issues of human rights, equality, and the broader question of discrimination: the KNCHR, the Gender and Equality Commission, and the CAJ. The three are independent commissions but with 'complimentary' mandates to fulfil the mandate of the KNHREC under article 59. This mandate seeks to ensure that Kenya's democracy is based on human rights protection and promotion without discrimination on any of the protected grounds, as well as ensure that there is redress when such violations occur.

The constitution provides that every person is equal before the law and has the right to equal protection and equal benefit of the law. This equality includes full and equal enjoyment of all rights and freedoms as provided for in the constitution. Further, the state or any other natural or legal persons shall not discriminate against anyone on the basis of a wide range of fields including race, ethnicity, gender, pregnancy, marital status and religion. It also requires the establishment of affirmative action programmes to address cases of disadvantage arising from past discrimination.

The constitution has a comprehensive progressive Bill of Rights that promotes equality and outlaws discrimination. The Bill of Rights applies to all and binds all state organs. It creates mechanisms for the promotion and enforcement of rights by all duty bearers and citizens, as well as ensuring that the courts play a role in enforcing the rights of individuals. It does not permit the state to claim that it does not have resources to implement or promote rights envisaged under the Bill of Rights. Should the state lack resources to implement a right, it would be required to demonstrate a prioritisation of resource allocation in order to facilitate the widest possible enjoyment of that right or freedom.

Additionally, the National Cohesion and Integration Act (2008) substantively addresses discrimination and, in particular, ethnic discrimination. The Act, one of the laws developed in the aftermath of the post-2007 election violence, specifically seeks to 'encourage national cohesion and integration by outlawing discrimination on ethnic grounds'. It also establishes the National Cohesion and Integration Commission (NCIC) to champion this cause. It outlaws discrimination through victimisation, harassment on the basis of ethnicity, and discrimination in employment. The coming to force of this law was an important milestone because ethnicity has never received direct legal, policy and political attention. No precedents exist for seeking direct interventions to address the challenge of ethnicity. The law also criminalises hate speech or instances in which people use threatening and abusive words against others. The NCIC profiled this law during the 2010 campaigns for the referendum on the constitution, resulting in several politicians being arrested and charged in court with making hate speeches. Although the cases were not successful at prosecution, the effort to arrest and charge them in court played a role in discouraging other politicians from using inflammatory statements. This also contributed to the toning down of ethnic bigotry during the campaigns for the March 2013 general election.

Finally, an important achievement under the Constitution of Kenya 2010 is the provision for the rights of inmates. Discrimination against the rights of inmates to vote has been addressed. Inmates were allowed to vote in the 2010 constitution referendum, after Kituo Cha Sheria, a Kenyan civil society organisation, litigated on the matter. The courts ordered the Interim Independent Electoral Commission (IIEC) toPublished in Kenya Gazette Supplement of 27 July 2007. oners in relation to political participation.

That judgment touched on article 51 of the constitution on the rights of persons detained, held in custody or in prison.

The constitution, thus far, has addressed the question of discrimination by providing for the establishment of institutions to promote equality, protect various groups and promote their rights while monitoring violations of such rights. Again, this is an improvement on the provisions of the old constitution; it contained anti-discrimination clauses but lacked enforcement mechanisms. The three institutions under the Kenya National Human Rights and Equality Commission are required to play complementary roles in fulfilling this mandate. They have legally binding enforcement mechanisms to ensure that they address the challenges experienced in enforcing the law under the old constitution.

Effort to introduce Affection Action

Efforts to introduce affirmative action and outlaw discrimination have not been very successful. For instance, the old constitution contained provisions that discriminated against women, particularly in the realm of personal law. Women's rights to property were unequal to those of men in Kenya. Illustratively, women's rights to own, inherit, manage and dispose of property were under constant attack from customs, laws and individuals. Concerned about this form of discrimination, in 2007, the 39th session of CEDAW expressed concern and urged Kenya to repeal these sections of the former constitution. There have also been concerns that the Independence Constitution's definition of discrimination fell short of the CEDAW one, which prohibits both direct and indirect discrimination. Amendments were, therefore, required to align the definition in the constitution with CEDAW. The Equal Opportunities Bill (2000) sought to domesticate the provisions of several international instruments on equality and non-discrimination, including the Convention on Civil and Political Rights, the Convention on Civil and Political Rights, the Convention on Economic and Social Rights, CEDAW and the Universal Declaration on Human Rights. The bill also sought to give effect to the outcome of documents from various international UN conferences, including the Rio Platform for Action (1992), the Vienna Human Rights Declaration (1993) and the Global Platform for Action (Beijing, 1995), all aimed at eliminating discrimination against women.

The bill described discrimination as 'an act or omission including any condition, requirement, policy, situation, rule or practice that has or is likely to have the direct or indirect effect of unjustly or unfairly causing disadvantage'. It specifically prohibited both direct and indirect discrimination against any person and made extensive provisions regarding discrimination in various sectors such as employment, education, professions and appointment to public office. The Equality Bill was not passed but was instead shelved to await the incorporation of its principles within the constitution.

The Affirmative Action Bill (2007) sought to have minimum reforms in support of special groups and specifically provided for '50 specially elected women members of the National Assembly'. These women were to be elected through the proportional representation system, whereby political parties participating in the elections were to submit to the Electoral Commission of Kenya (ECK) a list of 50 women candidates. The candidates were to be ranked in order of priority, taking into account special interests, including youth, disability and geographical distribution. Following the elections, the parties would be apportioned their respective number of seats based on the proportion of seats won in the National Assembly.

Even though there was insufficient support in Parliament for these laws, the reason they did not pass was because the government failed to anchor them on policy. These failures notwithstanding, gender equity remained a central focus in the struggles that fronted demands for comprehensive reforms. All the constitution review acts retained gender as an important element. The new constitution thus provided for gender equity and embedded affirmative action to promote this principle.

The constitution and representation of women

The constitution outlaws discrimination against women and other groups. It also provides for the improved status of women and requires the government to initiate affi action programmes and other policies to address historical disadvantages. In particular, women and men have the right to equal treatment, including the right to equal opportunities in political, economic, cultural and social spheres. Discrimination on grounds of sex, pregnancy and marital status, among others, is outlawed. As noted earlier, women have the right to confer citizenship on their children and foreign spouses. Recognising that society and individual persons are largely responsible for discrimination against women and the failure to respect women's rights, the constitution requires that all persons and the state protect and respect these rights.

The most important achievement of the Constitution of Kenya 2010 is guaranteeing the rights of women in respect of representation in elected and appointed offi in the public service. The National Assembly comprises 349 members, including 47 elected women's representatives. The Senate comprises 16 women representatives nominated by political parties according to their strength in the Senate. This is in addition to one woman representing the youth and another representing persons with disabilities. The constitution also provides for special seats for women in county assemblies by requiring that no gender should have more than two-thirds' representation.

There are other gains as well for women's participation in public life both in elected and appointed bodies. All bodies are required to be guided by the principle of promoting gender equality in the performance of their functions. The state is required to take measures to ensure that no more than two-thirds of the members of elective or appointive bodies shall be of the same gender. Specifi , with regard to representation, article 81 of the constitution requires that the electoral system shall comply with the principle that, among others, 'no more than two-thirds of the members of elective public bodies shall be of the same gender'. This principle is meant to guide the composition of the Senate, the National Assembly and the county assembly.

However, the constitution has also set the limit of seats for both the Senate (67) and the county assembly (349). Article 97 on the membership of the National Assembly sets the total membership at 349 while article 98 on the membership of the Senate sets the threshold at

Even though these are the limits, the constitution does not provide for an enforcement mechanism to ensure that the principle of 'no more than two-thirds' guides the composition of both houses. Past experience has shown that very few women are elected into various positions and it is thus possible that this gender rule will not be eff through direct elections. Political parties have also failed to comply with this provision but there is no provision to sanction them. It is possible that after elections, both the National Assembly and the Senate may be unconstitutional if they have more than two-thirds from one gender.

Nevertheless, the provisions on gender equity have increased the space for women's participation in public life in elected and appointed bodies at the local and national levels. They have guaranteed a minimum number of women in these bodies where key policy matters are decided. While this is an important achievement, there is a need to work towards refining the quality of representation in these bodies. There should be legislative measures to improve the quality of representation and prevent a situation where political parties support women candidates as part of their patronage machinery rather than to achieve quality representation.

Institutional and policy measures to promote gender equality

- At the level of Cabinet – the highest political decision-making organ in Kenya – women's issues were addressed by the Ministry of State for Gender, Children and Social Affairs The ministry set the policies while the Department of Gender in the ministry provided 'a technical base for gender mainstreaming through the national sectoral approach and implementation of recommendations of conventions'. The department's key functions include: Formulation and review of gender-responsive policies across all sectors for integration of women, men, girls and boys into the development process;

- Facilitation of domestication and implementation of resolutions made at the international and regional levels;

- Coordination and harmonisation of the implementation of the National Policy on Gender and Development, and other gender responsive interventions implemented by the government, non-governmental organisations (NGOs) and other agencies;

- Lobbying and advocating for gender mainstreaming in the development process and engendering the national budget; and

- Promoting the generation of gender disaggregated data/information on gender equality.

The government intends to set up gender divisions in all ministries so as to incorporate a gender perspective in all sectors. The government, in 2011, established the National Gender and Equality Commission (NGEC) pursuant to article 59(4) of the Constitution of Kenya 2010. The Commission is a successor of the National Commission on Gender and Development (NCGD). The NCGD was mandated to:

- Participate in the formulation of national policies;

- Liaise with government ministries on matters relating to gender and exercise general supervision over the implementation of the national policy on gender and development;

- Institute proposals and advise on the establishment and strengthening of institutional mechanisms which promote gender equity and equality in all spheres of life; and,

- Initiate legal reforms on issues affecting women in collaboration with the Attorney General's office

Concerns were voiced over the establishment and operations of these institutions. The International Federation of Women Lawyers Kenya (FIDA-Kenya) stated that:

> The establishment of the National Commission on Gender was not followed with a requisite operational plan. Subsequently, teething problems with regard to funding and relations with other bodies like

the Ministry of Gender, and specifically the Gender Department, were not clarified This scenario has left the Commission vulnerable and unable to meet [its] expected output.

Regarding funding, FIDA-Kenya noted that 'the commission was notably under-funded'. These concerns have also been echoed at the international level. The CEDAW Committee expressed concern over 'possible fragmentation of eff of [the Ministry of Gender and the NGEC] as well as their lack of resources'. The Committee recommended that Kenya expeditiously strengthen these institutions, fi and otherwise, so as to ensure a strong institutional mechanism for the promotion of gender equality.

As mentioned in the preceding part, the NGEC was set up in 2011 to succeed the NCGD, where the latter's mandate is also broad, and includes addressing inequality generally, not just gender-based inequalities – these include non-discrimination and protection of the marginalized groups and those living with disabilities. The NGEC is mandated to monitor, facilitate and advise on the integration of the principles of equality and freedom from discrimination in all national and county policies, laws, and administrative regulations in all public and private institutions ... [and also] act as the principal organ of the state in ensuring compliance with all treaties and conventions Ratified by Kenya relating to issues of equality and freedom from discrimination and relating to special interest groups, including minorities and marginalized persons, women, persons with disabilities, and children.

Women and participation in the political process
All Kenyans above the age of 18 years have the right to vote and to freely take part in the electoral process. Notwithstanding this constitutional guarantee, the full and free participation of women in the electoral process has been hampered by several factors, among them cultural attitudes, general lack of adherence to electoral laws, insufficient political goodwill in the enhancement of the participation Centre For Rights Education

And Awareness (CREAW) & 7 others vs Attorney General [2011] eKLR.

This situation is exemplified by the low number of women in Parliament and other elective bodies. Despite constituting slightly more than half of the total population, women have not marshalled their numeric strength for political gain: only 22 of the 222 members in the ninth Parliament were women. Out of these, 16 were elected while the remaining six were nominated by the political parties. It is noteworthy that an equal number of men and women were nominated to the tenth Parliament, demonstrating the ability to achieve equality in political participation.

Low as it is, the current number of women in the ninth Parliament was a marked improvement from the ninth assembly, where only ten women were elected and eight were nominated. In the December 2007 elections, 269 women contested parliamentary election compared to 44 in 2002, which was a phenomenal increase in the number of women participating. Notably, in the aftermath of the December 2007 elections, the offices of the president, vice president, prime minister and the two deputy prime ministers, were all held by men. In legislating on the appointment of the prime minister and the two deputy prime ministers, the National Accord and Reconciliation Act (2008) made no provision for the inclusion of women in these positions. And, indeed, no woman was appointed to these offices. There were only seven women ministers in a Cabinet of 42, and six women out of 51 assistant ministers.

The same scenario was exhibited in the diplomatic service, where women made up 23% of ambassadors and high commissioners (eleven women out of 48). In other levels of the public service, women were also poorly represented. Of the 42 permanent secretaries, only six were women. Additionally, there were no women provincial commissioners after the 2007 general election.

Table 3: Women in parliament, 1963-2007

Year	Women	Men	Total	Percentage of women
1963	0	124	124	0.0
1966[120]	0	28	28	0.0
1969	2	168	170	1.2
1974	6	164	170	3.5
1979	5	165	170	2.9
1983	4	166	170	2.4
1988	3	197	200	1.0
1992	7	193	200	3.5
1997	8	214	222	3.6
2002	18	204	222	8.1
2007	22	200	222	9.9

In the judiciary, the representation of women is higher in the lower cadres. Women constitute between 38% and 44% of all magistrates. The statistics are, however, dismal in the higher echelons of the institution. By 2009, the Court of Appeal, the highest court, had ten judges of appeal, and only one was a woman; she later left. The number of female High Court judges has risen considerably over the years. In 2005, women made up 12% of the High Court judges. Currently, 16 of the 47 High Court judges are women. This implies that women constitute slightly over a third of the High Court judges

Table 4: Women in public office 2008

Public Office	Women	Men	Total	% women
Ministers	7	35	42	16.6
Assistant Ministers	6	45	51	11.8
Permanent Secretaries	6	36	42	18.8
Provincial Commissioners	0	8	8	0.0

Ambassadors/High Commissioners	11	37	48	22.9
Court of Appeal judges	1	9	10	10.0
High Court judges	16	31	47	34.0

Concern has been expressed over the continued low representation of women in public and political life in the country. Kenya has been urged to take measures that accelerate women's full and equal participation in public and political life, especially at high levels of decision-making. The Constitution of Kenya 2010 has made provision for far-reaching affirmative action. It, for instance, provides for 47 elective positions for women in the National Assembly besides the nomination slots, and 18 nomination slots for women in the Senate. In addition to this, they are still free to compete with men in the remaining elective positions. The constitution also provides that not more than two-thirds of members of elective public bodies shall be of the same gender. The NGEC and other women bodies had been fighting for the immediate realisation of this provision. The Supreme Court, however, ruled that the two-third gender rule shall be realised progressively.

Further, the Centre for Rights Education and Awareness (CREAW) litigated against women discrimination in appointive offices. CREAW went to court after President Kibaki had nominated persons to the offices of Attorney General, Chief Justice, Controller of the Budget and also Director of Public Prosecutions in January 2011. Since President Kibaki had nominated only men to these offices, CREAW sought a declaration that any appointments that may be made in a like manner as the appointments to these offices made by the Office of the President on 28 January 2011 would be in violation of various articles, including article 27, and hence would be unconstitutional, null and void. Of course, the petitioners won and Kibaki had to recall all names and the nomination process started afresh, which eventually gave Kenyans the current occupants of the same offices.

Women have made substantive gains under the new constitution. As already mentioned, article 81(b) of the constitution requires the altered electoral system to comply with the principle that 'no more than two-thirds of the members of elective public bodies shall be of the same gender'. The government did not apply this principle to the March 2013 general election because the Supreme Court ruled that the principle will be applied progressively but not later than August 2015. Nonetheless, the electoral system comprises gender quotas for the houses of representatives. In this regard, the National Assembly has 47 seats reserved for women, who are elected from the 47 counties each representing a single member constituency. The Senate has 18 women's seats while the political parties in the county assemblies are required to nominate a sufficient number of women to meet this threshold if those elected do not meet the gender principle.

On the basis of the gains The main exception here was the nomination of Dr Richard Leakey in 1997, who had lost both limbs, and his replacement inof 67 members in the Senate. Even though the constitution is progressive in terms of providing for women's representation, only seven women were elected for the 290 single member constituency posts outside of the 47 reserved for women. Although this is the situation, these numbers of women's representation in the current Parliament are the highest that women have had in Parliament since independence in 1963.

Protection of persons living with disabilities

The constitution has defined disability to include 'any physical, sensory, mental, psychological or other impairment, condition or illness that has, or is perceived by significant sectors of the community to have, a substantial or long-term effect on an individual's ability to carry out ordinary day-to-day activities'. An estimated three million disabled people live in Kenya, accounting for about 10% of the country's population. Kenya is party to several conventions relating to disability, including the 2006 Convention on the Rights of Persons with Disabilities, although it is yet to ratify its accompanying protocol. The Persons with Disabilities Act, enacted in 2003, prohibits discrimination in various sectors including education, employment, health and the provision of services in the public and private sector.

The law provides for the establishment of the National Council for Persons with Disabilities as the focal point for all issues relating to persons with disability. The KNCHR has taken up disability as one of its key areas of concern. Interestingly, the Independence Constitution made no direct reference whatsoever to disability. Protection of the rights of persons with disability is, therefore, inferred from general human rights-related provisions. In this regard, the old constitution sought to protect the fundamental rights and freedoms of 'every person in Kenya', presumably including the disabled. However, that provision, and the outlawing of discrimination on the basis of 'race, tribe, place of origin, colour, creed or sex', made no express or overt mention of disability. It has been argued that other references to disability in the Independence Constitution are in themselves derogatory and discriminatory. The Report on the State of Disabled People's Rights in Kenyacites the example of the section of the constitution which allows for the removal of the president from the Office of the President in the event that he 'is unable by reason of physical or mental infirmity to exercise the functions of that office'. The report argues that this could be construed to mean that those with physical and intellectual disabilities cannot hold office. The report further highlights section 34 of the constitution, which outlined the qualifications for election as a member of the National Assembly, which requires that a person shall not be qualified unless 'he is able to speak and, unless incapacitated by blindness or other physical cause, to read the Kiswahili and English languages well enough to take an active part in proceedings of the National Assembly'.

This provision raises two fundamental issues. First is the suggestion that members of the National Assembly must be able to speak. It discriminates against those who, by their disability, are unable to speak. The provision also fails to recognise or make provision for sigar

In the ninth Parliament, just one member with disability was elected. Of the twelve nominated MPs, not one is a person with disability. This is despite the specification in section 33 that the twelve nominated persons should represent special interests. The reality has been that the twelve seats, for nomination, are usually reserved as a reward for those loyal to the president as well as the elites around the president. On the whole, the representation of persons with disability in Parliament has been dismal. Those with disability generally find it difficult to compete against other candidates in various elections. As one parliamentary aspirant candidly put it, 'If you thought that winning a seat in Parliament was difficult for the average Kenyan, ask someone with disability'. Several factors have hindered the participation of disabled persons in the political process. The political landscape has generally been hostile to persons with disability. There were no affirmative action provisions in the old constitution to favour participation by disabled persons. Second, the financial cost attendant to candidacy is extremely high and way beyond the means of most disabled persons. Campaign costs run into millions of shillings. The third is security. Campaigns are generally risky, but this risk is compounded for the disabled. Finally, the stigma associated with disability comes into play during political campaigns. The disabled are viewed as lesser-class candidates for political office, a fallacy that is often perpetuated by political opponents.

Aside from these factors, candidates in the 2007 general elections, for example, had to physically present their nominations to the ECK. Since the ECK announced that it would 'receive nomination papers on a first-come-first-served basis', the International. n to this challenge, political parties did not nominate disabled persons to Parliament even though there was a provision that required political parties to nominate people to represent 'special interest groups', one of which is the disabled persons group.

Discrimination against persons with disability is also rife in other sectors of public life. Save for the KNCHR in which representation of persons with disability is ensured, in no other instances has there been a deliberate effort to include them. This is true of the civil service, the judiciary, the diplomatic service and all other arenas of public service.

The Constitution of Kenya 2010 outlines various measures aimed at ending discrimination against persons with disabilities. Specifically, a person with disability is entitled to be treated with dignity and respect, and to be referred to in a manner that is not demeaning. S/he is entitled to access educational institutions and facilities for persons with disabilities, and to receive materials that aid in overcoming challenges associated with disability. The state is required by law to give effect to these principles.

The constitution has also put in place measures to address some of these challenges. With regard to representation, persons with disabilities are guaranteed at least two seats (one man and one woman with disabilities) in the Senate. Their representation in the National Assembly is also implied in the requirement that political parties shall nominate twelve members to represent special interests, including disability. Parliament is also required to pass a law to promote the representation of persons with disabilities. Similarly, counties are required to ensure that their assemblies include persons with disabilities. The constitution has furthered the rights of people with disabilities, generally, and has laid on the state the burden of not only respecting these rights but also promoting them and ensuring the protection of persons with disabilities. Indeed, article 55 on progressive realisation, which provides that at least 5% of persons living with disabilities (PLWD) are elected or appointed, is so far the most radical proposal of protecting and promoting the rights of PLWDs, while article 100 provides that legislation shall be enacted to ensure that

PLWDs find representation in Kenya's Parliament.

Protection of minorities and marginalised groups

Minority communities and other marginalised groups were neither recognised nor protected in Kenya, until the promulgation of the Constitution of Kenya 2010. Laws and policies were especially silent in providing for these categories. The national population census, conducted every ten years, provided the basis upon which groups were classified as minorities (numerically) and marginalised (on the basis of both numbers and the lack of access to basic services). For this reason, census results have become highly politicised.

Statistics are increasingly used to point at how smaller groups are historically disadvantaged while others use the census figures to argue for recognition as distinct ethnic groups. Because of this, the number Article 56. oups captured in the census has significantly changed since the first post-independence census in 1969.

There are discrepancies in various records on the number of ethnic groups, and even minorities, in the country. The 1989 Population Census identified about 42 ethnic groups but its successor, the 1999 Population Census, did not provide any information or statistics on ethnic groups. The Constitution of Kenya Review Commission (CKRC) Report on Culture, published in 2005, named 51 ethnic groups. The 2009 census identified about 50 groups, but the categorisation is not based on Kenyan African groups only – it also includes people from other races resident in Kenya.

Even where the specifics of the ethnic groups were given in previous censuses, no statistics have been attached to the minority groups. This significantly impacted on the recognition and protection of minorities and marginalised groups. The numerically minor groups and the marginalised generally are afraid of domination by the large groups.

The fears of the minorities and the marginalised groups have roots in how ethnic identities,

as well as other identities, such as race, religion, or such other 'protected grounds' have been manipulated in the past to provide advantages to individual leaders. Those from numerically

large groups have used their numbers in the first-past-the-post (FPTP) electoral system to win elections and to subjugate or marginalise those that do not support them. This brand of politics has been used to entrench corruption and patronage in the public sector. It has led to continued abuse of the electoral process and undermined policies that would otherwise promote democratic governance.

Minority groups have agitated for protection of their rights for a long while. For example, the Terik, in a Statement to the Working

Group on Minorities, stated:We recommend that the government officially recognise the Terik people as an ethnic group by indication of a code number assigned to them for the purpose of registration of persons and identity, as is the practice for all

The Independence Constitution made no direct reference to ethnic minorities and marginalised groups. There were, however, some provisions of interest, such as the one outlawing discrimination on the basis of 'race, tribe, place of origin, residence or residence or other local connection, political opinion, colour, creed or sex'. Broadly, the former constitution outlawed discrimination against ethnic minorities and marginalised groups. However, no law has been enacted to give life to and provide for the enforcement of these provisions. Enforcement was therefore left to the courts, in the event of litigation.

The former constitution provided that nominated MPs should 'represent special interest groups',but that was politically understood to be those that the normal electioneering process failed to capture and represent. That is, political parties filled these seats with members who did vie for but did not win the elections. In a cind, the deaf, the physically disabled and the youth ... We hold that the Electoral Commission of Kenya (ECK) has a responsibility of identifying all categories and to ensure that the lists reach the political parties and other organs with the power to appoint ...

A further case was that of the Endorois, which was filed at the African Commission on Human and Peoples' Rights (ACHPR), where the community, borrowing from the United Nations' Declaration on the Rights of Indigenous Peoples, including the African Charter, took the Kenyan government to task in terms of respecting communal indigenous rights. The ACHPR ruled that Kenya was in violation of various articles of the African Charter and urged the Kenyan government to 'recognise rights of ownership to the Endorois and restitute Endorois ancestral land'. The Independence Constitution made provision for the representation of ethnic minorities and marginalised groups through the devolved system of government. It particularly addressed fear of hegemony and domination of racially and ethnically smaller communities by large ones. A Senate was established to cater for the interests of all groups. But the erosion of the devolved structure in the Independence Constitution, and the creation of a strong central government, downgraded the representation of ethnic minorities and marginalised groups.

The Constitution of Kenya 2010 is, however, clear in terms of defining marginalised communities and groups. With regard to the latter, article 260 provides that: 'marginalised group means a group of people who, because of laws or practices before, on, or after the effective date, were or are disadvantaged by discrimination on one or more of the grounds in article 27(4)', which therefore expands the groups to include not only those discriminated against by account of gender, race, or sex, but all the other protected grounds provided for in the article. The constitution defines marginalised communities as those that are numerically smaller, pastoralists, nomadic communities (whether settled or not), indigenous communities based on hunter-gatherer systems of livelihoods, and also those communities that are traditional and seek to preserve their unique cultures from possible assimilation. Further, the constitution has addressed the plight of marginalised groups and minorities in several ways. The preamble recognises ethnic and cultural diversity and the determination to live in peace and unity within the context of this diversity. The state is obligated to promote and protect the diversity of language in Kenya. Protection of the marginalised is also identified as an essential national value and a principle of governance. Additionally, the Bill of Rights contains provisions for affirmative action for groups that have been discriminated against in the past. The state is required to address the needs of, among others, members of minority or marginalised ethnic, religious and cultural communities. The state is required to institute affirmative action programmes designed to ensure that minorities and marginalised groups.

- Participate and are represented in governance and other spheres of life;
- Are accorded special opportunities in educational and economic fields;
- Are given special opportunities for access to employment;
- Develop their cultural values, languages and practices; and
- Have reasonable access to water, health services and infrastructure

In addition to these provisions, the constitution requires the representation of all groups in elective and appointed bodies. It requires political parties to have a national character, and outlaws the formation of political parties on the basis of religion, language or race. Party lists for elective positions should also reflect the diversity of the Kenyan society. Although the above provisions safeguard and promote the interests of minorities and marginalised groups, the constitution has, once again, entrenched the majoritarian electoral system, which has contributed to increased use of ethnicised electoral politics. This implies that minorities will continue to be disadvantaged. Proportional representation is not catered for, yet it would have addressed the problems of minorities significantly. Further, the presidential system has remained centralised. It will continue attracting political competition based on the alliances of numerically large groups, especially if the constitution does not engender the politics of state transformation.

Immigrants and refugees

Kenya currently hosts approximately 280 000 refugees, and has hosted many more since independence. The country is a signatory to a number of international instruments that address the refugee question, among them the Convention Relating to the Status of Refugees (CRSR) and its Protocol, as well as the OAU Convention Governing the Specific Aspects of Refugee Problems in Africa. In terms of domestic legislation, the Refugee Act (2007) provides for 'the recognition, protection and management of refugees'. Prior to the enactment of this law, the rights of refugees were entrusted to two acts: the Immigration Act and the Aliens Restriction Act. These laws, however, do not accord refugees the rights enshrined in the various international instruments. The Refugees Act seeks to domesticate the provisions of international law. Aside from the law, the constitution is silent on matters relating to refugees.

According to the United National High Commission for Refugees (UNHCR), by September 2011, Dadaab, the largest refugee camp in the country, had received more than 140 000 new refugees, predominantly Somalis. The refugee population shot up to 450 000 during the period, yet the three camps in Dadaab have a capacity for only 90 000 persons. In the same month the overall population of refugees and asylum-seekers in Kenya was 559 000 people. Against this surge, Kenya had closed its border with Somalia in January 2007 following the resurgence of armed conflict between the Ethiopian-backed Somali Transitional National Government fighters and the Islamic Courts Union militia. The government claimed that the closure was intended to stop the movement of Islamic Courts Union fighters from entering into Kenya. Amnesty International condemned this action in a public statement dated 15 January 2007, saying the border closure had forced the return of about 400 000 refugees into an unstable environment. Amnesty International called on

Kenya to comply with its obligations under international law, particularly the principle of non-refoulement, which is enshrined in the 1951 Refugee Convention. The Convention provides that:

> No contracting state shall expel or return a refugee in any manner whatsoever to the frontiers or territories where his life or freedom would be threatened on account of race, religion, nationality, membership of a particular social group or political opinion

The benefit of the present provision may not, however, be claimed by a refugee who there are reasonable grounds for regarding as a danger to the security of the country in which he is, or who, having been convicted by a final judgment of a particularly serious crime, constitutes a danger to the community of that country.

In this regard, the OAU Convention provides that 'no refugee shall be repatriated against his will'. Concerning the Somalia situation, the Refugee Consortium of Kenya (RCK) has argued that the right to seek asylum from persecution and life-threatening situations is an inherent human right, and Kenya's actions directly violated this right. The Consortium further pointed to the OAU Convention on Refugees, which stipulates that 'the grant of asylum to refugees is a peaceful and humanitarian act and shall not be regarded as an unfriendly act by any member state'. On this basis, the Consortium argues that the grant of asylum should be regarded as a humanitarian act that is geared towards saving lives.

Conclusion and recommendations

Kenya's citizenship laws provides for non-discrimination towards all people. But the practice has been diff Women Kenya's citizenship laws provides for non-discrimination towards all people. But the practice has been different. Women could not pass citizenship to their foreign spouses or children born out of the country under the old constitution. Border communities have experienced challenges as well as explained in earlier sections.

The Constitution of Kenya 2010 has, even so, addressed these challenges. It states that men and women can pass citizenship to their spouses and that anyone married to a Kenyan citizen can become a citizen, but of course with limitations. Dual citizenship is also provided for but with limitations for state officers. Those who renounced their citizenship can become citizens upon application. Application of previous laws had denied many people citizenship rights. It is therefore recommended that legislation should be introduced to give direction on how people can claim back citizenship lost under previous laws.

The new legislative framework for providing citizenship comprises gaps that can lead to arbitrary administrative actions, especially in providing for citizenship by registration. The following recommendations are made. That:

> The government pass legislation and policies to make it possible to confirm one's nationality from birth as stipulated in article 53 of the constitution.

> The government urgently facilitate work towards effecting sections 15, 16 and 17 of the Citizenship and Immigration Act (2012) on the identification and elimination of statelessness in Kenya. In so doing, the government must provide information and education to affected groups so that they are able to make informed choices.

> Kenya implements the Africa Committee of Experts on the RiInterview with K24 TV, November 2008. ghts and Welfare of the Africa (IHRDA) and Open Society Justice Initiative on behalf of children of Nubian descent in Kenya vs the government of Kenya.

> The citizenship determination board and the ministry responsible for citizenship work towards the objective determination of citizens, and

that the government eliminate procedures that seek mass vetting for communities because they perpetuate arbitrary discrimination.

The requirement that Kiswahili or any other Kenyan dialect be used to determine whether a person who applies for citizenship by registration is qualified or not be withdrawn; the law should be amended because it is arbitrary and leaves public officers to use their discretion to determine who qualifies for approval.

Participation in the policy process

Until the early 2000s, Kenya's space for political participation had been severely constrained. Citizens' participation in policy-making was also limited. The executive, and especially the president, as well as powerful bureaucrats, influenced and decided policy without consultation. The greater majority of the population was excluded from the policy process. A systematic emasculation of Parliament, the judiciary, civil society and the media during the one-party regime, constrained the space for civic engagement. The government curtailed fundamental rights and freedoms, such as the freedom of the press and media, the freedom to receive and impart information or ideas, and the rights to assemble, associate, demonstrate, picket and present petitions. Government critics were detained without trial and jailed on trumped-up charges by a thoroughly compromised judiciary, especially during the period of the one- party regime of President Daniel arap Moi (1978–1991), before the re-introduction of political liberalisation in 1991.

The return of multi-party democracy in 1991 gradually began to restore some respect for rights, although the continued leadership of the previous regime prevented consolidation of democratic gains. Citizens could now participate in the policy process in a more free and meaningful manner than in the past. The media also flourished and the number of print and electronic media increased. Heavy-handed government censorship declined but state owned media, the Kenya

Broadcasting Corporation (KBC) continued to exclude the views of government critics and opposition politicians in general. On the other hand, the private media provided some space to those who could not access state media, although self-censorship guided their practice. But the enhanced space contributed to building a movement for reforms led by civil society groups, including human rights and religious groups.

The change of government in 2003 further enhanced the space for the enjoyment of rights. The rights of expression, assembly and association were most widely enjoyed in Kenya in the period after the change in government. The media flourished and were actively critical of governance. Official censorship dramatically reduced, although cases of self-censorship grew as the private media aligned with the different factions of the ruling, but disintegrating, coalition. Divisions in the ruling coalition eroded the foundation for democratic governance. Some of these gains, however, rolled back as some factions within government consolidated their hold on power. Freedoms and rights began to be restricted again and space for public participation became constrained. In some instances, journalists were physically attacked and media houses publicly censured for what they would broadcast.

The post-2007 election violence had consequences for fundamental rights and freedoms. The government restricted media freedom, and the freedoms of association and assembly among others. A gradual process to restore these rights began only after the signing of the National Accord in February 2008. The Constitution of Kenya 2010 has further strengthened fundamental rights and freedoms.

Participation of citizens in policy-making is a hall mark of democracy. In article 10 of the Constitution of Kenya 2010, democracy aof governance. Further, public participation is given emphasis throughout the constitution. The legislature is open to the public; article 118 provides that: 'Parliament shall: conduct its business in an open manner, and hold its sittings and those of its committees, in public; and facilitate public participation and involvement in the legislative and other business of Parliament and its committees'. Article 119, further allows that a 'person has a right to petition Parliament to consider any matter within its authority, including enacting, amending or repealing any legislation'. Given these provisions versus the mandate of Parliament, it is clear that the constitution is anchored on the provision that 'the people may exercise their sovereign power either directly or through their democratically elected representatives'. Among the human rights and fundamental freedoms likely to confer greater ability upon the citizens to participate more meaningfully in policy processes are guarantees for freedom from discrimination; freedom of conscience, religion, belief and opinion; freedom of expression; access to information; and the freedom of association, assembly, demonstration, picketing and petition. Generally, the constitution promises more space for citizens' political participation.

Freedom of expression and the media

Everyone has got the right to freedom of opinion and expression, according to the Universal Declaration of Human Rights (UDHR) adopted in 1948. This right includes the freedom to hold opinions without interference, and to seek, receive and impart information and ideas through any media. Freedom of speech is also granted unambiguous protection in international law by the International Covenant on Civil and Political Rights (ICCPR).

Kenya's old constitution also guaranteed the freedom of expression but did not mention freedom of the media specifi . In fact, it limited fundamental rights and freedoms under circumstances that may allow violations of these rights.

Numerous laws regulate the media: that is, from mainstream media, media that broadcasts in vernacular languages, community media and even new media such as short-text messages and to social media such as Facebook, Twitter or personal blogs. These laws include: the Penal Code (Cap. 63); Copyright Act (Cap. 130); the Preservation of Public Security Act (Cap. 57); the Public Order Act (Cap. 56); the Films and Stage Plays Act (Cap. 222 of 1962); the Chief's Authority Act (Cap. 128); the Offi Secrets Act (Cap. 187 of 1968); the Armed Forces Act (Cap. 199); the Communications Commission of Kenya Act of 1998; the Kenya Broadcasting Act (Cap. 221 of 1998), the ICT Act of 2007 and the Media Act (2007).

Other laws that constrain media freedom include the Public Order Act, the Defamation Act, the Preservation of Public Security Act, and the Books and Newspapers Act. Infl politicians and business leaders, for instance, used the Defamation Act to sue publishers and bookstores that sold publications which they claimed had defamed them. The courts rewarded the politicians and imposed heavy fi on the bookshops and the media. This encouraged self-censorship in the media. The media are also restricted from giving any information related to national security. Generally, the government tends to use the notion of national security to prevent the media from broadcasting information that the government does not want the public to access. For instance, the ban on live broadcasting during the post-election crisis was defended in government circles as 'preserving national security'.

Violation of media freedom

One important legal attack on the press in 1994 was the prosecution for contempt of court of Bedan Mbugua and David Makali, editor and reporter, respectively, of The People, and of lawyer GBM Kariuki. The weekly paper had published an article quoting Mr Kariuki as saying that a Court of Appeal ruling in a case involving striking university lecturers 'reeked of state interference'. Despite the fact that the case was already concluded, this comment was deemed to be in contempt by the Court of Appeal – the same court which had made the criticised ruling. The three were given heavy fines, which Bedan Mbugua and David Makali refused to pay. They served five and four months in prison respectively. Ironically, the rare use of criminal contempt charges against the press only served to reinforce the original allegation that the judiciary is susceptible to pressure from the highest levels of government.

The key media regulators include the Media Council of Kenya, the Communications Commission of Kenya and the Kenya Film Censorship Board, although the Ministry of Information also exercises influence in all three. The key policy currently is the Information and Communication Technology (ICT) policy and several other sessional papers intended to create policy. The ICT Act, policy and strategy (2007) does not also address the development of community media and broadcasting in local languages. A report on the role of the media in the 2007 elections and their aftermath suggests that the government has not supported community media because of its fear of empowering the citizenry in ways that would challenge its hold on power, especially in demanding good governance. The government also prepared the Freedom of Information Bill (2006), which could have countered the Official Secrets Act and improved access to official information and governance, but it is yet to become law. Kenya is also a signatory to the African Charter on Human and Peoples' Rights and the Declaration of Principles on Freedom of Expression in Africa, which stipulates that any restrictions on the freedom of expression must be provided for by the law and must serve a legitimate interest that is necessary for a democratic society.

The media plays a crucial role in shaping a healthy democracy. Indeed, a vibrant media is the backbone of a democracy. Media makes the public aware of various social, political and economic activities happening within the state and also outside. Many consider the media as a mirror, which shows the public or strives to show the state the bare truth and harsh realities of life. The media has undoubtedly evolved and become more active over the years.

With regard to elections, the media assists the public, especially the illiterate, in making choices in the elections. The media, especially the vernacular FM radios in Kenya, have made a significant achievement in improving the awarenen filling the gaps identified and making the system of governance more accountable, responsive and citizen-friendly. Finally, information technology has enhanced information flow to people in all walks and spheres. The perfect blend of technology and media has opened the state to public scrutiny especially on issues of corruption in politics and society. The Constitution of Kenya 2010 has provided for a comprehensive Bill of Rights that anchors freedom of expression and freedom of the media. Every person has the right to freedom of expression, which includes the freedom to seek, receive or impart information or ideas, freedom of artistic creativity, academic freedom and freedom of scientific research. In the exercise of the

freedom of expression, every person shall respect the rights and reputations of others. However the constitution prohibits hate speech and the advocacy of hatred, ethnic incitement, vilification, and incitement to violence or propaganda for war.

Freedom of the media is guaranteed under the constitution, but it does not extend to promoting hate speech or engaging in violence. The constitution also forbids the state from exercising control over media and from penalising people because of their views expressed in the media. These provisions create opportunities for the increased participation of the media and citizenry. They are in line with the new national values and principles of governance that embed democracy and public participation in civic affairs.

Broadcast and other forms of electronic media have freedom to establish, subject to licensing procedures that are designed to ensure the necessary regulation of the airwaves and other forms of signal distribution, and are independent of control by government, political or commercial interests. In addition, state-owned media are now required to be impartial and to afford fair opportunity for the presentation of divergent views and dissenting opinions. This will address concerns about biases by state-owned media, especially during elections. If effectively enforced, the new constitution will insulate the media from state interference. For instance, in the past, police have brutally attacked journalists in the course of their duties at important events. In other instances, government agents have physically attacked media houses and confiscated their equipment. The case of the Standard Group raid is such an example. In March 2006, government agents raided the offices of the Standard Group's television station, Kenya Television Network (KTN), confiscated software allegedly containing what was termed sensitive information, and set the following day's newspapers on fire.

This interference notwithstanding, the space for the enjoyment of freedom of the media has considerably expanded in the past two decades. From independence to the early 1990s, Kenya had only one television and radio broadcasting station, the Kenya Broadcasting Corporation (KBC). It is state-owned and state-run. The government also owned the Kenya News Agency (KNA), which employed correspondents widely distributed across the country operating as officials of the Ministry of Information. But the private sector owned several vibrant newspapers. After the political and economic liberalisation policies of the early 1990s, the government removed some of the restrictions on the operation of print and electronic media stations and internet portals, which resulted in increased players and activity.

The media has also played an important role in policy-making in Kenya. With the advent of multi-party democracy in Kenya, there has been rapid growth of the media. The existence of many media houses – both electronic and print – has been critical in not only disseminating information but also providing a forum for debate on important public discourse. The media, for instance, played a big role in civic education in the period preceding the 2002 and 2007 general elections. The media has also been opening debates on subjects such as sex and HIV/Aids in the country. The result of such media campaigns has been the improved participation of people in discourses around the issue of HIV/Aids. This has promoted awareness and reduced both the prevalence and the stigma that was once associated with the disease.

However, not all media have contributed to enhancing space for democracy or contributed to policy-making. Makokhaargues that the media have only been agents of democracy insofar as they have remained unfettered by government control and free of the influence or even interests of financial capital. Foreign media and the privately owned media in Kenya played an important role in Kenya's democratisation, but at a price. The Nation Media Group, for instance, was denied frequencies and a licence for radio and television broadcasting. Those close to the government also established their own media houses to articulate government and ruling party positions. Powerful and influential elites began to control the media by taking positions on boards as dirrity. Whether private rough the boards and indirectly th his family. The other large company, Royal Media

Services, has more than a 50% share of all radio frequencies as allocated at 2007. Other companies owning television and radio stations also belong to politically and economically influential individuals.

There is a coupling of business interests in the media and political elites. However, the elites involved in this relationship are quite few. This suggests that the media is in the hands of a narrow political and economic elite who usually use it to articulate certain positions. They can influence the media through direct orders to their employees or indirectly by employing loyal editors or even by constituting in them a leadership that can articulate political ideals desirable and acceptable to them. Thus, it is not interference by the government alone that can proscribe democracy in the media; poor internal governance and self-censorship are also challenges that privately owned media face

Media regulation

The legal framework in Kenya has constrained media freedom. Before 2008, there was no policy to guide operations and licensing. At the beginning of the post-election crisis in 2007, the government banned live broadcasting on the basis that the media transmitted information that contributed to violence. Subsequently, in January 2008, the government formed a media monitoring unit to track live media broadcasts and pass the information to the statutory Media Council of Kenya (MCK), but little action was taken. It later formed a task force to investigate the conduct of the media in the elections and the post-election violence besides threatening to withdraw its support for the MCK. The government later introduced the Kenya Communications (Amendment) Bill (2008), which sought, among other things, to regulate media content. It gave the Minister for Internal Security powers to search media houses and allowed the government, through a council, to prescribe media programme content. Although it was passed into law, the media protested and Parliament repealed the contentious provisions.

The media has often shown open bias during election campaigns. Both the state media and private print and electronic media have tended to play partisan roles or to show bias in favour of certain parties and candidates. Recognising that fairness in electoral competition requires that candidates receive reasonable access to state and other media to deliver their arguments to the voters, the Electoral Commission of Kenya (ECK) published guidelines on access to the media during elections. The Commission directed the state media, the KBC, to comply with the requirements of the law that set it up, that is, to operate as 'a responsible media service provider that provides fair and impartial media institutions published a guidebook on election coverage in Kenya, which delves into the salient principles of journalistic ethics, including accuracy, impartiality and fairness. These guidelines were established to protect freedom of expression as well as to inform and educate the public on elections and assist citizens to make informed choices.

At election time, media houses are encouraged to be impartial and to provide equal accessibility to all parties. Election observers, however, routinely find state media to be biased. In 2007, the European Union Election Observer Mission (EUEOM) reported that the elections lacked a satisfactory degree of equitable coverage of the political parties on a number of radio and television stations, clearly in breach of the MCK's code on the coverage of elections. The mission reported that the state-owned KBC's English and Kiswahili language services on radio demonstrated a high level of bias in favour of the Party of National Unity (PNU) coalition of partners. Local language radio stations' coverage demonstrated a tendency to grant greater access to the parties and candidates with close links to the tribal and political affiliations of their listeners. The report of the Independent Review Commission on the 2007 Elections (IREC) says the media contributed a lot towards civic education and a high voter turnout, though they were neither impartial nor did they uphold professional standards. Some media houses allowed the publication of anonymous campaign advertisements, and the ECK found it difficult to control what the print and electronic media published or broadcast. Some of the media published hate speech and messages, which fuelled the election violence, as the IREC report says:

> '[H]ate speech ... characterised the 2007 ... elections on party rallies: text messages, emails, posters and leaflets were other vehicles of incitement'. And when travelling around the country, the Commission observed that most radio stations lacked professional journalists able to control an audience or regulate talks ... Words and phrases such as 'settlers', 'let's claim our land', 'people of the milk to cut grass', 'mongoose has come and stolen our chicken', 'madoadoa'and 'get rid of weeds' aired by radio FM stations ... and songs such as 'talking very badly about beasts from the west'... also aired on FM radio stations were received by Kenyans with mixed feelings

Although the government established the Office of Public Communications in 2004 to provide information on critical policy issues, its holder has had a difficult relationship with an independent, assertive and watchful media. The media have also had difficulties with the government following the exposure of corruption cases such as the multi-billion-shilling Anglo Leasing and Finance Company scandal, in which public funds was allegedly lost in a security supplies swindle. Armed police raided the Standard Group headquarters in 2006, beating journalists, burning newspapers, destroying property and confiscating equipment on the pretext that the media house was a threat to national security. Following a humiliating defeat in the 2005 referendum, the Kibaki administration created the MCK in 2007 to regulate the conduct and discipline of journalists and the media, and as function because the law restricted it from receiving funds from any government – local or foreign. Subsequently, the government finances and appoints representatives to the MCK. Kenyan journalists are also not free from government harassment. A Human Rights Practices Report (2004) lists incidents of harassment, intimidation and arrest of journalists in 2004. For example, on 24 September 2004, approximately 20 masked gunmen claiming to be police officers ransacked the offices of two newspapers, the Weekly Citizen and the Independent. The gunmen, who showed no identification, seized or destroyed computers, disks, scanners, printers and other office equipment, allegedly to prevent the publication of a government investigation into land-grabbing. Another example is the court case against East African Standard editor David Makali, for the alleged theft of a police tape containing the confessions by suspects in the killing of University of Nairobi lecturer Crispin Odhiambo Mbai. Police occasionally dispersed demonstrators to prevent criticism of the government and journalists covering such events were often present during the dispersal. According to the report, the government did not restrict access to the internet.

Once, KISS FM (owned by Radio Africa) made critical comments about the Minister for Water, who in turn sued two of the station's presenters. In this case, the constitutional court, relying on section 79 of the former constitution, stated that the rights to expression

do have limitations, found the two presenters liable, and hence referred the case to the Civil Division to proceed. The then Minister for Information and Communications, Raphael Tuju, subsequently created a media review board to decide what was acceptable on the public airwaves. The board, headed by the chair of the Kenya National Commission on Human Rights

(KNCHR), recommended regulation of the media on exposing matters of violence or sexually explicit content, but not other types of expression. The government reportedly rejected the report. Neither the lawsuit nor the work of the media review board resulted in any concrete changes. The Kenya Union of Journalists (KUJ), an umbrella trade union for journalists and civil society organisations, criticised the establishment of the review board as an attempt to restrict freedom of the press.

Towards the end of 2007, there were reports of an increased use of criminal libel laws by individuals closely associated Interview with Wanjiku Kiiru from Transparency International and Jane Marine from the CJPC, November 2008. s brought by the then Keiyo South MP Nicholas Biwott and State House Comptroller, Matere Keriri. Printers and distributors, as well as retail stores, were equally responsible and cautious with publishers and authors for libellous content. Individual journalists practised self-censorship because they experienced pressure or received bribes from influential persons to avoid reporting on issues that could harm the interests of persons or expose their alleged wrongdoings. There also were credible reports that journalists accepted payments to report or withhold certain stories, some of which were fabricated. The Books and Newspapers Act (Cap. 111, Laws of Kenya) requires publishers to post a bond of US$ 12 800 (approximately KSh 1 million) before printing any publication and to deposit copies of their newspapers and books with the Registrar of Societies within two weeks of publication. The law criminalises the selling and distribution of publications for which a bond has not been posted, and prescribes a fine of US$ 256 (approximately KSh 21 000) or six months imprisonment when in breach. Some members of the media were concerned that the government would use this law, as well as the Official Secrets Act, to stifle freedom of expression. However, the law is generally not strictly enforced. The regulatory framework for broadcast media continues to permit abuse and manipulation in the issuance, withholding and revocation of broadcast permits and frequencies. Despite licensing the East African Television Network (EATN) to broadcast, the government continued to block it from using its frequencies, as a case was pending in court at year's end. However, the government revised regulations and procedures during the year to streamline and regularise cumbersome licensing. Government then issued additional licences during the year, including an additional frequency to owners of the popular, but controversial KISS FM radio station.

Mbekeproposes a firm entrenchment of progressive laws governing the media and

communications in Kenya to provide impetus for steady growth of the media sector. He also proposes a language policy that deals with the use of hate speech in the media and particularly during the electioneering periods. He also recommends the need to integrate community media, public and private commercial broadcasting principles and regulatory frameworks in the broadcasting policy. A comprehensive communication policy would also need to address such issues as media ownership and control, programming and local content, education and training, and capacity-building for community media.

Freedom of association

FKanyinga, K, Mitullah, W et al. (2007) The Non-Profit Sector in Kenya: Size, Structure and Financing. Nairobi: Institute fordom of association is also recognised in the UDHR and International Labour Organisation (ILO) Conventions, and is also included in the constitution. The riers on every person the right to freedom of association, which extends to the formation, operation and continued existence of organisations. However, a person shall not be compelled to join an association of any kind.

For registration of associations and political parties, the constitution requires that any law that required for registration of any association should not be withheld, or withdraw that registration unnecessarily. It also provides for the right to a fair hearing if deregistration is an option. Further, article 36 provides that 'every person has the right to freedom of association, which includes the right to form, join or participate in the activities of an association of any kind' and prohibits any person from being compelled to join an association of any kind. One notable deviation from the former constitution is article 37 on the right to assembly, demonstration, picketing and petition – so long as such persons are peaceable and unarmed.

The Independence Constitution details the procedures for the registration of trade unions and associations, which include reasonable conditions relating to the requirements for entry into a register, the minimum number of persons necessary to constitute a trade union or association, and their qualifications. The law lays out conditions upon which registration may be refused. The Industrial Relations Charter, executed by the government, gives workers the right to engage in legitimate trade union activities. The Trade Unions Act (1952) regulates the formation and management of trade unions and employer organisations. The law provides that all workers, including those in the export processing zones (EPZs), are free to form and join unions of their choice. Workers numbering seven or more in an enterprise have the right to form a union by registering with the trade union registrar. If the registrar denies them registration, a union may appeal to the courts. However, the Kenya Civil Servants' Union, de-registered in 1980, was only re-registered on 10 December 2002.

The armed forces, the police, prisons service and administration police were explicitly prohibited from forming or joining unions. The security forces could not bargain collectively but had an internal board which reviewed salaries. Other groups that cannot bargain collectively, such as health sector workers, have associations, not unions, which negotiate wages and conditions that match the government's minimum wage guidelines. The law permits workers to go on strike, but they must notify the Ministry of Labour 21 days in advance. The ministry always refers disputes for mediation, fact-finding, or binding arbitration to the Industrial Court. In that period, any strike is illegal, thus removing legal prohibitions on employer retaliation against strikers.

Other civil servants can strike following the 21-day notice period (28 days for essential service workers, such as water, health, education, or air traffic control workers). The third law is the Labour Relations Act (2007), intended to regulate the formation and operations of workers' and employers' associations. The law streamlines the registraticonstitution. The constitution also attempts to recognise to a certain degree, civil society organisations (CSOs) and faith-based organisations (FBOs). It is, however, not clear on the representation of all religious groups in policy debates. The law, according to Criminal Justice Policy Coalition (CJPC), is selective on the issues that citizens can organise and/or represent. Civil societies in Kenya are required to pay taxesg with those issues they believe in and advocate for.

Access to information

Under the former constitution, a majority of Kenyans were excluded from accessing information deemed sensitive by the state. Such information included the health status of the head of state, numbers of the armed forces, troops lost in combat and findings of numerous commissions of inquiry. The main impediment to the release of this information is the Official Secrets Act, which prohibits dissemination of classified information to the public. However, the constitution stipulates that every citizen has the right of access to information held by the state; and any information that is held by another person that is required for the exercise or protection of any right or fundamental freedom. In addition, every person has the right to demand the correction or deletion of untrue or misleading information that affects that person. The state must also publish and publicise any important information affecting the nation.

Kenyans now have more access to information than ever before. The only existing gap involves what are referred to as 'official secrets' as provided for in the Official Secrets' Act and the only organs with the muscle and legitimacy to compel government to disclose the contents of such secrets are Parliament and the courts. This law should be repealed, or reviewed, to give constitutional impetus to the right to access information. Recently, the naming in Parliament of politicians and government officials involved in the illegal drugs trade, opening up the scandal of the National Health Insurance Fund (NHIF) in May 2012, the Mars Group pointing out budget inconsistencies and other incidents may be seen as a breakthrough in public access to sensitive information. In general, civil society (including the media) have used access to information to point out cases of corruption, and also use this information to enhance the accountability of the state to its people.

Civil society's participation in public policy development

In Kenya, civil society broadly refers to the autonomous and voluntary non-state associations. These associations are voluntarily formed to solve communal problems; their activities are voluntarily organised and are aimed at promoting social well-being – they are involved in the public good. These associations are widely spread and are, indeed, an important part of Kenyan culture. The country has a strong tradition of communalism in which people join together to address communal problems. Indeed, this spirit of doing things collectively is well recognised in the national development process and policies. Communities contribute resources to support local development initiatives and the government comes in to complement their efforts. But Harambeeappears not to play this role any more. The declining capacity of the state to deliver development, starting from the early 1980s, led to the state hijacking Harambee development projects to claim credit for delivery. This resulted in the increased politicisation of Harambee especially after local politicians started patronising local development projects. Nonetheless, communalism is the foundation of civil society development efforts in the country.

Civil society in Kenya is heterogeneous. It comprises non-governmental and autonomous groups organising outside of the control of the state. Operating in this space are non-governmental organisations (NGOs) undertaking development work, community based organisations (CBOs), religious or faith-based organisations (FBOs), trade unions, professional associations, self-help and numerous other voluntary organisations. Thus, civil society in Kenya is heterogeneous in composition and interests. These multiple interests also imply potential for divisions, especially with regard to engagement with the government.

Civil society's contributions to national development and the democratisation process in Kenya are enormous. Civil society groups are involved in service delivery activities, for instance, providing water, health care, and supporting community development efforts in addition to many other roles. There is no single sector of the economy that does not have the presence of CSOs. The government recognises NGOs as important partners in the development process. A national policy on NGOs' role in development is also in place. The policy seeks to facilitate the work of NGOs in the development space and to improve coordination in the sector. In the period between the early 1990s and the 2002 general elections, civil society was synonymous with the democratisation process in Kenya. From the early 1990s, civil society

fiercely fought against one-party repression in the country and led intense struggles for a return to multi-party democracy. It is during this period that the Kenya Human Rights Commission (KHRC) and the Citizens Coalition for Constitutional Change (4Cs) were formed to provide leadership in the struggle for democratic reforms. In providing leadership in the democratisation initiatives, civil society groups acted as the training ground for opposition politics and political leadership in general. Many political activists joined with civil society to articulate demands for change but later competed for elective posts to become MPs. The first leaders of opposition politics in the 1990s had a strong civil society background. Some were members of the National Conventional Executive Council (NCEC), formed in the earlier 1990s by different groups to front the struggle for constitutional reforms. As already mentioned, the NCEC later collaborated with different progress groups led by progressive MPs to intensify the campaign for constitutional reforms before the 1997 general election. This organic relationship with opposition politics continued throughout the 1990s until early 2000 when civil society urged and facilitated opposition parties that were keen on reforms to form a coalition so as to defeat the ruling party, the Kenya African National Union (KANU), which had been in power throughout the post-independence period. Civil society and opposition parties hoped to pursue democratic governance reforms once they got KANU out of power. It is this alliance of parties and civil society that won the December 2002 general election.

The coming to power of a new government with a strong civil society backing had several consequences for civil society. The government recruited experienced leaders from civil society thus weakening the sector. Recruitment of individuals who had sharpened skills for advocacy, lobbying and mobilising for reforms, depleted the sector of experienced leadership developed over many years. While a much more youthful leadership took over, it lacked experience to immediately lead the sector in the new political environment. Secondly, the government began implementing reforms and undertaking activities similar to those that CSOs were undertaking. The government spoke the language of rights, justice and equality. This hastened the formulation of several policies and the enactment of legislation that would promote and protect rights.

But the new opening contracted shortly thereafter. Incoherence within the new NARC government created space for the ancient regime to regain control of key institutions in government. Anti-reformers from the old regime and the bureaucracy re-grouped and captured the attention of the powerful faction within NARC. To get a parliamentary majority that would assist the government with passing legislation, this faction sought the assistance of the conservatives and the anti-reformers within Parliament. Gradually the language of rights, people's participation and democratisation receded into the distance Consultations with civil society diminished as did the engagement of civil society actors in government-led events. Civil society itself began to withdraw and/or to experience internal divisions over whether to engage with the government or not. Ethnic divisions soon emerged within the leadership. Some of these divisions, though ethnic, however, were also ideological. It was a division on whether to engage the state or remain autonomous. It was about whether to partner with a besieged state or criticise its new mission. Working with the government meant working with the faction that was influential and identified with one ethno-region part of the country the Mt. Kenya region. Yet working with the faction that was marginalised through these power struggles meant working with other ethnic groups or the Luo and Kalenjin who were most visible in this new struggle. This considerably weakened civil society's collective efforts that had contributed to the formation of the new government.

Kenyans for Peace with Truth and Justice

During the post-election violence, civil society played an important role in stopping the conflagration. CSOs influenced, through research and analysis of data, the making of important decisions under the KNDR process. Notably, Kenyans for Peace with Truth and Justice (KPTJ) undertook neutral and objective analysis of the situation and shared it broadly.

The KPTJ, a grouping of over 30 organisations and individual academics and researchers, began by observing that sustainable peace would be obtained only when the country resolved the question of justice and truth about the election result, truth and justice about the violence spreading in the country, and justice for victims of police brutality and the prevalent militia. The KPTJ provided strategic leadership on how to articulate the relationship between peace, justice and truth. Small groups such as Citizens for the Re-Counting of Votes and individual leaders of human rights and governance organisations joined to generate strategic synergy in the search for peace, truth and justice. The statutory human rights body, the KNCHR, provided the resources required, including space for meetings. 172 The organisation has since continued to monitor and engage with all mechanisms and processes arising from the crisis, with a particular focus on establishing truth and justice about the elections and the violence. Alongside the birth of the KPTJ was an equally progressive private sector grouping under the Kenya Association of Manufacturers. Its members comprised individuals who did analysis based on solid and objective data on the impact of the crisis on private businesses. Their analysis and views generally tended to coalesce with the views of the KPTJ. 173

KPTJ members also engaged in high level international advocacy to inform on the Kenyan crisis. This ensured that the international community was objectively informed about the happenings. As a result, the international community acknowledged neither the presidential election results as legitimate, nor the newly elected government until the coalition was formed.

During the mediation, the KPTJ also played an important part. Together with other civil society members such as the Kenya Civil Society Congress, religious groups and the international community, the two parties were compelled to mediate. The KPTJ later made recommendations on what the mediation process would prioritise to stop violence, bring justice to the victims and punish the off These informed the development of agendas for discussion at the KNDR

Beyond the KPTJ, there were other civil society initiatives too. Women's organisations formed an inter-ethnic caucus known as the Vital Voices. Ordinary citizens formed Citizens for the Recounting of Votes while the Centre for Multiparty Democracy (CMD), a political parties' formation, formed the National Salvation Forum to advise and buttress the political parties' efforts. Some of these groups coalesced around the progressives or had their efforts subsumed by the above initiatives. There were other groups that existed before the crisis. They too participated in responding to the crisis. They included the National Civil Society Congress and the Kenya Red Cross, among others.

There is a long and established tradition of civil society organisations engaging on diverse issues ranging from human rights to social justice and economic rights. The country has good examples of well-organised networks and collaborative efforts, such as the network on land issues, and the collaborative effort on constitutional reform. The Kenya Land Alliance (KLA), a coalition of several NGOs and CBOs working on land rights advocacy, mobilised various constituencies to collect views for an appropriate national land policy. Through advocacy and lobbying, the policy generally incorporated the KLA recommendations. Later during the constitution-making process in 2009, the KLA lobbied for the adoption of these recommendations. Chapter 5 on land and the environment broadly features articles from the National Land Policy.

Citizens have also impacted on the budget-making process in a significant way. They have played an important oversight role especially by scrutinising the budgeting process and final budget, a role which Parliament should be playing. In 2008, the Mars Group identified errors in the 2008 supplementary budget. The Ministry of Finance had to revise the budget. Two oversight committees of Parliament immediately ordered a probe and later recommended a forensic audit of the government budgeting and expenditure. Citizens have remained vigilant on the budgeting process. Related to this is the role of the Institute for Economic Affairs (IEA), which is a key institution in the national budget analysis in Kenya. The Institute, a non-profit policy think tank, has been involved in research on economic and public financial management policies. Their work contributed to the passing of the Financial Management Act (2008) and to the establishmet Office.

CSOs have influenced government policies in many respects. In 2009, a group of civil society mobilised under the 'Goro Goro Campaign on Food and Fuel Prices'. The campaign included street protests or advocacy, petitions to the relevant government bodies as well as threats of commodity and product boycotts. The government immediately called for the reduction in stable food and fuel prices and even began to consider the re-introduction of price control as a policy. Although the government is yet to introduce price controls, the impact of advocacy led to the reduction in prices.

In 2008, human rights groups led by the KHRC and the KNCHR called for a policy on heroes and memorialisation. The Ministry of Heritage formulated a policy which reflected some of the thinking of these two institutions. These institutions and many more have been involved in the formulation of the National Policy on Human Rights.

From the above examples, one may conclude that the space for engagement with civil society has experienced various challenges in the recent past. Notably, the failure of the government to implement fundamental reforms has resulted in some CSOs withdrawing their engagement from policy-making. All the same, the government continues to involve other actors in policy-making through consultations. However, there is no coherent and structured approach for engaging all actors. This appears to depend on the ingenuity of individual ministries and government departments. The space has thus remained open but the approach to engagement is ad hoc, both on the part of non-state actors as well as the government. Civil society participates in the process through lobbying for fairness, efficiency and inclusion in the allocation and distribution of public resources. In other instances, it is the practice to print draft bills, policies and budgets where the input of CSOs is invited.

Conclusion and recommendations
The state has dominated the policy-making arena. However, one of the major achievements of the 2010 constitution is the provision for public participation as an essential national value and principle of governance. Freedoms of association, expression and the media, although provided for in the

constitution, have been abused in many ways. Citizens' rights to protest are sometimes curtailed while government's intervention in the media industry through influential board members or even the owners of the media industry, contribute to self-censorship. Journalists

have been harassed and intimidated while on duty. Therefore, the recommendations include that:

- Kenya introduce and implement a policy framework to provide direction on people's participation in public affairs beyond participation through elected and appointed public officials at the national and county level of government. The policy framework should guide how citizens' views are collected and integrated into national policies, how the government provides feedback to the people, as well as what would be termed active, meaningful and effective participation of people in public affairs. The policy framework should establish organs through which people would participate in the making of key decisions at the local level.

- Government provides mechanisms for engaging civil society organisations in the policy-making processes.

- The executive introduces to Parliament a legislation promoting the enforcement of article 10 of the constitution on values and principles of governance. The legislation should provide guidelines on what the effective adherence to the values and principles of governance would be

- Government repeals laws that undermine media freedom and freedom of expression. These laws include the Official Secrets Act, the Public Order Act, the Preservation of Public Security Act and the Police Act, among others.

- The executive introduces a strong freedom of information law, and in particular a law that promotes media freedom and freedom of information. The law should also be forward-looking to address emergent issues such as social media, the use of hate language and speech, and the abuse of information communications technology, among others. The law should provide sanctions for public officers who do not provide the public with access to information.

- The executive introduces legislation giving effect to article 34(5) establishing a body (independent media commission) that is void of control by the government, political interests or commercial interests and a body to regulate the media industry. The legislation should guard the media industry from monopoly by a few individuals and corporations.

- Development partners provide support to civil society to monitor the government's efforts in promoting public participation in public affairs, and provide support for

- public litigation in this respect.

Elections

Elections are key to citizens' participation in political processes. In order for elections to be credible, legitimate and a meaningful exercise of choice by citizens, they have to take place in an environment in which fundamental rights are protected. Kenya has held regular and periodic elections since independence in 1963. At independence, an independent election commission was established to preside over elections. However, this commission's power was subsequently taken over by the executive arm of the government. Elections held between 1969 and 1988 were, therefore, presided over by a civil servant in the Attorney General's office who held the title of 'supervisor of elections'. The Section 41(9) of the former constitution of Kenya.

Despite sections 41(9), 99(3) and 104 of the former constitution of Kenya, the ECK was disbanded. Visit http://www. Commission of Kenya (ECK) presided over elections between then and 2007. Following the post-2007 election violence, the Independent Review of the 2007 Elections Commission (IREC), established to investigate the electoral basis of the violence, recommended that the ECK be disbanded and another one be established in an accountable and transparent manner. The coalition government disbanded the ECK in November 2010 and formed the Interim Independent Electoral Commission (IIEC). The IIEC conducted the by-elections and the referendum on the new constitution held in August 2010. As already mentioned, the constitution provided for establishing a new and independent electoral body. The Independent Electoral and Boundaries Commission (IEBC) was established in November 2011.

Kenya's uses the first-past-the-post (FPTP) electoral system. Each political party is entitled to put forward candidates to contest in an election year. The candidate who gets the most votes is declared the winner. A candidate can thus win by a single vote.

There have been eleven general elections in independent Kenya – in 1963, 1969, 1974, 1979, 1983, 1988, 1992, 1997, 2002, 2007 and 2013. The 2013 election was the first election under the 2010 constitution. A common thread running through these elections is their regularity, which has been used by successive regimes to legitimise their reign.

The first polls held in 1963 were multi-party elections, while the subsequent five elections between 1969 and 1991 were held under a de facto (1969–82) and de jure (1982–91) one-party system. Overall, five elections were held (1969, 1974, 1979, 1983 and 1988) which were basically 'KANU-only' elections. Under these circumstances, no presidential contest was held. The leader of the sole party was always assured of automatic nomination. Hence the only electoral contest of consequence was over who would represent each parliamentary constituency and civic locality. Consequently, mobilisation during this period was essentially local and hence fashioned along tribal and clan lines. The candidates' electoral arithmetic began and largely ended with calculations of tribal and clan support. During this period, most voters rated their members of Parliament (MPs) on how well they conveyed their views to the government as well as on their capacity to initiate development projects and attract government benefits for the constituency.

Generally, the one-party era elections oscillated from being semi-competitive to non- competitive. The elections held between 1969 and 1988 under the one-party regime were semi-competitive with elections that could pass as the party primaries serving as general elections. These elections were not free: they were conducted by a supervisor of elections from the Attorney General's office, assisted by the Provincial Administration whose officers tended to assist government-friendly individuals to win. They only allowed free and fair election in constituencies where the government did not have an interest in any candidate.

The multi-party elections that followed in 1992, 1997, 2002, 2007 and 2013 have generally taken an ethnic and regional anround locally defined ethnic communities), the transition to multi-party politics brought a shift to a regional pattern of ethnic bloc-voting and alliance-building. This can mainly be attributed to the contest over the presidency, which was not a factor in any elections until 1992.

Legal and institutional framework

The principle of free and fair elections is legally enshrined in Kenya's constitution and provided for in the Elections Act (No. 24 of 2011), and, among other laws, codes of conduct and regulations set up by the Electoral Management Body (EMB). In addition, Kenya has signed and Ratified international and regional treaties which contain standards on the conduct of democratic elections – the Universal Declaration of Human Rights,the International Covenant on Civil and Political Rights,the Convention on the Elimination of All Forms of Discrimination

Against Womenand the African Charter on Human and Peoples' Rights. Furthermore, Kenya has agreed to, and endorsed, the AU Principles Governing Democratic Elections in Africa. Previously, there were numerous laws in Kenya relevant to the conduct of elections. In addition to the former constitution, elections in Kenya were governed by the National Assembly and Presidential Elections Act,the Local Government Act,the Election Offences Act,the Kenya Broadcasting Corporation Act,the Public Order and the Preservation of the Public Security Act,the Registration of Persons Act,the Police Act,the Societies Actand the Penal Code. The now dissolved ECK also issued supplementary regulations on the registration of electors, election petitions and election procedures. In general, this patchwork of election-related laws provided a workable basis for holding elections by the end of 2007.

The former constitution established the ECK and stipulated its functions. It also provided for the election of the president and members of the National Assembly, as well as citizenship, which provides the basis for recognition as an elector. The National Assembly and Presidential Elections Act provided for registration of electors, declaration of vacant seats, elections and election petitions and expenses. The Local Governmentge and nationality. The Societies Act provides for the registration and control of societies and is the legislation under which political parties were registered prior to 2008. The Political Parties Act (No. 11 of 2011) provides for the registration, regulation and financing of political parties. It succeeded the Political Parties

Act (No. 10 of 2007), which had succeeded the Societies Act in respect to how parties were registered and regulated.

Article 81 of the constitution lays a firm legal and institutional foundation for the electoral

system in Kenya. It outlines the general principles for the electoral system, with include free and fair elections conducted by an independent body and administered in a neutral and accountable manner. Article 88 of constitution also provides for the establishment of the IEBC, whose key mandate is: to conduct and supervise referenda and elections to any elective body or office established under the constitution; the delimitation of electoral units; the registration of voters; voter education; and the facilitation of election observation and evaluation. All election laws were consolidated into the Elections Act (2011). The Independent Electoral and Boundaries Commission Act (2011) provides for the functioning of the new electoral management body.

Election administration

The ECK was created to manage and conduct elections. Before the 1992 elections, the electoral process was steered by a department in the Attorney General's Office and a civil servant, the supervisor of elections, managed elections. However, in 1992, the former constitution and the elections law were amended to establish an Election Management Body (EMB) that is independent of the Attorney General's office, with powers to direct and manage the entire electoral process. The ECK had a chairman and between four and 21 members appointed by the president for renewable five-year terms. Further, the constitution described the role and functions of the ECK to ensure that it would be the only body legally mandated to conduct elections. Accordingly, the ECK was responsible for the registration of voters, including the maintenance and regular revision of the register, and directed and supervised the presidential, National Assembly and local government elections. It promoted voter education throughout Kenya and was required to have such other functions in law necessary to conduct 'free and fair' elections. The ECK, created in 1992, was envisaged as an independent body. A set of legal provisions accompanied the establishment of the ECK which assured its independence.

The old constitution states that 'in the exercise of its functions, the commission shall not be subject to the direction of any other person or authority'. While the defunct National Assembly and Presidential Elections Act required members and staff of the ECK to serve impartially and independently, andIREC (2008) Report of the Independent Review Commission on the General Election of 2007 held in Kenya on 29 December 2007,, any public officer, any political party, any candidate participating in an election, or any other person or authority', the ECK of 2007 was severely influenced by the Party of National Unity (PNU) and its candidate, former President Mwai Kibaki. Whereas there were other provisions to secure the tenure of the commissioners and protect them from arbitrary removal from office, it has been observed above that the ECK commissioners were fired unilaterally in November 2008 through a parliamentary process supported by the executive, following recommendations from the IREC report. The ECK's reliance on the government for funds undermined its independence. Indeed, the law establishing the ECK did not state the sources of finances for the ECK, nor did it say

whether it had powers to raise funds for itself from any other source. The government decided how much to give the ECK, thus greatly jeopardising its independence. Inadequate funding from the government often resulted in serious ineffectiveness.

Another hindrance was that the ECK did not have physical coordinating offices at the district or constituency levels, thus derailing efforts to update itself on the electoral environment. The implication here was that field staff recruitment was done on a part-time basis, that is, for the election year only. The ECK, to this end, trained staff in the field on a crash programme, thus creating opportunities for mistakes. To address some of these challenges, a proposed law contained in section 3(1) and (2) of the Statute Law (Repeals and Miscellaneous Amendment) provided for the ECK to recruit its own staff.

The manner in which ECK commissioners were appointed also undermined its independence. By the time the country was going to the polls in 2007, the ECK had 22 commissioners who could take decisions by a simple majority. While President Kibaki acted in line with the constitution at the time when appointing new commissioners before the 2007 elections, he went against the spirit of the Inter-Parties Parliamentary Group (IPPG) agreement by not consulting with the opposition parties. According to the IPPG of 1997, the opposition was entitled to appoint ten commissioners to the ECK. Kibaki himself had helped to negotiate the IPPG agreement with Moi in 1997 in order to guarantee a more balanced ECK.

President Kibaki did not honour this agreement. Part of the 'gentleman's agreement' was for political parties with representation in Parliament to choose members for appointment to the electoral commission according to their strength in Parliament. The president's decision to appoint the commissioners without consulting the opposition between 2003 and 2007 undermined public confidence in the electoral authority. The new commissioners were perceived as biased in favour of the president. In addition, most of them lacked experience in election administration. Kibaki's unilateral decision to appoint ECK commissioners thus undermined the public's confidence in the electoral body.

Constituency delimitation

Because of the FPTP electoral system and voting patterns that follow ethnic lines, the delimitation of electoral areas is politically sensitive. The former constitution and the law empowered the ECK to review parliamentary constituencies and civic electoral wards. Yet, Parliament retained the power to determine the minimum and maximum number of constituencies into which the country could be divided. There were 210 parliamentary constituencies in Kenya before the promulgation of the 2010 constitution. Although the former constitution provided that the constituencies should, as near as possible, have equal numbers of residents, it also allowed the ECK to consider certain peculiarities such as community interests, population size, and physical infrastructure among others. The 210 single member constituencies varied greatly in population and size. The least populous constituency then, Lamu East, in Coast Province, had 12 866 registered voters while the most populous, Nairobi's Embakasi, had 249 903.

The ECK could review constituency numbers and boundaries at intervals of not less than eight years and not more than ten years or whenever directed by Parliament through a law. At the end of the review, the ECK could make an order to alter the number, boundaries or names of constituencies to the extent that it considered desirable, as long as it remained faithful to the constitution. In May 2002, the High Court ruled that the constituency boundaries as determined by the ECK were not in accordance with the principles set forth in the constitution and asked the ECK to address them. The ECK proposed that the number of constituencies be increased for the 2007 elections, but Parliament failed to approve that proposal. On 3 December 2007, the ECK announced that the realignment of 15 constituency boundaries had been concluded in line with administrative boundaries, but this exercise only concluded some administrative adjustments and could not substitute a constituency boundaries review. Consequently, the 2007 elections were conducted using the same constituency boundaries as those in 2002, thus violating the constitutional principle as well as the ICCPR standard of equal representation of voters. Without that approval, there was nothing that the ECK could do. Evidently the ECK's ability to competently handle the electoral process in 2007 was brought into disrepute as a result of the anomalies that arose. The most glaring evidence of the ECK's incompetence in handling the 2007 elections were the statements by the ECK chairman to the effect that, first, he had no control over the activities of his staff, and, second, that he was unable to get in touch with them when delayed results seemed not to be forthcoming. Furthermore, following the ECK announcement of the presidential election results, on 31 December 2007, four ECK commissioners (Jack Tumwa, David Alfred Ndambiri, Samuel arap Ng'eny and Jeremiah Matagaro) called for an independent inquiry into whether any of their colleagues tampered with the presidential election results before they were announced. The position taken by these commissioners, coming so soon after the announcement of the results further eroded the credibility of the ECK. In addition, on 2 January 2008, ECK chairman Samuel Kivuitu admitted that he had announced the results under pressure from the PNU and the Orange Democratic Movement-Kenya (ODM-Kenya), and that he was not sure whether President Kibaki had won the election fairly.

Voter registration and participation

Every Kenyan citizen 18 years of age and older, who possesses an identity card or Kenyan passport, may apply for registration as a voter. Persons can be disqualified from registering as

a voter if they suffer from insanity, are bankrupt, or have been convicted of an election offence. Only those citizens who produce national identity cards or Kenyan passports and voter identity cards can be allowed to vote at presidential, parliamentary and civic elections.

For the first multi-party elections in 1992, the ECK conducted a national registration drive. The data of registrants was entered in the black book, from which mimeographed lists were derived for use at the polling stations. In 1997, the ECK computerised the registers using optical mark recognition forms. The 2002 elections were based on the 1997 register, updated in registration drives in 2000, 2001 and 2002.

In June 2002, amendments to the constitution introduced a permanent or rolling voter registration. Although continuous voter registration is carried out throughout the year at district level, the ECK organised a yearly 30-day drive with voter registration taking place in centres and registration units where polling stations would be located on election day.

The ECK carried out the 2007 voter registration drive in March, followed by a 30-day inspection period in April. The ECK conducted a second voter registration initiative from 11 June to 31 July 2007. These two voter registration drives produced an additional 1. 8 millioIED (2008) Pre-Election Observation: Registration of Voters in 2007: An Audit, 2007; IREC (2008) Report of the Independentdiness for the upcoming elections. The Vijana Tugutuke Ni Time Yetu (Arise, young voters, it's our time) voter education campaign, in which the ECK, the Institute for Education in Democracy (IED), the Redykyulass Group and Trublaq Limited were partners, contributed significantly to the heightened levels of awareness – especially among youth under

35 years of age, who now form a significant percentage of the national voters register.

A study published by the IED commended the ECK for the increased number of voter centres that had enhanced people's access to registration. The study revealed that the ECK had done a commendable job in creating and increasing polling stations that not only enhanced accessibility to registration stations but also eased the accessibility of polling booths. The number of registered voters has increased each election year since the re-introduction of multi-party politics in 1991, while voter turnout has been on the decrease, only registering an increase in 2007 as a result of the competitive nature of those elections. In 1997, a total of 8 967 569 Kenyans registered as voters. In the 2002 elections, only 70% (10 451 150) of the eligible voters (15 959 484) registered, and of those, only 5 969 181 (57%) voted. Men constituted 53. 78% (5 620 634) while women were 46. 22% (4 830 003). A total of 14 296 180 voters registered for the 2007 elections, with 7 559 570 (52. 9%) men and 6 736 610 (47. 1%) women. A large percentage of the registered voters (68. 8%) ranged between 18 and 40 years, which represented 71% of the total eligible voter population (19. 8 million aged 18 years and older who had been issued with national identity cards). In 2013, a total of 14 388 781 registered as voters. This represented about 80% of the total number that the electoral management body had projected to register.

The voter registration for the 2013 general election was the first to use new technology, the biometric voter registration toolkit. The use of the technology helped in compiling a relatively clean voter register compared to the previous ones. Double registration and the existence of dead voters in the register were some of the problems eliminated through the use of the new technology. Still, it did not mean the registration was without a problem. A petition against the presidential results was filed immediately after the election was held on 4 March 2013, and the petitioner identified the lack of a final register as a challenge that faced the election. The electoral body had failed to produce the final register, yet a final register was critical for a closely contested election in which a winner was required to have 50% plus one vote.

Table 5: Voter turnout in elections

Elections	Registered voters	Voter turnout	Percentage
1992	7 956 328	5 437 769	68
1997	8 967 569	6 173 171	64
2002	10 451 150	5 969 181	57
2007	14 296 180	9 877 028	69
2013	14 388 781	12 330 028	86

It is instructive that the ECK was not responsibNAPEA, section 5. cards, yet those are requisite documents for one to register as a voter. That duty fell on the Ministry of Immigration and Registration of Persons. The fact that the ECK had no control over the issuance of ID cards means that it had no control over one of the most critical stages of ensuring that the elections were free and fair, namely the registration of voters, which would have accorded every eligible person a chance to take part in that important civic exercise. Delays in the issuance of identity cards greatly affected the registration of voters.

The lack of national identity cards remains a major impediment to voter registration for persons aged between 18 and 22. The limited resources and extremely bureaucratic organisation of the Registrar of Persons led to serious delays, which mostly affected young applicants. In general, the average waiting time for a new identity card was reported to be three months. Certain minority groups also experienced difficulties in acquiring identity cards that would have enabled them to register as voters. The Kenyan electoral system also disenfranchises other voters who already have identity cards and voter's cards, including prisoners, officers serving in the Kenya Army, the Kenya Police, and persons living abroad, because of the absence of electronic voting.

Prior to election day, the ECK recognised that there were high instances of multiple registrations and took corrective action, resulting in a significant reduction of such entries. However, despite their commendable effort, over 400 000 duplicated names remained on the list. These names were identified and placed on a special list, which was to be sent to each polling station. The problems of multiple registrations were attributed partly to the failure of the registration machinery to cancel the former registrations of people who had been transferred and those who had made corrections to their particulars

Voter turnout is the commonest means of assessing participation in a democracy. The 27 December 2007 elections were the most seriously and closely contested in Kenya's history. According to official election results, 9 886 650 Kenyans voted. This figure is equivalent to a 69% national voter turnout and represented the highest turnout ever experienced in Kenya until 2007. It was an increase from the previous years, which had registered a continuously declining figure since the re-introduction of multi-party politics in 1992. In 1992, the voter turnout was 67. 5%, 64. 2% in 1997 and 57. 2% in 2002. The 2005 referendum witnessed the lowest turnout, at 54%.

A new voter register was prepared after the post-2007 election violence upon the recommendation of the Kriegler Commission (IREC). That recommendation followed the IREC's finding that some people had voter's cards but couldn't find their names in the register, while some had died but their names were still on the list of voters. 10.

The newly-formed IEBC, established after the passing of the new constitution, attempted to compile a new voter's register using biometric voter registration (BVR) technology. However, by early November 2012, they had not begun the process. The process to procure the BVR kits begun in June 2012, but the IEBC cancelled the tender process in August of the same year after their tender committee members disagreed on which company to award the tender.

The IEBC had shortlisted four international companies but members disagreed on which company to award the tender, amidst allegations that some of the companies had bribed government officials. Some of the shortlisted companies had been banned from doing business with the government because of having been involved in corrupt practices, but were shortlisted nevertheless. The IEBC cancelled the tender process and announced it would resort to a manual voter registration process instead.

There were public protests and complaints that the manual voter register would not guarantee credibility of the elections because it was vulnerable to manipulation, as had been found out by the Kriegler Commission. Following these complaints, the executive held a meeting with the IEBC after which both agreed that the government should assist the IEBC to procure the BVR kits. The government contracted a Canadian firm to provide the kits. But that was not without controversy and allegations of corruption involving the IEBC and other government officials. There were allegations that initial attempts to provide the BVR kits had failed because officials had demanded payments from the firm that won the tender. There were also allegations that the kits were provided at a high cost. They were supplied later than originally scheduled, which left little time to train officials on how to use them. Following the use of BVR, the IEBC used electronic poll books during election day in the March 2013 general election. However, many of those failed to function at some point. The domestic Elections Observation Group (ELOG) reported that its parallel vote tabulation indicated that the electronic polling book malfunctioned or failed at some point during the voting in over half (55%) of polling stations in the country. Where the polling book failed, the polling stations resorted to manual voting, which was what the country had been trying to avoid.

Voter education

The ECK was mandated by the former constitution and the law to promote voter education. The electoral body undertook that responsibility with government funding and in strategic partnership with the international donor community as well as civil society. Civil society groups, political parties and candidates, media and religious institutions also take up the task to carry out civic education, even though the onus, by law, lies with the ECK.

The 1992 elections were the first since independence to be held after concerted efforts to conduct civic education. Since then, CSOs, NGOs, political parties, religious organisations and the media have been involved in voter education. In 1992 and 1997, the ECK instituted voter education campaigns, but these initiatives were supplemented by more elaborate programmes mounted by local NGOs, CBOs and religious organisations. The 2002 and 2007 voter education drives were undertaken in collaboration with the ECK. In the run-up to the 2002 elections, voter education was implemented under the aegis of the National Civic Education Program (NCEP): both NCEP I and II were two-year projects that started in 2001 up to 2004. Some 69 CSOs were involved. The NCEP promoted general awareness of democratic principles, good governance and constitutionalism while contributing to the consolidation of a mature political culture. In the run-up to the 2007 elections, the ECK conducted a very comprehensive voter education programme funded by the government and the United Nations Development Programme (UNDP). The programme aimed to and succeeded in increasing participation in the electoral process, particularly among women and other marginalised groups. The programme also sought to inform voters' choices, reduce electoral violence and increase voters' knowledge as to when, where and how to vote. The ECK contracted CSOs countrywide to carry out its voter education campaign. Some 40 CSOs (NGOs and faith-based organisations) were selected to facilitate the programme. These CSOs targeted the general public, women, young people and religious leaders. For instance, the IED launched an ambitious voter education campaign – Vijana Tugutuke – targeting youth who had previously shown extreme apathy towards elections. Consequently, a large percentage of the new voters that registered in 2007 consisted of young people. Despite these comprehensive voter education programmes, there has been limited impact since elections continue to revolve around known personalities, and Kenyans tend to value ethnic affinities above civic virtue.

Several players provided voter education for the 2013 general election. These included the Uraia Trust Programme focusing on civic engagement, and the Kenya National Integrated Civic Education Programme (K-NICE), which was a partnership between civil society groups and the government, with support from development partners. The programme succeeded in motivating citizens to participate in the implementation of the constitution. Others included media campaigns such as Uongozi, an initiative of Inuka, the Nation Media Group in partnership with USAID, UK-Aid and a number of other donors. The programme played a major role in encouraging Kenyans to participate in the electoral process in a positive way. Besides these initiatives, there were regular IEBC talk shows in the media.

The electoral system

Kenya uses the first-past-the-post system (FPTP), which is essentially a winner-takes-all scenario. Elections are, therefore, won or lost by a simple majority, regardless of the number of registered voters in a constituency who turn out on polling day to cast their ballots. FPTP belongs to a class of electoral systems with similar characteristics that are referred to as majoritarian or plurality- majority systems. It is the least complicated of all electoral systems. Individual candidates are nominated and voters invited to place a mark against one name on the ballot. The candidate who receives the highest number of votes is declared the winner.

According to the Independence Constitution, the president could only be directly elected by a popular vote, and had to fulfil three criteria before being duly declared as elected: first, he/ she had to be elected as a member of the National Assembly; second, he/she had to receive the highest number of votes in the presidential contest, and third, he/she had to receive a minimum of 25% of the valid votes cast in at least five of the eight provinces. If no candidate met all these requirements, a second round would take place between the two candidates with the highest number of valid votes. In addition, presidential candidates were to be citizens of Kenya, at least 35 years old and registered in a constituency as a voter for elections to the National Assembly. No person could be elected as president for more than two terms. In the parliamentary elections, voters elected one person per constituency by a simple majority. There were 210 electoral constituencies. Another twelve MPs would be nominated by political parties, proportional to their strength in the new Parliament. Candidates for member of the National Assembly had to be Kenyan citizens who had reached the age of 21 years, had been nominated by a political party, registered in a constituency as a voter, could speak and, unless incapacitated by blindness or another physical disability, read Kiswahili and English to a proficient level to take an active part in the proceedings of the National Assembly. Although the requirements were largely reasonable, there were some overly restrictive qualification criteria on certain categories of persons. Independent candidates, for example, were not permitted to stand for any election in Kenya, a regulation that was at variance with international standards.

A person was not qualified to be elected as an MP if, at the date of his or her nomination for election, he or she owed allegiance to a foreign state, had been sentenced to death or imprisonment for a term exceeding six months. People judged to be of unsound mind through a judicial process, undischarged bankrupts and those who had an inteElectoral Commission of Kenya (1998) 1997 General Elections Report. Nairobi: ECK. rest in a contract made with the government of Kenya or held an office in the public service, armed forces, or a local government authority, were also not be eligible for candidature FPTP electoral systems have been favoured on three grounds: first, single member constituencies retain a link between voters and their representatives; second, they funnel the party system of a country, and thus voter choice, into a competition between two broadly-based political parties; and third, they give rise to a strong opposition in Parliament. Despite their widespread use, however, FPTP systems are often exclusionary: they exclude smaller parties and communal minorities from fair representation and lock women out of Parliament. In new democracies, FPTP systems are also criticised for encouraging the development of political parties based on ethnicity or region. In Kenya critics have argued that FPTP has entrenched ethnic patterns of voting to such an extent that results of presidential elections tend to mirror ethnic settlement patterns, and that those who win neglect numerically smaller groups because they do not have the numbers to help in tilting election results. Political parties themselves are not institutionalised because they form and fragment along ethnic lines. Because of this, there have been arguments for mixed member proportion (MMP) and proportional representation (PR). MMP or PR will influence the way parties and political elites behave because the system will encourage them to seek support in many regions. This has the potential of institutionalising political parties. The system also gives incentives to party leaders to couch their political discourses in a manner that endears them to many regions and groups.

Between 1993 and 1997, there was concerted effort on the part of CSOs and sections of the political opposition to have more changes introduced in the electoral system to make it fair. The system could not allow the opposition to win because the ruling party used state resources to divide the opposition. With many opposition political parties competing against the ruling party, the latter was guaranteed to win. This did not allow the opposition to feel it could win at any time. On the whole, the movement for change in electoral laws was a reaction to the experience the political opposition had gone through during the first multi-party elections in 1992 and which had demonstrated that, unless changes were introduced before the 1997 elections 'to level the playing field', there would be no meaningful contest between the opposition and the ruling party during the second multi-party elections.

Largely due to a lack of consensus on key issues among CSOs and the opposition parties, no changes had been effected four months prior to the 1997 elections. And when the said changes did come, they would turn out to be compromises reached between MPs and the less radical CSOs. Therefore, as would be expected, the changes were not as comprehensive as the radical civil society movement had been pushing for. This Inter-Party Parliamentary Group (IPPG) Accord, nonetheless, produced some laws and introduced important administrative reforms that supported the 1997 general elections. The ruling party won again and the opposition and civil society began, once more, the struggle for comprehensive constitutional reforms

The gentleman's agreement 'in lieu' of constitutional reforms

The Inter-Party Parliamentary Group (IPPG) introduced some fundamental changes that greatly altered the electoral playing field. The reforms were of a constitutional, statutory, penal and administrative nature and were intended to level the political playing ground and repeal laws that hitherto denied Kenyans liberty. Among the changes introduced prior to the 1992 and 1997 elections include:

- Membership of the Electoral Commission was increased from eleven to 21; the president was to fill the ten vacancies from a list submitted to him by political parties proportional to their parliamentary strength.

- The twelve nominated MPs hitherto appointed by the president were to be named from a list submitted by parliamentary parties proportional to their parliamentary strength.

- Campaigns were to be managed exclusively by the Electoral Commission with no interference from the Provincial Administration.

- The Public Order Act was amended as follows:

- All political rallies and processions in public places would henceforth require only prior notification to the local police.

- Meetings of political party organs called exclusively to discuss party matters would not require notification. 'Meet-the-people' tours would not require notification.
- The police would only stop a meeting or a procession where there was clear, present or imminent danger of a breach of peace or public order.
- Detention without trial was scrapped.
- The section of the Public Security Act dealing with sedition was repealed.
- The Kenya Broadcasting Corporation (KBC) Act was amended to ensure that the Corporation kept a fair balance in all respects in allocation of broadcasting hours between different political viewpoints.

The effect of the IPPG reforms was put to the test on numerous occasions. In the majority of the cases, its provisions were implemented. The behaviour of the then ruling party, KANU, towards the opposition did not change even after the IPPG reforms package. KANU continued to behave as if the opposition parties had no right to free political participation. The government ensured that the provisions of the IPPG package, which had the effect of levelling the playing field, were wilfully ignored. For instance, equal coverage was not provided to all political parties during the 1997 and 2002 elections. The KBC continued to operate as the mouthpiece of the ruling party and even denied the opposition the opportunity to air paid-up advertisements.

When NARC came to power, with many members who were the pioneers of the IPPG reforms, it was expected that the provisions of this agreement would be respected. However, the NARC regime behaved in exactly the same way as the KANU regime before it. The KBC continued to be the mouthpiece of the ruling party while President Kibaki unilaterally appointed commissioners to the ECK without consulting the opposition parties in the run-up to the 2007 elections.

The constitutional and legal reforms undertaken under the IPPG framework also focused on delinking the bureaucracy, especialection 6(d). vants to support party campaign efforts

Without constitutional reforms, therefore, the government and elites in power continued to renege on the promiser every election, new struggles for comprehensive change would begin because the leaders in power preferred the status quo; they preferred to govern and to conduct elections using old laws because the government had effective control over the application of these laws.

The 2010 constitution introduced significant changes to the electoral system while retaining the FPTP system. The constitution sought to give Kenya a fairer electoral system through the establishment of a two-round system in the presidential elections. It also introduced a FPTP system with quotas in the House of Representatives.

The two-round system requires that the winning presidential candidate receive more than 50% of the votes cast in the election and, at the same time, garner at least 25% of votes in each of more than half of the 47 counties in the first round of the election. And if no candidate achieves this threshold in the first round, the top two candidates enter into a second round of voting within 30 days. These requirements are meant to ensure that the country has a presidential leadership with broad support across the country. But the two-round system, anchored on the FPTP system, appears to have some weaknesses. Primary among its shortcomings, it makes leaders focus on ethnic blocs and encourages cooperation along the main ethnic cleavages. Unfortunately, the system is still not fair because at least two numerically large ethnic regions can form a voting bloc that win if they get the support of a few other groups and can exclude others from power. And if the electoral system is not fair and does not allow the opposition to feel it can win in another election, then it forces the losers to work outside the existing system. It also breeds violence during elections, as has happened before, beginning in 1992.

Electoral malpractices

In 2008, the Kriegler Commission stated that the 2007 elections were so fraudulent that it was impossible to know who had won the presidential poll. In the description of electoral fraud, the Commission stated:

> Numerous, implausibly high turn-out figures reported in the strongholds of both main political parties evidence extensive perversion of polling, probably ballot-stuffing, organised impersonation of absent voters, vote buying and/or bribery. This inference is supported by numerous
>
> eyewitness accounts given to the IREC of various forms of manipulation as well as election observers' observation reports and ECK submissions. Indeed, vote-buying and ballot-stuffing appear to be such extensive and universally condoned practices in Kenyan elections that the question can rightly be asked whether genuinely free and fair elections are at all possible.

Code of conduct

The Electoral Code of Conduct was introduced in 1997 as an amendment to the elections law. While the country's criminal laws and the Election Offences Act apply to election activities, the code specifically deals with campaign activities. It binds political parties, candidates and the government to refrain from any action involving violence or intimidation. It also binds political parties to refrain from publishing or repeating false, defamatory or inflammatory allegations about persons or parties connected with the elections. To this end, the code of conduct applies to political parties, candidates and the government of the day. Its overall objective is thus to promote conditions conducive to conducting free and fair elections and a climate of tolerance in which political activities may take place without fear of coercion, intimidation or reprisal.

The electoral dispute resolution process in 1992 was highly inefficient. Most allegations of misconduct were presented to the Kenyan judiciary system, but the ECK and the courts were not prepared to respond to the large volume of electoral complaints. The chaotic nature of the 1992 elections forced the ECK to engage political parties with a view to negotiating the code. However, since the code was enacted late in the election year (7 November 2007 and signed by political parties on 27 November 1997), there wasn't ample time to put in place a mechanism to ensure effective compliance for that year's elections. As a result, most, if not all, political parties violated the code. The Code of Conduct Committee, comprising three ECK commissioners to monitor compliance, failed to play an effective role as it lacked the requisite powers. The ECK was empowered to enforce the code and impose sanctions by way of warnings, fines, limiting campaign activities or seeking a candidate or party's disqualification through the courts. It could also, through a court order, bar a party or candidate from taking part in the election. The code was first enforced during the 2002 general election when the ECK set up the Electoral Code of Conduct Enforcement Committee, chaired by its vice-chairman. The committee summoned political parties and candidates to hear evidence concerning complaints from opponents or as provided through observation by electoral officials and the press, that is, of vote-buying and electoral violence.

The then ruling party was fined, and so was a candidate of one opposition party. It was reported that the ECK held eight hearings in cases of alleged breaches of the code. These cases pertained to electoral offences, including violence, intimidation, use of abusive language, civil servants campaigning for candidates or parties, and bribery and cheating. This resulted in six cases in which the ECK issued formal warnings and two cases in which it sanctioned parliamentary candidates and political parties. KANU was fined KSh 100 000 for an assault by its supporters on a former Cabinet ministerand Raphael Wanjala of NARC was fined KSh 50 000 for assaulting a returning officer. It must be stated, however, that the most important factor was probably the deterrent effect of the publicity generated by the ECK and its judgments. In 2007, another code of conduct enforcement committee was similarly responsible for ensuring compliance with electoral guidelines. It had powers to issue formal warnings, impose fines and prohibit a political party from campaigning and/or from using state-owned media. The committee could also ask the special electoral police force, comprising 17 units of five policemen each, to investigate any violation of the code or to enforce its sanctions. However, despite these positive measures, the committee had limited competence and its range of corrective measures was not adequate to resolve disputes between parties or prevent violent incidents. Consequently, and despite numerous violent incidents and deaths, the committee received a very limited number of complaints. The committee rejected most of these on technical grounds, and many cases were not addressed with the promptness they deserved. However, even when the committee dealt with cases and took decisions, the decisions were not obeyed, demonstrating the weakness of the mechanism in place. Specifically, the committee heard four cases filed by complainants in the Ikolomani, Malava, Maragua aation. In the cases of the Ikolomani and Malava constituencies, former MPs were accused of instigating violence against Orange Democratic Movement (ODM) supporters and destroying campaign materials. The former MP for Malava had also failed to inform the police of his intention to stage a rally, with the full knowledge that his opponent had scheduled a rally in the same area.

The above-mentioned instances led to a clash between the ODM and New FORD-Kenya supporters, resulting in deaths and the destruction of property. The two former MPs were found guilty of violating the provisions of the electoral code of conduct and fined KSh 100 000 (about EUR 1 000) to be paid within 30 days. In the Maragua case, the former MP was accused of using abusive language and instigating violence against his opponents. The committee fined him KSh 100 000, also to be paid within 30 days. In the fourth complaint, a parliamentary candidate in Kilgoris constituency made allegations of an illegal transfer of election returning officers and the blatant unprofessionalism and lack of impartiality amongst presiding officers. His claims could not be substantiated, however. The former MPs involved in these proceedings publicly stated that they would not pay the fines. As the above cases show, the ECK's regulatory functions were fairly limited since they were not backed by robust legal provisions. Much was said, for instance, about the ECK's 'toothless' nature when faced with errant parties and candidates flouting the electoral code of conduct in the lead up to the 2007 elections. The electoral commission lacked adequate powers to enforce even its own decisions during instances of such infractions. Overall, it was not easy to enforce the ECK code for two main reasons. First, the campaign period was usually so tense and activities moving so fast that organising the hearing of disputes and getting witnesses was problematic. Second, taking the matter to court in order to bar a party or candidate from taking part in the election or campaign was difficult given the slowness of court processes. The ECK has since been dissolved and replaced with the IEBC, which was constituted in 2011.

Abuse of state resources

Abuse of state resources, generally, includes the use of material and property of the state (read public) for any political parties' campaign purposes, which may include human resources and time, physical resources such as vehicles or office space, including software and hardware, and also the use of public funds (withdrawn or otherwise) from state coffers. Although multi-party elections in Kenya in the years 1992, 1997 and 2002 were judged as generally free and fair, there was credible evidence that the incumbent regime abused or misused state power to tilt the electoral outcome in its favour. Since the re-introduction of multi-party politics in 1992, the party in power has been prone to abusing state resources to ensure electoral victory. This has been the case for the KANU and the NARC (PNU) regimes. The major areas of incumbency abuse include the engagement of public servants in campaigns, incumbent candidates and supporters benefiting from preferential access to public facilities, use of state resources and facilities for political rallies, and slanted coverage of campaign activities in favour of the incumbent by the state-owned broadcaster.

A number of cases rise to the fore in the 1992, 1997 and 2002 elections. In 1992, the ruling party KANU and retired President Moi enjoyed the use of state property and personnel on a massive scale during campaigns. On his tours throughout the country, Moi took with him leading civil servants and other established figures from each area. Often, he paraded such persons before the attendant crowds as evidence of how much he had rewarded local people. The Provincial Administration consistently and publicly campaigned for the ruling party and harassed the opposition. In the 1997 and 2002 elections, KANU blatantly continued to use state resources for its campaigns. The party's candidates used government personnel and vehicles during nominations, campaigns and even on polling days. The Provincial Administration was always actively involved in KANU rallies. Despite numerous reports by various watchdogs, especially the Kenyan National Commission on Human Rights (KNCHR), this practice has continued unabated and was widespread during the by-elections held between 2003 and 2007, the 2005 referendum as well as the 2007 elections.

Pubic officers, including senior government officials and Cabinet ministers, widely used state resources during the campaigns for the 2007 general elections as they campaigned for the president and his party as well as candidates loyal to the president, in breach of the Electoral Code of Conduct and in violation of the Public Officers Ethics Act (2003). The KNCHR reported 141 cases of the use of government vehicles and two cases of the use of government helicopters. Public servants, heads of parastatals and the Provincial Administration officials were overtly involved in campaign activities. A notable example is the Presidential Advisory Board (PAB) and the Presidential Elections Board (PEB), strategy groups for President Kibaki's re-election campaign, which comprised numerous high ranking public officers including Joe Wanjui (chancellor, University of Nairobi), Nathaniel Kang'ethe (director, Kenya Revenue Authority), George Muhoho (managing director, Kenya Airports Authority), Eddy Njoroge (managing director, KenGen), Titus Mbathi (chairperson, KenGen), James Kimonye (managing director, Kenya Meat Commission) and Professor Nick Wanjohi (vice-chancellor, Jomo Kenyatta University Agriculture and Technology). The head of the civil service, Francis Muthaura, was also involved in the presidential campaigns. In addition, Mwai Kibaki used his presidential powers for campaign purposes when he announced the creation of a substantial number of new districts during campaign rallies. There were also cases where police officers were recruited as agents of President Kibaki's PNU during the disputed 2007 general elections. Despite being provided for in the 2010 constitution, the government is yet to promulgate comprehensive regulations to control the use of state resources by public officers, especially during elections. In addition to the Public Officers Ethics Act (2003) there is the Political Parties Act (2011), which bars political parties both from accepting or using public resources other than those allocated to the party through the Political Parties Fund, and using state resources for partisan campaigns. In addition to this, the Independent Ethics and Anti-corruption Commission Act (2012) provides that a 'member or employee shall conduct their private affairs in a manner that maintains confidence in the integrity of their office and the Commission as a whole' and that the member should not engage in political activity that may compromise or be seen to compromise 'the neutrality of their office or the Commission'. Parliament passed the Campaign Financing Bill (2012), although it is not comprehensive in regulating the use of public resources. In general, there is a legislative framework that the government can utilise to regulate these resources. However, there is lack of political commitment to enforce these laws and is not confined to the use of state resources alone; it is an endemic problem running through all public institutions.

Violence

Since the advent of multi-party politics in 1991, the past four multi-party elections in Kenya have witnessed recurrent political violence that has been replicated in almost every province. These violent episodes in the country have left over 5 200 people dead and almost 950 000 displaced. Most of these conflicts have either directly or indirectly been associated with ethnic animosity. This is partly explained by the fact that different communities in Kenya continue to consciously or unconsciously rely on ethnicity to express their political dominance and hegemony in an atmosphere largely characterised by scarce resources, fear and prejudice. The proliferation of ethnic conflicts in election years has been so widespread that it has affected most of the country's eight provinces. Some known hotspots include Western (the districts that flank Mt. Elgon, namely, Trans-Nzoia, Bungoma and Mt. Elgon), the Rift Valley (districts of Nakuru, Molo, Kericho, Nandi, Uasin Gishu, Trans-Mara and Marakwet), Nyanza (Gucha, Kuria), Coast (Kwale, Kilifi), North Eastern (Mandera, Wajir, Marsabit), and Nairobi (Mathare, Kibera) Provinces.

The ethnic conflicts in Kenya during the 1990s vividly illustrated the use of such politicisation by the in-group to remain in power. In the run-up to the 1992 and 1997 multi-party elections, what were generally regarded as politically instigated ethnic conflicts took place. They were evidently intended to protect the interests of the in-group by destabilising the opposition support bases in Rift Valley Province and parts of Nyanza Province in the run-up to the 1992 elections, and in Mombasa in Coast Province in the run-up to the 1997 elections.

The 1991 clashes were preceded by inflammatory statements by Kalenjin leaders in Majimbo rallies that called for the eviction of non-members of the Kalenjin, Maasai, Turkana and Samburu (KAMATUSA) communities from the Rift Valley. On the other hand, the 1997 violence in Mombasa occurred at the height of the opposition and civil society agitation for constitutional reform that preceded the second election under the new multi-party system. And immediately after the 1997 elections, violence erupted again in Kikuyu strongholds in Rift Valley Province, that is, the Laikipia and Nakuru districts, which were seen as meant to counter the legal challenge mounted against the election of Moi by opposition leader Kibaki. In other wordsored violence unattractive. KANU politicians had a two-way battle – for their own political survival and for the survival of KANU as a party. This left them with little time to organise any violence. Thirdly, there were intense campaigns in the media and on other forums by the ECK, NGOs, churches, CBOs and politicians on the need to have violence-free elections. This greatly helped the electorate to shun electoral violence. Fourth, the experience of the previous two general elections, as far as violence was concerned, was still fresh in people's minds. It was an ugly experience that they wanted to put behind them.

Peace committees in the 2002 elections

The 2002 elections witnessed a much lower level of violence as a result of the campaign by the ECK, civil society and the media. The Central Depository unit had personnel in most parts of Kenya where there was potential for violence to monitor and report on those responsible or affected by it. The ECK set up peace committees in all the constituencies to assist in conflict management and resolution and to tackle differences among political parties. The committees comprised the returning officer, three religious organisations (one leader per organisation), one youth leader, one elder, an officer commanding a police station (OCS), and an officer commanding a police division (OCPD). These committees were intended to further enhance the capacity of the ECK to enforce the Electoral Code of Conduct and promote non-violent campaigns. The peace committees were in place and operational for about a month before, during and after elections. They met at least once a week and were effective in most parts of the country. They gathered intelligence in their respective constituencies and took preventive measures if and when violence or some other act that would disturb the peace was about to be committed. Where candidates contravened provisions of the Electoral Code of Conduct, they were reported to the ECK. Where complaints were filed with the ECK regarding breaches of the code, it dispatched its investigative team to the area and took the observations of the peace committee very seriously.

2007 general elections

The level of violence that followed the 2007 elections was unprecedented. Apart from the widespread violence that was witnessed during parliamentary and civic party nominations, and when supporters of the ODM and PNU clashed during campaign rallies, the fighting that followed the release of the election results was of a degree that had not been experienced since 1992. About 1 500 people died and 300 000 were displaced as a result of the election-related violence. Marauding, armed, rag-tag militia – and the police – unleashed terror on Kenyans in many parts of the country. As in 1992 and 1997, the violence was mainly between people from different tribes. In parts of Nairobi, Nyanza, Rift Valley, Coast and Western Provinces, the main victims were people from Kikuyu, Embu and Meru communities, and to a lesser extent the Kisii, who were being targeted because of their perceived support for President Kibaki. In other parts of Nairobi, Nakuru, Naivasha and areas of Central Province, the main victims were people from the Luo community, who were attacked in reprisal for what was happening to Kikuyus and their related ethnic groups elsewhere. The Luo were, in this case, targeted for their perceived support for Raila Odinga, who was the main challenger to Mwai Kibaki for the presidency.

Electoral violence in Kenya has always been exacerbated by the impunity of the perpetrators – the result of the inability and/or failure by the government to put to account those implicated in fomenting it. No action was taken against those implicated in the 1992 and 1997 ethnic clashes despite the presentation of evidence to a parliamentary select committee and a judicial commission of inquiry. A further case in point occurred in 2007 when no action was taken against the then Minister for Roads, Simeon Nyachae, for his role in the violence meted against ODM leaders on 12 September 2007 in Kisii, or against assistant minister Raphael Wanjala when his government vehicle was impounded in Naivasha carrying 100 pangas, whips, bows and arrows and 70 Somali swords, a few days before the 2007 elections.

With Kenya on the brink of the precipice, the international community was forced to intervene and set up a framework for engaging the antagonistic parties. An African Union Panel of Eminent African Personalities led by former United Nations Secretary General, Kofi Annan, brokered a settlement which heralded a government of national unity between the main political parties and a common commitment to urgent constitutional reform. The settlement included the appointment of two commissions, one to examine the violence and the other to examine the December 2007 elections from various perspectives. In its findings, the Commission of Inquiry into the Post-Election Violence (chaired by Justice Philip Waki, and therefore popularly referred to as the Waki Commission) pointed out that the violence that shook Kenya after the 2007 elections was, by far, the most deadly and the most destructive ever experienced in Kenya. Also, unlike previous cycles of election-related violence, much of it followed rather than preceded elections. The 2007–2008 post-election violence was also more widespread than in the past, affecting all but two provinces, and was felt in both urban and rural areas. Previously, violence around election periods had been concentrated in a smaller number of districts, mainly in the Rift Valley, Eastern and Coast Provinces.

One of the main findings of the investigations was that the post-election violence was spontaneous in some geographic areas. It was also the result of planning and organisation in others, often with the involvement of political and business leaders. Some areas witnessed a combination of the two forms of violence, where what started as a spontaneous violent reaction to the perceived rigging of elections, later evolved into well-organised and coordinated attacks on members of the ethnic groups associated with the incumbent president and his party, the PNU. This happened where there was an expectation that violence was inevitable whatever the results of the elections. Similar sentiments had been echoed by the KNCHR. The Waki Commission identified several suspects including senior politicians as the main perpetrators of violence and recommended that an independent special tribunal for Kenya be established to try the suspects. The Commission also recommended that the International Criminal Court (ICC) take up the matter if the government failed to establish a special tribunal.

In 2009, Parliament failed on two occasions to agree to establish the special tribunal, and the Chair of Eminent African Personalities handed the list to the ICC. The ICC later indicted six persons, including incumbent president, Uhuru Kenyatta, and his deputy, William Ruto, former head of the Civil Service and Secretary to the Cabinet, Francis Muthaura, and radio journalist, Joshua Sang, former Tinderet MP Henry Kosgei, and former Commissioner of Police, Hussein Ali. Three of those have since been acquitted due to insufficient evidence – Muthaura, Ali and Kosgei.

It is apparent that the government and senior politicians lack the commitment to investigate and try perpetrators of violence. Even though the ICC will try senior politicians, the government is yet to establish a complementary mechanism to try lower level perpetrators. The government has maintained that there are over 3 500 cases to be tried, but there have been limited attempts to try any of the suspects. Because of this failure, more than 60% of Kenyans consider the ICC intervention as a good way to deal with high forms of impunity, especially because the government has not shown any commitment to effectively investigate and prosecute post- election violence cases involving both senior and ordinary Kenyans.

Election observation

The ECK Guidelines for Election Observers set out the role, rights and privileges of observers comprehensively and offered a summary of principles and practices for election observers which, by and large, were in consonance with international principles. The Presidential and Parliamentary Elections (Amendment) Regulations (2002) mandated the ECK to accredit individuals and organisations to act as election observers, and to issue guidelines accordingly. Election observation in Kenya began with the 1992 elections. That election was observed

by local observers under the consortium of the National Elections Monitoring Unit (NEMU), which trained and deployed some 8 000 domestic observers throughout the country. About 200 international observers also participated, including the International Republican Institute (IRI), the Commonwealth, and national delegations from Denmark, Egypt, Germany, Japan and Switzerland. In spite of some irregularities experienced during the elections, both the domestic and international observers concluded that the elections reflected the general will of the people. Likewise, in the 1997 elections, the Domestic Observation Project was jointly run by the IED, the Catholic Justice and Peace Commission (CJPC) and the National Council of Churches of Kenya (NCCK). It trained and deployed almost 30 000 observers together with a number of international ones, including the IRI, the Norwegian Team for Observation of

Election in Kenya and the Donors for Development and Democracy Group (which comprised 22 Western

cataloguing the various shortcomings of the 1997 elections and noting the institutional bias of KANU, concluded that the elections on the whole reflected the wishes of Kenyan voters. In 2002, the ECK accredited 45 000 election observers, 40 000 of whom were domestic and 5 000 foreign. During the elections, domestic observers again coalesced around a single entity named the Kenya Domestic Observation Programme (K-DOP). K-DOP mobilised a team of 64 regional coordinators, 420 constituency observers, 210 organisers and 18 366 poll watchers in the 18 366 polling streams countrywide. The international observers included the Commonwealth Observer Group, the European Union Elections Observation Mission (EUEOM), the Carter Centre, USAID/US Embassy, the British High Commission, the African Union and the Donors for Development and Democracy Group, all of which collaborated in their efforts. Despite some minimal irregularities, they all returned a verdict of a free and fair election.

However, the 2007 elections witnessed a decrease in the number of observers, both local and international, as it was deemed that Kenya had already crossed the Rubicon in the holding of free and fair elections. The ECK accredited 24 063 election observers, who included 15 000 local observers under the Kenya Domestic Observation Forum (KEDOF). The domestic teams were funded under the 2007 Election Assistance Programme managed by UNDP-Kenya and supported by Canada, Denmark, Finland, the Netherlands, Norway, Sweden, the European Union, the United Kingdom and the United States of America.

The main aim of the programme was to strengthen the overall capacity of the ECK, civil society, media and other agencies critical to the achievement of free and fair elections, and to improve citizens' participation in the electoral process and their understanding of their rights and duties. The international observers included the EUEOM, IRI, the East African Community, the Common Market for East and Southern Africa and the Commonwealth. The observers were deployed well in advance of polling day and remained thereafter.

The various observers were united in their findings that the conduct of the electoral process up to election-day was credible. They opined that the administration of the 2007 elections in Kenya was largely professional on a technical level up to and including voting and counting in the polling stations. However, as far as tallying, tabulation and announcement was concerned, the observers said the election administration did not meet key international and regional standards for transparency in the conduct of elections. The same is true in regard to the independence of the election administration as emphasised in the ICCPR (HRC GC 25, paragraph 20) and (AU CPGDEA II [4]). They, therefore, returned the verdict that the 2007 elections were not free and fair. There was also a general agreement that the ECK was not an independent institution and was subordinate to the executive branch of the government. Monitoring reports also highlighted that observers and party agents were denied full access to the tabulation of results at national and, partly, at constituency levels. They gave the recommendations that

- All laws relating to the operational management of elections be consolidated under one statute;
- The current rules and regulations on the procedures of election petitions be repealed and replaced with new rules that would ensure petitions are heard in a just and timely manner;
- A results process be set up that guarantees full transparency at every stage and which enables the publishing of results at constituency level upon the

completion of tallying and posting of polling station results on the ECK website;

- The selection and appointment of ECK commissioners be in a manner that ensures the confi of all election stakeholders;

- A review of the processes for the transmission and announcement of results be imperative;

- A national voter registration database and computerised constituency registration offi be set up;

- A regulatory framework be a requisite need for the audio-visual media and the restoration of the independence and public accountability of the KBC; and

- The ECK be disbanded.

Validity of results

Since the re-introduction of multi-party politics in 1992, no election results, apart from the 2002 ones, have been accepted by all parties to have met the threshold for being free and fair. It is only in the 2002 elections that the losing parties and their candidates endorsed the results as a refl of the will of the people. In 1992 and 1997, despite the numerous anomalies reported in the electoral process which painted the election as short of democratic standards, most election observers concluded that the election results refl the wishes of Kenyans. However, in the 2007 elections, all international observers, a majority of the Kenyan public and one of the main political parties – the ODM – pointed out that the elections did not meet the threshold for a free and fair election and did not refl the will of the voters. The domestic observers, including the Law Society of Kenya, KEDOF, the KHRC and the KNCHR gave a similar verdict.

The manner in which the president was sworn in, privately, in the absence of members of the diplomatic community, dignitaries, including political leaders of other countries and the general public, and the time it was done (at 18h00, after working hours) further contributed to the widespread perception that the elections lacked credibility. The Constitution of Kenya 2010 provides a cure to this malady by providing that:

The swearing in of the President-elect shall be in public before the Chief Justice, or, in the absence of the Chief Justice, the Deputy Chief Justice. The President-elect shall be sworn in on the fi Tuesday following the fourteenth day after the date of the declaration of the result of the presidential election, if no petition has been fi under Article 140; or the seventh day following date on which the court renders a decision declaring the election to be valid, if any petition has been fi under Article 140.

According to the IREC report, the conduct of the 2007 elections was so materially defective that it is impossible – for the IREC or anyone else – to establish true or reliable results for the presidential and parliamentary elections. The report argues that although there was room for disagreement as to whether there was rigging of the presidential results by the ECK, the process was perverted at the polling stage and so inaccurate as to render any reasonable accurate, reliable and conclusive result impossible. Subsequently, the IREC called for the total overhaul of the ECK, the taming of political parties and the amendment of electoral laws and systems. The declaration of a presidential winner in the absence of all the original result certify and the external pressure on the ECK to prematurely announce the presidential results was an indication of a breach of the constitution and the electoral law. Furthermore, before the announcement of the presidential election was made, the media was ordered to leave. Almost immediately, the government, through the then Internal Security Minister, John Michuki, ordered broadcasters to suspend live broadcasts. This was not only an infringement of the freedom of the press, but it also contributed to considerable tension across the country. All domestic and international observer missions swiftly issued statements condemning the tallying process and casting doubt on the results of the presidential election.

Election petitions

Election petitions have emerged over the years as characteristic post-election phenomena in Kenya. Petitions have come to be viewed as off the only safety valve for confl and enmities engendered by the electoral process. However, there is a scant history of success with electoral petitions. At the presidential level, election petitions were instituted in the 1992 and 1997 elections. In 1992, Kenneth Matiba, who had run as the FORD-Asili presidential candidate, petitioned Moi's election, but the case was struck down because he had not personally signed the petition; his advocate had signed it for him. In 1997, Kibaki's petition against Moi was also dismissed on the grounds that Moi was not personally served with the petition. In 2002, there was no petition at the presidential election as the loser conceded defeat. It is against this background of distrust of the judiciary that ODM leaders decided not to petition the results.

At the parliamentary level, every election has been followed by numerous petitions. However, over the years, only a few have succeeded. The period within which petitions must be fi and served is very short, and there are no timelines for the determination of such petitions. In most cases, the fi parliamentary term ends before a petition is determined. In 1997, many of the 27 election petitions lingered in the courts until late 1998, and at least fi were not concluded until late 1999. In 2002, 25 petitions were fi but twelve of them were struck down in the early stages. At least ten other petitions remained unresolved as Kenyans went to the polls in the 2007 elections. In one unique case (one of the three cases that was concluded in 2007), Magarini legislator Harrison Kombe's election was nullifi and a by-election held, but he won back his seat.

After the 2007 elections, 38 petitions were fi against members of the tenth Parliament disputing parliamentary elections. Four petitions were dismissed – those against Magarini MP, Jeff Kingi; Kitui West MP, Charles Nyamai; Dagoreti MP, Beth Mugo; and Garsen MP, Danson Mungatana.

The 2013 elections had a total of 188 election petitions fi Twenty-four petitions challenged the election of governors, 13 were about senators, 70 National Assembly members, nine county women representatives in the National Assembly, and 67 county assembly members. There were another fi petitions challenging the election of speakers of county assemblies.

The electoral system under the Constitution of Kenya (2010)

Following the disputed 2007 presidential election and the eventual formation of the grand coalition government, the ECK was disbanded and replaced by an Interim Independent Electoral Commission (IIEC). After its formation, the IIEC compiled a new voter register as well as conducted the referendum on the then proposed new constitution. In addition, the IIEC conducted several parliamentary and civic by-elections in various parts of the country. With the passage of the constitution, the IIEC was replaced with an Independent Electoral and Boundaries Commission (IEBC). The constitution makes provisions to cushion the electoral body from government interference and seeks to address some of the loopholes that made the ECK unable to discharge its mandate eff and with impartiality.

The IEBC is responsible for conducting or supervising referenda and elections to any elective body or office established by the constitution. According to the constitution and the

Elections Act, the IEBC has the following functions:

- The continuous registration of citizens as voters;
- The regular revision of the voters' roll;
- The delimitation of constituencies and wards;
- The regulation of the process by which parties nominate candidates for elections;
- The settlement of electoral disputes, including disputes relating to or arising from nominations but excluding petitions and disputes subsequent to the declaration of elections results;
- The registration of candidates for election;
- Voter registration;
- The facilitation of the observation, monitoring and evaluation of elections;
- The regulation of the amount of money that may be spent by or on behalf of a candidate or party in respect of any election;
- The development of a code of conduct for candidates and parties contesting elections; and
- The monitoring of compliance with the legislation required by article 82(1)(b) relating to the nomination of candidates by parties.

Whereas these are functions established by law, the IEBC is robustly more independent than the ECK, through:

- Having commissioners competitively recruited through a transparent and public process;

- The IEBC process of budget formulation and defence being more a public process than just the mere allocation of funds from Treasury; and

- The IEBC having a fairly independent staff (commissioners and Secretariat). The ability of the IIEC and later the IEBC, to hold all the by-elections successfully and without any petition arising is a clear pointer to the independence and competency of the EMB, unlike the defunct ECK.

Conclusion and recommendations

Kenya has held periodic elections as provided for in the former constitution. The elections have been competitive but results for presidential elections have tended to refl national ethno-regional settlement patterns. The electoral system, FPTP, has undermined the potential of electoral elections to enhance democracy. The FPTP system leads to intense confl over access to state power because it focuses on mobilising the numeric strength of various communities. The constitution has not radically altered the electoral system, which explains why violent confl are bound to occur around election time, primarily because of the pitfalls of the system, but also because of heightened impunity in Kenya over electoral violence. The ICC intervention may reduce the potential of violence in the short term but complementarity mechanisms must be established to try other perpetrators in order to demonstrate a commitment to addresing impunity and electoral violence. The masterminds of electoral violence and crimes remain at large.

The government has shown limited commitment to enforcing existing laws on elections and political practice. There are several laws in place to regulate the use of public resources, among other areas, but these are poorly enforced. For this reason, the IEBC, through the Registrar of Political Parties and the political party leadership, should enforce the Political Parties Act by adhering to the relevant provisions in the 2010 constitution.

The following recommendations are made. That:

- The relevant bodies undertake the strict enforcement of electoral laws (the Political Parties Act, the Elections Act and other related legislation).

- The Director of Public Prosecutions seeks support from the Attorney General and the judiciary to establish a permanent department to investigate and prosecute cases on election violence. This department should support the establishment of a complementary mechanism to try other perpetrators of post-election violence. These eff should be undertaken with the support of the judiciary as it has already established a committee to advise on election matters.

- Civil society closely monitors the electoral process and the implementation of existing legislation. This should be done with a view to undertaking public interest litigation when a breach of electoral laws is found.

- The government provides enough resources to the IEBC and the Registrar of Political Parties to eff enforce existing electoral laws. The IEBC should seek support from the Attorney General, Director of Prosecutions, the judiciary and the police for this purpose. The Commission should also establish a department to coordinate eff with these institutions.

- The government allocates more resources to the IEBC on an annual basis to enable it to roll out voter registration and voter education on a continuous basis to ensure that these activities are not linked to any particular election.

Political parties

Kenya gained independence under a multi-party system but soon became a one-party state that lasted for nearly three decades. During this period the divide between the ruling party and the state was thin – a factor that has persisted to date, the return to multi-party politics in 1992 notwithstanding. Since independence, the political parties formed in Kenya have been institutionally weak. The main parties have revolved around wealthy individuals and relied on ethnic coalitions or singular ethnic groups as their bases of support. Due to their institutional weakness, parties in Kenya have been functionally ineff as democratic and democracy- promoting institutions in the political process. This has been primarily a function of poor leadership, lack of eff programmes, lack of human and fi resources and weak societal linkages. Many parties do not espouse a coherent or sound ideology or doctrine upon which to base their articulation of interests, mobilise supporters and shape or structure public opinion. They also lack eff programmes aimed at achieving their objectives. For those that have manifestos, they have been strikingly similar in form and content, the discernible diff being only in the details.

The repeal of the constitutional provision that made Kenya a one-party state in 1991 was a milestone because it facilitated the country's return to multi-party politics. However, Kenya failed to include direct provisions in the constitution to guide the formation of political parties, including their organisation, funding, roles, functions and operations. The registration of political parties was, unfortunately, left under the authority of the Societies Act, whose stipulations encompassed societies/organisations in general. The government's previous liberal attitude in the registration of political parties resulted in the country being littered with numerous parties. As at the 2007 elections, there were 160 political parties in Kenya, most of which were formed for speculative purposes. The majority have no fi abode, paid up membership or party structures. They are barely active in between election years.

Kenyan political parties are diametrically opposed to what political parties ought to be. Political parties symbolise the development of democracy. That is, the development of modern parties has been linked to the development of democracy, marked by the extension of popular suff and parliamentary power. In this regard, political parties constituted, and still constitute hitherto, an important element, particularly considering that, previously, governments were organised on the basis of cliques, factions or blocs, and were not representative of the public. Kenyan political parties, which later form governments, tend to be closer to this notion.

Political parties are equally considered as mechanisms for the political elite to seek state power, consolidate it, and use it even as it is conceded that they have to seek people's approval. Thus, political parties are crucial in any democracy, not only because they are avenues within which modern governments are formed but also because of their role in linking the public to the government. That is, among other things, parties will be found preparing for general elections, formulating electoral platforms, mobilising the electorate, structuring the vote and, thereafter, forming governments. In summary, the main areas of linkages between parties and citizens are the following:

- Campaign linkage: parties recruit candidates and set the parameters of the electoral process;
- Participatory linkage: parties activate citizens during elections and mobilise them to vote;
- Ideological linkage: parties inform voters about policy choices in elections and voters strongly base their voting preferences on these policy alternatives;

- Representative linkage: elections achieve a good congruence between citizen policy preferences and the policies of the parties represented in Parliament and government; and,

Policy linkage: parties deliver on the policies they advocated in the election.

From the foregoing, political parties are organisations with the explicit and declared purpose of acquiring, consolidating and maintaining state power, either singly or within coalitions that form government. As such, political parties diff from unorganised and amorphous groupings of citizenry such as interest groups, since the former seek not just to infl government policy, but equally undertake the responsibility of forming and implementing government policy.

Generally, the potential functions of political parties could be summarised into fi broad areas: the integration and mobilisation of citizens; the aggregation and articulation of citizens' interests; the formulation of public policy; the organisation of parliaments and governments; and lastly, the recruitment of political leaders. Thus, as captured by Reginald Austin and Maja Tjernström:

Parties are expected to reflect the concerns of citizens, aggregate and mediate diverse interests, project a vision of a society and develop policy options accordingly. They are supposed to inspire and attract supporters to their cause, their membership being of key importance in their claim to represent citizens. Parties may well not live up to expectations regarding their services to citizens or quality for leadership. They, nevertheless, continue to be entrusted with what is, perhaps, the most strategic responsibility of modern democracy – to prepare and select candidates for parliamentary and presidential elections and then to support them into positions of leadership and government.

But until recently, Kenyan political parties have rarely performed the fi broad functions identified above, and if they seem to be doing so, the only motivation is to capture state power, after which they abandon the lofty ideals and promises that get them elected in the fi place. In April 2012, some of the political parties in Kenya have been literally forced, through the operationalisation of the Political Parties' Act (No. 11 of 2011), to recruit 1 000 registered voters from at least half of the 47 counties, among other conditions. As of 30 April 2012, 24 political parties had gained registration certifi while 22 others had applied for registration. Other operational issues facing political parties in Kenya are discussed hereunder.

Legal framework

Until July 2008 when the Political Parties Act (No. 10 of 2007) came into force, there was no specific law regulating parties in Kenya. Political parties were registered under the Societies Act, and their operations regulated by other legislation touching on elections such as the Local Government Act, the Election Offences Act, the National Assembly and Presidential Elections Act. The absence of a specific political party law and the fact that parties owed their existence to the Societies Act meant that party affairs were, for the most part, confined to the realm of 'private matters'.

Within this legal framework, political parties were registered as societies in a routine and simple manner. The only requirements to qualify for registration were having a party constitution, a formal address, a list of ten members, and a fee of KSh 2 000. Under the Societies Act then,

registration could be denied if the registrar 'has reasonable cause to believe that the interests

of peace and welfare of good order are likely to suffer prejudice by reason of the registration of the society'. This rule was used arbitrarily for political purposes to deny, delay or register party factions to the advantage of the ruling party. The delayed registration of the United Democratic Movement (UDM) in 2002, which was a threat to the then ruling party in Kenya's expansive Rift Valley Province, and the registration of the Orange Democratic Movement (ODM) to little known officials in order to deny the then popular Orange Movement that had just caused a defeat of the government at the referendum the right to the name, are some examples of how ruling parties

– Kenya African National Union (KANU) and National Rainbow Coalition (NARC) – sought to use the Registrar of Societies to their political advantage.

The parties that have been in power variously have also been adept at registering feuding factions of rivals they perceive to be threats to their hold on power. The ruling parties have occasionally registered splinter groups of the same parties in order to neutralise the opposition. Moi and KANU, for instance, registered two factions of the Forum for the Restoration of Democracy (FORD) – FORD-Kenya and FORD-Asili – in 1991 when the formidable movement looked all set to win the following year's elections. KANU too had a taste of its own medicine once out of power when a Kibaki-friendly KANU faction, New-KANU, led by Nicholas Biwott was registered at a time KANU chairman, Uhuru Kenyatta, had teamed up with the Liberal Democratic Party faction of NARC to threaten Kibaki's hold on power. The Kibaki regime also registered Malava legislator Soita Shitanda's New FORD-Kenya, which splintered from Musikari Kombo's FORD-Kenya, that was a key partner of the then fractious government, thus weakening its bargaining power.

The law also requires parties to prepare books of accounts and file them for inspection by the Registrar of Societies, hold annual general meetingsand file returns with the Registrar. However, political parties have rarely adhered to these rules, and the registrar of political parties has not also been particularly keen on enforcing the regulations. It is against this background of overwhelming weakness of the law to regulate political parties, as well as its failure to propel them to be vehicles of institutionalising democracy, that informed the enactment of the Political Parties Act (No. 10 of 2007).

However, this law operated between 2008 and 2010, where, after the promulgation of the constitution in August 2010, it was reviewed to give rise to the new Political Parties Act (No. 11 of 2011) which is now in force. This law seeks to give a legal regulatory framework specific to party issues and create an institution specifically responsible for the regulation of political parties. The Registrar of Political Parties, who was housed within the Independent Electoral and Boundaries Commission (IEBC), is charged with the registration of political parties as well as keeping and maintaining a register of parties and their particulars.

In the past, however, under the 2007 law, the Electoral Commission of Kenya (ECK) ran the show since it was charged with making the regulations that gave life to the law, especially detailing the manner in which political parties were to be registered and how funds were to be administered. Further, whereas the 2007 law was silent on the manner in which the registrar was appointed as well as his or her relations with the ECK, the current law is clear that the office of the registrar is a State Office in accordance with article 260 of the constitution, and also 'the Office of registrar shall be independent and shall not be subject to direction or control of any person or authority'. The current law further provides that the registrar's functions include: to 'register, regulate, monitor, investigate and supervise political parties to ensure compliance with this Act', and to 'ensure and verify that no person is a member of more than one political party, and notify the Commission of [such] finding'. These powers are anchored on the provisions of the 2010 constitution. By April 2012, it was evident that some political leaders preferred the status quo or 'business as usual' for political parties because politicians and parties were flouting the law without facing any consequences for their actions. For instance, the law provides that no one should belong to more than one political party at the same time and that anyone campaigning in favour of another political party shall be deemed to have resigned from the party that sponsored him/her to Parliament.

A group of individuals under the name Friends for Raila (FORA) or Friends of the Prime Minister filed a case in the middle of 2012 in court challenging the registrar to act on MPs who had been elected through the Prime Minister's ODM party, but were instead openly supporting other parties. The registrar, responding to that challenge, as well as to those from other petitioners who had presented similar cases before the Registrar's office, argued that only courts can determine the fate of some 100 MPs who have ditched the parties that took them to Parliament ... [since] it was difficult for my office to crack the whip on the politicians, especially since none of them had said in writing that they had left the party on whose ticket they were elected However, the Political Parties Act (2011) read together with the constitution, requires action by the registrar in such instances. The constitution, in article 103, outlines that those MPs who resign from the party that sponsored them to Parliament, or those 'deemed' to have resigned, shall lose their seats. Section 14 of the Political Parties Act (2011) provides that 'a person shall not be a member of more than one political party at the same time'. Further it is stated that any person who 'forms another political party, joins in the formation of another political party, joins another political party, in any way or manner publicly advocates for the formation of another political party or promotes the ideology, interests or policies of another political party' shall be 'deemed' to have resigned, even if one has not done so in writing to the party, the clerk of Parliament and so on.

Further, the current law provides for a procedure for the appointment of the registrar and three deputies. However, in March 2012, political parties in the tenth Parliament were unable to agree on the process – despite the provisions and procedures being clear in sections 35 and the Sixth Schedule. This is yet another indication of the unwillingness of MPs and the majority of the political parties in Kenya to reform parties in accordance with the constitution and other laws.

The current law outlines conditions under which the formation of a party can be prohibited. The registrar 'shall not register a political party which does not fit any of the conditions set out in article 91 of the constitution'. These conditions include: a political party shall be of national character and shall 'abide by the democratic principles of good governance, promote and practice democracy through regular, fair and free elections within the party', and also a political party shall not 'be founded on a religious, linguistic, racial, ethnic, gender or regional basis or seek to engage in advocacy of hatred on any such basis'. These are some of the basic requirements for political parties under the law and the constitution. Generally, political parties addresses challenges that prevent the institutionalisation of political parties. It seeks to make parties stronger institutions and to ensure that they have a national character.

The law also provides for provisional and full registration. For provisional registration, a political party shall provide mundane issues such as the application, minutes of meetings, name and abbreviation of the party, and so on. However, for a party to qualify for full registration, it

should have met the following conditions:

- Recruited as members, not fewer than one thousand registered voters, from each of more than half of the counties;
- The above members should reflect regional and ethnic diversity, gender balance and representation of minorities and marginalised groups;
- The composition of its governing body (mostly, the national executive council) should reflect regional and ethnic diversity, gender balance and the representation of minorities and marginalised groups;
- Not more than two-thirds of the members of its governing body should be of the same gender; and
- It should have demonstrated that members of its governing body meet the requirements of chapter 6 of the constitution and the laws relating to ethics

These provisions are considered radical, and will serve in transforming political parties in Kenya if the law is strictly followed and the registrar has the political wherewithal to 'crack the whip'. If a party fails to meet any of the above conditions, and any other as provided for in the law, it shall lose its registration certificate. The registrar's decisions are not final, since they could be challenged under the Political Parties Disputes Tribunal (PPDT), whose mandate and jurisdiction is set out in section 40 of the law to include resolution of disputes within parties, across parties, between coalition partners, between independent candidates and political parties, and between parties and the registrar, among others.

Finally, the Political Parties Act (2011) provides a series of schedules to guide the operations and management of the same, such as a code of conduct, the contents of parties' constitutions, methods of appointing the registrar through a selection committee, and also oaths for assuming office.

Principal parties contesting for office

The formation of new parties that contest for political power. The number of political parties has also rapidly increased with each election year. In 1992, there were nine registered political parties, all of which fielded a varying number of candidates in the presidential, parliamentary and civic elections. In 1997, the number of registered political parties had risen to 27 and of those, 22 fielded candidates in that year's election. By 2002, the number of registered political parties had swollen to 51, with 42 fielding candidates in the elections. In 2007, there were 160 parties, with 118 of them presenting candidates for election. This increase in political parties is attributable to a number of factors, most notable being the number of individuals who form political parties with a view to running in an election without competing for party tickets with other candidates, and especially candidates in parties that have a broad and large membership. Thus they form parties for self-interest. There are others who form parties for financial gain, that is, they form parties with the expectation of issuing party tickets during elections for a fee. Consequently, some of the parties are formed for commercial reasons, because those who lose out in competitions for party tickets usually vie for seats using fringe political parties, usually formed by individuals without a strong social basis of political support.

KANU has contested in all of the four multi-party elections since 1992. In 2007, however, the party did not field a presidential candidate as it had formed an alliance with the Party of National Unity (PNU), whose candidate was the incumbent, Mwai Kibaki. Under the alliance, KANU was allowed to field its own parliamentary candidates wherever they won in the joint nominations. The Forum for the Restoration of Democracy-

Kenya (FORD-Kenya) is the one party that has also contested in four multi-party elections but with diminishing significance.

In 2002, FORD-Kenya did not field candidates as it had joined the umbrella NARC, where its party leader, Wamalwa Kijana, under the memorandum of understanding, was appointed vice president. In 2007, it joined the PNU alliance, fielding the majority of its candidates under the latter's banner, with another 43 under the FORD-K banner. Of its candidates who won parliamentary seats, six were under the banner of the PNU, with the exception of Kimilili constituency where the candidate on the party's own ticket won. In the 2002 and 2007 elections, parties that won the presidency as well as the parliamentary majority were all new on the political scene. These were NARC, the PNU and ODM, signalling the fact that parties in Kenya are not institutionalised. In fact, NARC was formed barely two months prior to the 2002 elections, the PNU three months to the 2007 elections while the ODM was taken over by the Raila Odinga faction with barely four months to the 2007 elections.

In 1992, there were four major parties that contested for political office. These were the then ruling party KANU, FORD-Asili, FORD-Kenya and the Democratic Party (DP). KANU, taking advantage of a splintered opposition, and also using the state largesse at its disposal, not only won the presidential race but also won 100 of the 188 seats in Parliament. FORD-A and FORD-K tied with 31 parliamentary seats while the DP won 22 seats. Four seats were won by fringe parties. The next multi-party elections were held in 1997. The ECK had reviewed constituency boundaries and came up with an additional 22 constituencies that took the total number of constituencies to 210. During these elections, there were five major parties – KANU, FORD-K, the DP, National Development Party (NDP) and Social Democratic Party (SDP). Just as in the 1992 elections, the incumbent Moi and

KANU once again benefited from a splintered opposition and were victors. KANU won 107 seats of the 210 seats. Mwah Kabuki's DP bagged 39 parliamentary seats. The NDP secured 21 seats, FORD-K 17, while the SDP won 15 seats. The remaining eleven seats were won by fringe parties.

The 2002 elections were unique in that the incumbent president, Moi, was not running as he was barred by the constitution after serving two terms as per the constitutional provision that had come into force at the advent of multi-partyism. The election also witnessed the main opposition parties uniting for the first time. The main parties during this election were KANU, NARC (which was a coalition of parties) and FORD-People. During the election, NARC secured 125 seats, KANU 64 and FORD-P 14. The remaining seven seats went to fringe parties.

The 2007 elections were also unique owing to the fact that all the three main parties were coalitions of sorts. These were the ODM, PNU and Orange Democratic Movement-Kenya (ODM-K). Although the ODM was a single party, it had within its ranks former KANU and Liberal Democratic Party (LDP) legislators and members. The PNU had several constituent parties, including NARC-Kenya, KANU, FORD-P, Shirikisho, the DP and FORD-K, while the ODM-K had the Labour Party of Kenya (LPK) as a constituent party. The latter had welcomed disgruntled LDP followers who, taking the cue from presidential aspirant Kalonzo Musyoka, decamped to it. The election results were disputed but the ECK all the same arrived at a verdict. The PNU secured 43 seats while its affiliate, KANU, garnered 14 seats. The ODM won 99 seats while the ODM-K obtained 16 seats. The remaining 38 seats were won by fringe parties.

As is evident from the foregoing, the major parties that have contested elections since 1992 include KANU, FORD-A, FORD-K, the DP, SDP, NDP, NARC, FORD-P, ODM, PNU and ODM-K. KANU, Kenya's oldest party, was formed in 1960, forming the country's first government at independence in 1963. The following year, it absorbed the opposition, the Kenya African Democratic Union (KADU), making Kenya a de facto one-party state until 1966 when an internal split led to the formation of the Kenya People's Union (KPU). The party, led by Kenya's first vice president, Oginga Odinga, was, however, banned in 1969 and the country reverted to being a de facto one-party state. This state of affairs prevailed until 1982 when Parliament passed a law to make Kenya a one-party state, with KANU as that sole legal party. The party's long history in power gave it the strongest structure and branch network of all the political parties during the first three multi-party elections. This invincibility collapsed after Moi's term ended. Overall, KANU had ruled without interruption from independence to 2002 when Moi, on his final year in office, picked first President Jomo Kenyatta's son, Uhuru, as his successor. The decision precipitated a split that saw KANU lose hold of poweg its own parliamentary candidates who won the joint alliance nominations. KANU only managed to win 14 seats compared to the 64 it had won in the 2002 elections. The truth is that the dominance of KANU in the Kenyan political terrain had begun to wane FORD-Kenya is an offshoot of the original FORD movement that successfully pressurised the government to amend the constitution to provide for a multi-party political system. The movement thereafter was weakened by internal conflicts over the method of selecting a presidential candidate which split it down the middle to yield FORD-Kenya and FORD-Asili. The FORD-K faction was registered as a political party on 8 October 1992. It was led by the country's first vice president, Oginga Odinga, who had also been the leader of the banned KPU. The party had, among its ranks, the crème of the day's 'Young Turks', some of whom are today leaders as well as major players in the dominant political parties. They included Paul Muite, now leader of the Safina party; Kijana Wamalwa, who later became party leader of FORD-Kenya, and died in office as the vice president in 2003; Raila Odinga, currently the leader of the ODM and Kenya's prime-minister from 2008–2013; and cabinet ministers Kiraitu Murungi, James Orengo and Peter Anyang'-Nyong'o, who were all part of FORD-Kenya at its peak.

In 1992, FORD-K was the only party that had at least an MP in all the country's eight provinces. After the death of the elder Odinga in 1994, FORD-K faced internal dissent that finally saw Raila Odinga shift to the then moribund NDP. This affected the party in the 1997 elections and it returned only 17 MPs to Parliament, with its leader receiving a paltry half a million votes in the presidential election. In 2002, the party entered into an alliance with the DP and the National Party of Kenya (NPK) to form the umbrella party National Alliance Party of Kenya (NAK). This alliance would later be joined by KANU renegades (under the banner of the LDP) to form the National Alliance Rainbow Coalition (NARC), which saw Kibaki elected as president. He appointed FORD-K leader Kijana Wamalwa as vice president. Just before the 2007 elections, a faction of the party split away to form New FORD-K, further weakening the original FORD.

FORD-Asili is the other faction that split from FORD, under the leadership of Kenneth Matiba and Martin Shikuku as chairman and secretary general respectively. It was registered on 16 October 1992. During the 1992 elections, the party drew its support mostly from Central Kenya and the Kikuyu-settled areas of the Rift Valley as well as parts of Western Province, the strongholds of its two leaders. In 1997, however, and Matiba did not contest the presidency due to ill health. Most of his supporters turned to the other Kikuyu candidate in the race, Mwai Kibaki. FORD-Asili ended up winning only one parliamentary seat. The party has since then diminished in significance and has not been a major contender in the subsequent elections.

The DP was registered on 17 January 1992, founded by Mwai Kibaki, Njenga Karume, John Keen and Eliud Mwamunga, who left KANU after the return of multi-party politics. At its inception, the party was rooted in Central Province, especially Nyeri and its environs, from where its leader, Kibaki, hailed. It also elicited support from the Meru and Embu areas as well as the areas occupied by the Kamba. In 1997, the DP benefited from Matiba's absence from the elections, a development which saw the party win all the votes from Central Province and in the KikuCentre for Governance and Development (2004) Money and Politics: The Case of Party Nominations in Kenya. Nairobi: CGD. e run-up to the 2002 elections, the DP joined forces with FORD-K and the NPK to form NAK, which subsequently coalesced with the LDP to form the NARC. Mwai Kibaki was the presidential candidate, and he won the elections but disowned the DP once in office. This marked the beginning of the DP's diminishing influence in the political arena.

Although it was one of the corporate members of the PNU, the DP wielded the least influence in the coalition as most of its MPs under the NARC umbrella had defected to NARC-K.

The SDP was registered on 5 February 1992, with Johnstone Makau as its chairman. Soon after, Makau defected back to KANU and was elected to Parliament on its ticket. The party thus remained dormant until Peter Anyang' Nyong'o, Apollo Njonjo and Charity Ngilu revived it ahead of the 1997 elections. The party fielded Ngilu as its presidential candidate in a move that appeared to undercut the dominance of ethnicity in the electoral arena through gender. However, this strategy did not succeed as Ngilu mainly attracted votes from her Kamba community. In the post-1997 elections, internal differences in the SDP saw Ngilu leaving to found the NPK. In the meantime, James Orengo joined the SDP and was soon embroiled in factional fights with a group led by Apollo Njonjo. The Orengo faction triumphed and he became the party's presidential candidate. However, he performed dismally in the 2002 elections, coming a poor fourth with less that 1% of the votes cast. The party also did not win any parliamentary seat. The party has since been dormant.

The NDP was registered on 6 May 1996, under Stephen Omondi Oludhe as founding chairman. However, it was relatively inactive until Raila Odinga took over the party after leaving FORD-K. After the 1997 elections, the NDP entered into a cooperation pact with the ruling party, KANU. This cooperation saw its leader Odinga and Adhu Awiti appointed to the Cabinet as ministers, and two other NDP MPs (Peter Odoyo and Joshua Orwa Ojode) named as assistant ministers. The cooperation evolved into a merger between the NDP and KANU, with the former being dissolved and being obliterated from the books of the Registrar of Societies.

FORD-People was registered on 3 October 1997 in an attempt to give Kenneth Matiba – who was involved in a leadership wrangle with his secretary general, Martin Shikuku in FORD-A – a ticket on which to contest the presidency. In the end, Matiba declined the offer and instead formed Saba Asili. The party contested the 1997 elections and won three parliamentary seats. For some time, the party was in the hands of trade unionist, Kimani Wanyoike, but it remained lacklustre until former KANU minister Simeon Nyachae took it over and breathed life into it. In the run-up to the 2002 elections, the party entered into a short-lived working relationship with Paul Muite's Safina. The party later opted for the super-alliance that would give birth to NARC. This, too, was short-lived as Nyachae led his party out of the coalition after he disagreed with the method used to settle on Mwai Kibaki as the presidential candidate. The party fielded Nyachae as a presidential candidate, and he came in a poor third. The differences in NARC gave FORD-People an opportunity to join the government to help tame the LDP wing of the coalition. Nyachae was appointed Cabinet minister while two other MPs (Kipkalya Kones and Henry Obwocha) were named assistant ministers. Obwocha would later become a full Cabinet minister after the LDP group was ejected from the governECK (2004) 2002 General Elections Report. Nairobi: ECK. he 2005 referendum. In 2007, FORD-People was one of the constituent parties of the PNU. However, it performed dismally, with its leader Simeon Nyachae losing his parliamentary seat.

NARC was formed in October 2002, two months prior to that year's election. It was an umbrella party that brought together NAK (which was a grouping of the DP, FORD-K and NPK) and the LDP, comprising renegade KANU MPs and their followers who had left after

Moi imposed Uhuru Kenyatta as the party's presidential candidate. NAK and the LDP signed a memorandum of understanding committing both parties to share power in a future NARC government. The NAK wing of the party, led by Kibaki, however, failed to honour that agreement, thus precipitating the fallout with its LDP counterpart. Kibaki had also, immediately after his election, made attempts to make NARC a grassroots party, with individual members as opposed to its corporate status. The coalition partners rejected that move. After the 2005 referendum, in which the LDP teamed up with KANU to oppose the draft constitution, Kibaki offloaded LDP members from his Cabinet. In reaction, the LDP officially pulled out from the NARC coalition. Further attempts to have NARC register individual members, mostly from former MPs allied to the DP, met resistance from FORD-K and Charity Ngilu, who was the registered chair of NARC. It is the latter's resistance that forced former DP-allied MPs to form a new party, NARC-Kenya, in 2006. In the run-up to the 2007 elections, there were further attempts to persuade Ngilu to relinquish control of NARC as a coalition for parties that were willing to support Kibaki's re-election bid, but she declined, thus precipitating the formation of the PNU. NARC, under Ngilu, eventually entered into an alliance with the ODM to support the party's presidential candidate, Raila Odinga, while at the same time fielding parliamentary candidates. The party, however, performed dismally, winning only three parliamentary seats.

NARC-Kenya was registered in April 2006. It was formed after Ngilu refused to allow NARC's party constitution to be changed to allow for individual members. Its key members were former DP members. For a time, the party was touted as the vehicle Kibaki would use in his 2007 re-election bid. However, after the president snubbed it, it became a corporate member of the PNU coalition. All the same, some of its members contested the elections directly on the party's ticket. After the 2007 elections, NARC-Kenya pulled out of the PNU coalition and declared intent to field its own candidates in the 2012 elections. Its chairperson, Martha Karua, contested the 2013 presidential election but came in a distant fifth.

The ODM was registered immediately after the 2005 referendum by lawyer Mugambi Imanyara. The name ODM had been popularised during the 2005 referendum on the draft constitution in which the 'NO' side was assigned the symbol of an orange and the 'YES' a banana. The orange campaign brought together members of the LDP and KANU. In one of the rallies in Kisumu, Mvita legislator Najib Balala had hinted that they would transform the movement into a political party. However, before they could act, Imanyara registered a party under the name. This forced the LDP and KANU to register a new party called the ODM-Kenya. Following wrangles between Kalonzo Musyoka and Raila Odinga, both of whom wantDaily Nation, 2 September 2007. East African Standard, 1 September 2007. East African Standard, 2 September 2007. inal ODM to the Odinga group. The ODM went into the election as a single party but entered a pact with NARC that saw the latter's leader, Ngilu, sit in the party's top decision-making organ – the Pentagon. After the 2007 general election, the ODM was the single largest party in Kenya with 105 legislators in the 222-member National Assembly. It also formed a working partnership in Parliament with NARC and the UDM.

ODM-Kenya was registered in 2007. Originally it housed both KANU and the LDP.

However, it was soon embroiled in wrangles that ranged from who were its genuine officials to whether the party was a corporate entity or a single party as well as over the method of selecting its presidential candidate. The wrangles left the party wounded after the Raila camp left to take over the ODM with most of the key players and KANU's Uhuru Kenyatta pulling away with his wing of KANU. The ODM-K was thus left with renegade LDP legislators who had remained loyal to Kalonzo Musyoka and the feeble LPK belonging to Julia Ojiambo. In the thick of the post- election crisis that followed the disputed 2007 election results, the party entered into a pact with the PNU that saw Kalonzo Musyoka appointed as the country's vice president while its chairman, Samuel Poghisio, was appointed a Cabinet minister. After the signing of the National Accord that ended the post-election violence, its secretary general, Mutula Kilonzo also joined the Cabinet, and the government appointed a number of assistant ministers from the party.

The Party of National Unity (PNU) was registered in October 2007 with the sole aim of providing a vehicle for Kibaki's re-election bid. The PNU, just as NARC before it, started as an umbrella party that accommodated constituent parties such as KANU, NARC-K, FORD-P, the DP, Shirikisho and FORD-K. Thus, in 2007, Kibaki was the only direct member of the party. After the election, and in order to fend off the pressure from the ODM over the disputed presidential election results, the party entered into a pact with the ODM-K. Additionally, the party courted the small parties that were represented in Parliament to vote alongside it.

Table 6: Political parties represented in Parliament in 2007 (by end of 2009)

Party	Seats	Seats %
ODM	99	47.14
PNu	43	20.48
ODM-K	16	7.62
KANU	14	6.67
SAFINA	5	2.38
NARC-K	4	1.90
FORD-P	3	1.43
NARC	3	1.43
New FORD-K	2	0.95
Chama Cha uzalendo	2	0.95
PICK	2	0.95
DP	2	0.95
Sisi kwa Sisi	2	0.95
Mazingira, uDM, PPK, FORD-A, KENDA, NLP, KADu-A, PDP, FORD-K	(Total 10 seats) one seat each	4.8

The process to form new parties and alliances for the 2013 general election was not any different from the previous ones. The IEBC and the Registrar of Political Parties were not strict in enforcing the law, and individuals and political parties continued to behave as before. There was no clear break with the past. Leaders also switched from one party to another until a few days before the election. Of significances as well is that the elections law, under the 2010 constitution, allows for *pre-election alliances and coalitions. It allows parties to merge before elections and deposit their agreement with the Registrar of Political Parties before the election. For the purpose of the 2013 elections, there emerged two major alliances – the Coalition for Reform and Democracy (CORD), comprising two political parties (the ODM and ODM-K) and the Jubilee Alliance, comprising mainly the United Republican Party (URP) and The National Alliance.*

Table 7: Political parties' representation in various elective posts, 2013

	Governor	Senator	National Assembly	Women
Orange Democratic Movement (CORD)	16	11	78	15
Wiper Democratic Movement (CORD)	4	4	19	6
The National Alliance (Jubilee)	8	11	72	14
united Republican Party (Jubilee)	10	9	63	10
Others	9	12	58	2
Total	**47**	**47**	**290**	**47**

Internal party democracy

In Kenya, political parties are poorly organised, poorly resourced and lack distinct ideological grounding. Because most, if not all, political parties are active only during election years, one is tempted to categorise them under the 'electoralist genre'. This is because they subscribe to most of the characteristics that Gunther and Diamond ascribe to this category: as political vehicles used by the elite to win an election and exercise power; they are organisationally shallow and/or weak, have a superficial and vague ideology, and are overwhelmingly elections-oriented. Furthermore, the overriding (if not sole) purpose of these parties is to maximise votes, win elections and govern. As would be expected, these parties are fluid, and in their effort to expand their appeal to a wider variety of groups, their policy orientations are eclectic and shift with the public mood. For a political party to be internally democratic, at a minimum, there are four key aspects that it must fulfil: (i) development of a member-centered party document; (ii) establishment of an accountable and effective party structure; (iii) the holding of free, fair and peaceful party nominations and elections; and (iv) the establishment of an effective internal mechanism for conflict resolution. Kenyan political parties cannot be said to be internally democratic because the achievement of these four minimum ingredients of internal democracy remains elusive. Implicitly, the lack of internal party democracy could be attributed to the many years that most of the party leaders spent under the one-party regime, as well as to the financial muscle that most of them have over their parties. These leaders have developed elaborate patronage linkages with their ethnic communities, which have enabled them to control the parties' activities and most,

A remarkable feature of Kenyan parties is that they have been marked by little institutionalisation. Most of them do not have proper party structures, and a majority lack offices outside the major urban centres. One of the big threats to the institutionalisation of political parties in Kenya has been the lack of a disciplined party membership. From the 1992 elections up to the 2007 elections, there has been a dearth of distinct party membership, coupled with very few card-carrying members; this could be the reason most parties have failed to have a sustainable lifespan. Where 'members' have cards, those cards have in most cases been bought for thDaily Nation, 29 November 2007. Daily Nation, 17 November 2007; The Standard, 17 November 2007. Daily Nation, 19 November 2007. Ibid. e than one party membership card for different political parties. The practice of internal democracy has also been hampered by the fact that most parties lack funds. Most parties are thus run by an individual or group of leaders' funds. Investment in major political parties is by a few wealthy individuals who, by virtue of their financial power, control them and determine their affairs. This makes the parties dependent on the whims and ambitions of these leaders. Such was the case that FORD-A took a downward slide after Kenneth Matiba withdrew his patronage. On the other hand, other parties came to life when they were taken over by financially endowed politicians, for example, Raila's takeover of the NDP and Nyachae's takeover of FORD-P. The patron-client tradition that bestows upon certain individuals who control parties the power and authority to overrule decisions suggests that members have no stake in their parties. This lack of space for membership interventions is clear evidence of the general lack of internal democracy in most parties. This creates doubt about the ability of parties to institutionalise democracy at the national level when they cannot achieve internal democracy. Many Kenyan parties are also oligarchic in nature. Party elections are rarely held. For the few that have been held, they are mostly coronations for the party leader and his or her lieutenants. In others, such elections have been hampered by maladministration, confusion, incivility, widespread allegations of rigging and even violence. In addition, party structures and lines of command often appear to be unclear, inefficient or haphazard.

It is against this background that most parties in Kenya have experienced internal wrangles as members seek to create the democratic space to exercise their rights. Such wrangles have, in the end, led to splits or defections. Examples abound and include, FORD, the movement that in 1992 looked poised to dethrone KANU from power. Internal wrangles led to its split into FORD-K and FORD-A and five years later another offshoot, FORD-P, was formed. Second, FORD-K in 1996 split over leadership wrangles between Kijana Wamalwa and Raila Odinga, with the latter decamping to the NDP. Third, the battle for the control of FORD-A between Kenneth Matiba and Martin Shikuku led to the former founding Saba Saba Asili. Fourth, KANU, in the countdown to the 2002 elections, split when Moi imposed Uhuru Kenyatta as the presidential candidate and renegades decamped to the LDP. And in 2007, the ODM-K split because of wrangles over bona

fide officials and contests around who would be the presidential nominee, with Odinga's faction

decamping to the original ODM. These examples are vivid indicators that internal democracy is lacking in most parties. This is the main explanation for the back and forth movements between and within parties.

Furthermore, although party constitutions and manifestoes outline relative democratic practices and progressive ideals, virtually all parties have failed to hold fully democratic elections for party offices. Party leaders and top party organs seem bent on interfering in internal elections. In most parties, particular posts are assigned to popular individuncies in the party. Competition, if any, is thus confined to the region in question. This is the situation that prevailed during the 2005 KANU elections.

The nomination of party candidates is another area where internal democracy in parties can be faulted. Party leaders and top party organs routinely control who gets nominated. Intimidation, violence, vote buying and even sidestepping the process have been seen in all the major political parties' nominations. All political parties have, in theory, laid down procedures for identifying candidates for the various elective positions. These procedures and the rules governing them are, however, rarely adhered to.

All the pre-election nominations by political parties since 1992 have been dogged by the interference of the top leadership at every level of the contest, especially nominations for parliamentary and local council elections. There have been cases where a contest produces a winner, only for a loser to be declared the party candidate. In 2002, Suleiman Murunga beat Mukhisa Kituyi in the NARC nominations in Kimilili, only for the party's top organ, the Summit, to settle on Kituyi. So was the case in Nairobi's Starehe constituency, where the Summit overturned the election of Jimnah Mbaru and settled on Maina Kamanda. There have also been cases where winners have been shunted aside and direct nominations handed out by the party leadership. In some cases, figures have been tampered with and the winners' voters assigned to the losing contestant. The problem has been getting worse from election to election. In 2002, there were a total of 26 double nominations that affected all the three main parties as a result of interference by the parties' top decision-making organs. Overall, the situation has been so messy that in some cases, more than two candidates would claim to have been nominated, some directly by the party's headquarters, others by regional or district coordinators. This would be in addition to those who were nominated by the voters according to the agreed formula – either by secret balloting or queuing.

The 2007 party presidential primaries were largely reflective of the primaries of the previous election years, whereby the candidates were known well before the nomination exercise was carried out. The primaries turned out to be a mere formality. The three main political parties the PNU, ODM and ODM-K – did not exist during the 2002 elections and were hurriedly cobbled together, from among the parties that participated in the 2002 elections, some months before the 2007 elections. This is a clear indicator that parties remain very much the preserve of strong individual politicians who hold sway over them and who stand above the parties institutional structures. This is evident from the fact that immediately after the leaders left their original parties to go into the PNU, ODM or ODM-K, their supporters moved along with them. It is this same lack of institutionalisation that led to the split in ODM-Kenya. The PNU's candidate, by virtue of incumbency, was unopposed while the ODM and ODM-K's candidates were elected through the delegates system.

Both the ODM and ODM-K held their primaries for presidential candidates on consecutive days at the Kasarani Sports Complex in Nairobi. Both parties settled for a secret ballot as tpool of 4 200 delegates, with each of the 210 constituencies contributing 20 members. But how these delegates were selected remains unclear as none of the two parties held any elections. There was also a lack of transparency in the selection of delegates as neither parties had registered members.

On 31 August 2007, the ODM-K conducted its party nomination to elect its presidential candidate. Kalonzo Musyoka polled 2 835 votes against his sole opponent, Julia Ojiambo, who garnered 791 votes. On 1 September 2007, the ODM also conducted its nominations. Raila Odinga won in seven out of eight provinces with a clear margin after bagging 2 656 votes against his closest rival, Musalia Mudavadi, who had 391. William Ruto received 368, Joe Nyaga 30, while Najib Balala, who had stepped down in favour of Odinga, got four votes. Odinga named Mudavadi as his running mate and the rest of the presidential aspirants teamed up to form the Pentagon as a steering body for the party's election campaigns. Charity Ngilu was later incorporated into the Pentagon, besides being the chairperson of NARC.

In both primaries, there was an apparent effort to portray all steps of a democratic nomination, including transparent ballot boxes – complete with counting that was done on an open table. But there were some hitches in the voting, with officials in the ODM-K admitting that some non-delegates got to vote while some delegates voted twice. At the Eastern stand, delegates received up to three ballot papers each, as officials ferried more ballot papers to delegates in the stand. There was also no indelible ink to mark those who had voted, thus creating a possibility for delegates to vote twice. Confusion also reigned as some delegates demanded more ballot papers from various stands, prompting officials to bring in more. Journalists witnessed Kalonzo Musyoka's supporters stuff ballot boxes. At one time, the ballot box for Eastern Province was returned into the crowd long after voting was closed and stuffed with ballot papers. But the process ended smoothly with Kalonzo ultimately clinching the party's ticket. In the ODM, the presidential nominations were delayed for two hours as party officials made a last minute rush to sort out a problem with the delegates' list.

Generally, the election of the presidential candidates of the two ODM parties was a great improvement from the previous election years when the leaders ended up being the automatic party flag-bearers.

A further inhibition to the exercise of internal democracy was the fact that the three main political parties were hurriedly cobbled together and as such had no stable membership. They could hardly marshal appropriate systems and mechanisms to manage the demands of a countrywide nomination process. The national election eboards (NEB) of the PNU and ODM were simply overwhelmed by the exercise, which had attracted thousands of candidates at the parliamentary and civic levels. The necessary logistics and infrastructure for the successful execution of the nomination exercise was, in most cases, either not in place or poorly implemented. The ODM-K, on the other hand, had an easy time as its nominations mostly attracted candidates in its Kamba-inhabited stronghold of Eastern Province. For one to participate in the nominations, conducted through the secret ballot, one had to produce a national identity card and a voter's card. Candidates were required to pay a nomination fee of KSh 100 000, as well as a membership fee of KSh 30 000 for the PNU, KSh 20 000 for the ODM and KSh 10 000 for the ODM-K. Additionally, a candidate had to pay another KSh 10 000 for 1 000 membership cards for the signatures required from supporters.

The unpreparedness of the national election boards in the three parties was to blame for the chaotic nominations. This, coupled with massive rigging and blatant vote buying among a host of other electoral malpractices, triggered violent protests. The headline of The Standard newspaper, 'Rungudemocracy', aptly captured the state of parliamentary and civic nominations in the three main political parties. The nominations were characterised by mismanagement, runaway chaos and the destruction of property, as well as assault, protests and defections. Gangs and angry supporters of rival candidates clashed in virtually all of the country's eight provinces as security forces struggled to restore order. There were protests from numerous aspirants in the three parties over irregularities in the nominations. Claims of rigging were most pronounced in Western, Rift Valley, Nyanza, Central and Nairobi Provinces. Voter bribery was also rampant during the exercise, especially in the strongholds of the three main parties. In total, political parties and candidates spent nearly KSh 1 billion in voter bribery during the nominations. A survey conducted by the Coalition for Accountable Political Financing found that politicians and their parties spent more than KSh 5 million in each of the 210 constituencies by the end of the nominations week. The findings painted a damaging picture of the party nominations outcomes: it showed that all party nominations exercises were effectively about vote buying and voter bribery, as four out of every five voters were bribed to participate. The mode of conducting the PNU nominations was a bone of contention among the constituent parties. The first method suggested joint nominations where all parties would compete under the PNU banner. The second was that each party hold its own nominations but back the incumbent for the presidency. The latter method was viewed as divisive since constituent parties would be competing against each other. The PNU thus settled for joint nominations in 140 constituencies, individual parties competed in 30 seats and about 40 slots were filled through direct nominations. KANU was given an exemption to field its own candidates where they won in the joint nominations to enable it to retain its identity. The 'corporate' entity that KANU bargained for within the coalition made other parties decline from participating in the joint nomination. They chose, instead, to field their own candidates independently. In this category candidates independently in select constituencies in its stronghold of the Gusii-occupied areas of Nyanza Province.

Other parties fielding their own candidates were Sisi kwa Sisi, Agano and the Mazingira Party. The transparency of the ODM's elections board was also brought into question by somere, for example, a former legislator, who all along had the open support of one of the elections board members, transported ballots, and literally manipulated the entire nomination process. In Eldama Ravine, former MP, Musa Sirma, drew a gun to scare away angry party supporters who were baying for his blood after ballot papers were found in his car. In Kisii, an ODM nomination returning officer in Bonchari constituency was taken hostage for several hours by supporters of four aspirants whose names had been dropped from the list of candidates. These sorts of anomalies, and the ones that continued to trickle in as the nominations proceeded, forced the party to set up an appeals board to handle complaints arising from the exercise. However, in the majority of cases, the appeals board was unable to address the anomalies and the party's highest decision-making organ – the Pentagon – was forced to intervene.

Tampering with the ODM nomination results was more widespread in Nyanza, Western and Rift Valley Provinces. In Nyanza, one-time Ugenya legislator, James Orengo, outgoing legislators, Philip Okundi and Peter Odoyo, lost in the nominations but were cleared to run on the party's ticket. Others included Enock Kibunguchy and George Khaniri. In Rangwe, an angry mob stormed the home of Philip Okundi and damaged property to express their anger at the ODM's decision to issue him with nomination papers despite losing. His nomination was later rescinded. In Nyakach, youth barricaded roads and lit bonfires after word spread that former legislator George Khaniri had been trounced by newcomer Maurice Makomere. Hardly twelve hours later, the elections board overturned the decision and handed Khaniri the ticket, arguing that some votes had not been counted. Makomere later defected to FORD-K, but Khaniri won the elections. In Khwisero, Barrack Muluka had emerged the clear winner in the nominations only to be replaced by Evans Akula. While the nominations of Okundi, Odoyo and Kibunguchy were reversed after violent protests by the winners and their supporters, those of Khaniri, Akula and Orengo stood, forcing the affected politicians to defect. The ODM-K's nominations were the most peaceful of the three main parties, reflecting the low passion they stirred in many areas. In many cases, the ODM-K candidates were unopposed except in the party's stronghold of the lower Eastern Province. Outside Eastern Province, the primaries were not competitive and, therefore, not well attended. Little was reported on the Nairobi elections, and most candidates are believed to have run unopposed. In Rift Valley, Coast, Western, Nyanza, Central and North Eastern Provinces, the majority of the ODM-K candidates were selected rather than elected. The ODM-K was, however, the only party that fingerprinted voters with indelible ink to prevent double-voting. Unfortunately, this did not prevent members from other parties participating in its nominations.

The much-touted appeals outfits set up by the respective parties were overwhelmed by the complaints that came their way. In the end, the appeal bodies failed to fulfil their mandate and the parties' top decision-making organs were forced to intervene. Again, the inability of the appeal boards to address the electoral malpractices during the nominations, as well as the consequent intervention by the top decision-making organs, paints a grim picture of internal party democracy as well as institutionalisation.

The chaos that prevailed in the three main parties' nominations resulted in last minute defections from major parties to the fringe ones, a damning indictment of low institutionalisation. The main victims of defections were the PNU and ODM. PNU candidates defected to constituent parties once they missed the joint nomination certificates, while ODM losers joined the ODM-

K, NARC, KADU or other fringe parties. The ODM-K, which received most of the defectors, also faced defections as those who had been dislodged sought alternatives elsewhere. In its stronghold in lower Eastern Province, the ODM-K suffered a few defections from members who were dissatisfied with the way the nominations had been conducted. For instance, in Machakos Town, outgoing legislator, Daudi Mwanzia defected to the LPK and, in Kitui West, Francis Nyenze boycotted the nominations and moved to The Independent Party (TIP). Last-minute defections have been a perennial problem since the country reverted back to multi-party politics

Direct nominations

Interference in nominations by the parties' bureaucracy also demonstrated the gaping lack of internal democracy. Cases of direct nominations were rife in all the three major parties, more so in the PNU and ODM, which gave about 46 and 50 direct nominations, respectively, for one reason or another. There were also cases where certificates were awarded to losers, forcing the winners to defect to other parties. The respective parties argued that those who had been given direct nominations were the only applicants for the seats in question. However, this was only in a minority of the cases.

After analysing the 2007 parliamentary and civic nominations by political parties, the Centre for Law and Research International (CLARION) observed that numerous direct nominations were awarded to candidates – mainly in the PNU and ODM – forcing other contestants in these parties to seek alternative parties or pull out of contention altogether. The report argues that some candidates got certificates because of their 'good connections' with the party headquarters, the election boards and/or the leaders.

In the PNU, the majority of the direct nominations involved individuals who were said to be either preoccupied with the presidential campaign or party affairs. However, in reality, most of

them got nominations by virtue of their 'connections' with the key decision-makers in the party. A total of 14 Cabinet ministers, including Vice President Moody Awori (Funyula), Maina Kamanda (Starehe), Suleiman Shakombo (Likoni), Mutua Katuku (Mwala), Mutahi Kagwe (Mukurweini), John Michuki (Kangema), Njenga Karume (Kiambaa), Musikari Kombo (Webuye), Mohammed Abdi (Wajir East), Rapahel Tuju (Rarieda), John Munyes (Turkana North), Paul Sang (Bureti), Joseph Munyao (Mbooni) and Kivutha Kibwana (Makueni) received direct nominations. Of these, only Michuki, Munyes and Saitoti retained their seats in the elections. Outside Central and Eastern Provinces, the party gave direct nominations to candidates in many constituencies. In the majority of cases, the PNU candidates who got direct nominations lost in the elections.

These direct nominations created animosity among the constituent parties in the alliance, with some accusing the PNU leadership of favouring particular candidates in areas where they were unpopular. This forced some candidates to seek nomination certificates from their original parties. In some cases, like the Kiambaa, North Imenti and Mukurweini constituencies, candidates beat PNU rivals at the elections in the PNU strongholds.

Just like the PNU, the ODM handed direct nominations to candidates mainly from the PNU in Central Province and the ODM-K strongholds in Eastern Province. In these two regions, the ODM's chances at the parliamentary elections were almost nil. The party chose, therefore, not to hold any nominations. Selected candidates were simply awarded the party's certificate to contest elections. Pentagon members, some party officials and a few others involved in the presidential campaign were also given direct nominations. These included Raila Odinga, William Ruto, Najib Balala, Joe Nyagah, Musalia Mudavadi, Peter Anyang'-Nyong'o, Omingo Magara and Henry Kosgey.

However, direct nominations in some constituencies in ODM strongholds provoked great fury, with some candidates and their supporters protesting violently. A case in point was in Kisumu Rural, where the ODM had handed party secretary-general Anyang'-Nyong'o a direct nomination. His rivals held a demonstration and accused the headquarters of cheating them out of their nomination fee. Protests also rocked Isiolo North, Isiolo South, Moyale and Saku where the ODM anSection 25 of the Political Parties Act (2011). Ibid, section 26. already picked their preferred candidates.

Initially, the ODM-K had ruled out direct nominations for both parliamentary and civic nominations. However, this rule was broken when the party began receiving defectors from their rivals. It gave them direct nominations, even in areas where candidates had been elected or nominated unopposed. These candidates were asked to step down in order for the defectors to receive the party's parliamentary nomination. For instance, Elijah Bor stepped down in favour of former minister John Koech, who moved to the party after losing in the ODM nominations. In other examples, like in the Makueni constituency in Eastern Province, no nominations were conducted and the 15 parliamentary candidates, including party chairman Daniel Maanzo, were asked to step down for Peter Kiilu. Maanzo was promised nomination as an MP. It was, however, not clear on what basis Kiilu was picked and why the nominations were never conducted. Judging from the foregoing, it is evident that political parties in Kenya fail the internal democracy test. They, for the most part, do not adhere to their own operational procedures.

Constitutions that contain rules and regulations for conducting the affairs of parties exist on paper, but are never adhered to.

The Political Parties Act, which came into effect in August 2011, has provisions that have gone a long way towards addressing the problem of internal democracy in political parties, but only partially so. These provisions also find expression in the current constitutions of various political parties, but are yet to find full adoption.

Policy development and implementation

Internal party democracy can also be enhanced through the development of documents that incorporate members' input. The most important documents to this end are the party constitution, manifesto and any party position papers. Ideally, before these party documents are written and adopted, leaders and members should brainstorm and discuss the party ideology, philosophy, aims and objectives, values and principles, internal organisation and structure, and decision-making protocol. They should debate the powers and limitations of each office bearer. On the contrary, political parties in Kenya since independence have always lacked a connection with the masses that do not influence the policy-making process. Members are rarely called upon to endorse specific policy positions. These are left in the hands of technocrats linked to the various political parties or a platform committee. The commitments are then endorsed by party conference delegates.

Most parties are also not formed along ideological lines but rather on a given leader's ambition to win elections. A critical look at the various party manifestoes and other policy documents in Kenya reveals striking and remarkable similarities. Most, if not all, political parties in Kenya espouse the tenets of social democracy. However, these tenets are rarely put into practice and remain only on paper – as neither party leaders nor members stick to the professed ideology. Furthermore, even where such party manifestoes exist, they never form the backbone of the campaign strategies and platform. Overall, only the major parties in each election year develop manifestoes outlining the policies and programmes that they intend to implement once in office. A majority of the parties, most of which never field presidential candidates, have perennially no reference policy documents, which brings into question their readiness to govern. Ruling parties have also perennially ignored the policies that they outline in their manifestoes once in power. KANU, for example, promised in 1963 and in every election year thereafter, that it would eradicate poverty, disease and ignorance. These promises wIbid, section 28(2). Ibid, section 300. Ibid, section 31(5). ndence, but the state lacked the capacity and resources to meet them. They were generally unrealistic promises and were aimed at simply showing that the colonial state had left a burden on the newly independent state. Thus, four decades later, when it was removed out of power, these societal problems had increased rather than been reduced. When NARC came to power in 2002, it also had lofty promises that included a new constitution in 100 days and zero tolerance towards corruption. The party not only failed to provide a new constitution in 100 days, but actually spent the better part of its time in power trying to sabotage the will of the masses for a people-driven constitution. It thus came as no surprise when the Kenyan people rejected its version of a new constitution during the 2005 referendum. On corruption, the party found itself entangled in the Anglo-Leasingscandal, in which Kenya stood to lose KSh 53 billion in fraudulent security-related contracts.

Party financing

From independence in 1963 up to the 2007 elections, political parties in Kenya did not receive state funding. The Societies Act did not have specific restrictions on political parties. There was no provision regulating parties' sources of finance. There also was no restriction on donations that parties could receive. They could accept contributions from businesses, unions, foreign sources, as well as their own businesses. There were also no limits to political party or candidate spending during election and non-election periods. A law imposing a spending ceiling of KSh 40 000 on candidates was repealed in 1992. Political parties and candidates were also not required to file reports disclosing their funding sources. Parties were, however, required to submit financial statements to the Registrar of Societies for audit. However, there has not been large-scale compliance. The foregoing situation is bound to change with the coming into force of the Political Parties Act.

Most parties in Kenya have, therefore, only remained significant on the political scene insofar as wealthy individuals remained at their apex. Parties have risen and fallen at the whims of these individuals. Among the parties that became major players after their takeovers by wealthy individuals include the NDP when it fell under the control of Raila Odinga, and FORD-P after Simeon Nyachae took it over. Others have lost ground after their chief financiers lost interest in them – such was the case with Kenneth Matiba and FORD-A, and Kibaki with the DP. The absence of public financing for political parties in Kenya has had a negative impact on parties in general and opposition parties in particular. Ruling parties have often exploited the advantage of incumbency to extract state resources to finance their election campaigns at the expense of the opposition. This financial disparity between the ruling party and the opposition has derailed the democratisation process in Kenya because the political playing field has been uneven. Abuse of state resources by an incumbent party undermines democratic contestation for state power and in turn impedes meaningful participation in political processes in a democratic society. Membership fees are not a large part of political party financing because these are hardly ever collected. Many Kenyans join political parties expecting to gain materially from the party and its leaders. The financial resource base for most parties often comprises a few friends or associates of the parties' leaders. Many parties in the study undertaken by the Coalition for

Accountable Political Finance (CAPF) reported that they did not bother with membership fees;

instead they allowed only those who could afford their own campaigns to run as candidates. The Political Parties Act does not limit campaign finance.

Over the years, election campaigns in Kenya have been financed through donations from individual candidates and well-wishers, who mostly include wealthy party leaders and their friends, business entrepreneurs and, in some cases, foreign-based organisations and citizens. Public resources have not been spared either, even though the use of state resources in elections, as already noted, is expressly outlawed by the Electoral Code of Conduct and the Public Officers Ethics Act (2003). In spite of these two laws, political parties that have been in power have unlawfully utilised state resources at their disposal to the disadvantage of the opposition parties. Both KANU and its successor, NARC, have abused the advantage of incumbency. There have been numerous cases of the misuse and misappropriation of state resources or public facilities by candidates for the ruling party, especially the presidential candidate and Cabinet ministers. The most prominent financial scandals were the Goldenberg affair when KANU funded its 1992 election campaign from public coffers, and the Anglo-Leasing scandal that was overseen by the NARC regime with the goals of influencing the constitution-making process, fund the party elections as well as the 2007 general election. The Anglo-Leasing scandal was, however, nipped in the bud by the then permanent secretary in the president's office in charge of ethics, John Githongo.

Anglo-Leasing scandal

The Anglo-Leasing financial scandal was one of many corruption scandals that the NARC government inherited from KANU after winning the December 2002 elections and forming a new government. The scandal involved the newly appointed senior Cabinet ministers and senior civil servants who were already in office. After taking office, the government began to source equipment for passports and a forensic laboratory to facilitate the work of the police. The KANU government had started these prn had been quoted at EuR 6 million by a French company but NARC awarded it to a British company, Anglo-Leasing Finance. The tender itself had not been advertised anywhere and, therefore, the government had single-sourced, unable to conceal the scandal, a junior civil servant blew the whistle. He alerted the permanent secretary for ethics and governance, Mr John Githongo, whom President Kibaki had picked from a leading anti-corruption civil society organisation, Transparency International Kenya, to spearhead the fight against corruption. Mr Githongo notified the Cabinet ministers in whose ministries these two scandals were taking place: the Ministry of Internal Security whose minister, Mr Chris Murungaru, was President Kibaki's loyal and close adviser; and the Ministry of Home Affairs under Vice President Mr Moody Awori. This ministry was in charge

All the elections since the return of multi-party politics have seen opposition presidential candidates pump millions of shillings of their own money and the money of their wealthy friends into the campaigns. In the 2007 elections, the main political parties raised funds from party nomination fees, fundraising dinners, foreign entities and Kenyans in the diaspora, as well as corporations and chief executives of state parastatals. The PNU, using the advantage of incumbency, mobilised state resources for its campaign amounting to KSh 445 million. The ODM was, however, the biggest recipient of donations, amassing more than KSh 1.3 billion through this route. Small political parties became a phenomenal success after the party nominations fiasco in the three main parties. They collected KSh 340 million mainly from nomination losers in the three main parties. Among the major beneficiaries of this success were Safina, KENDA, KANU, KADU and TIP. The CAPF monitoring survey was unable to link the money collected by these small parties to any campaign expenditure. of immigration and, therefore, the passports project. In spite of informing them that Anglo-Leasing Finance was a phantom company and that the government was losing money, the two ministries authorised payments to Anglo-Leasing.

After questioning why the government had made payments for goods not delivered and to phantom companies, the Minister for Justice and Constitutional Affairs who was supposedly working with the permanent secretary to deepen the fight against corruption, pleaded with him to slow down on his investigations. He pointed out that Anglo-Leasing was 'our people' – alluding to people close to the minister as well as the president – meaning the political friends of the minister as well as the president. To scare the him, the minister brought to his attention a legal case involving the permanent secretary's father and an Asian businessman. Apparently, the 'businessman' was the front for Anglo-Leasing. The minister also informed Mr Githongo that the Minister for Internal Security was very much aware of the matter.

Aware that 'our people' or the Minister for Internal Security and the Vice President were behind the phantom companies, the permanent secretary decided to alert the president. No action was taken. In early 2005, Mr Githongo resigned from government and went into exile.

He had established that Anglo-Leasing had been turned into a cash cow for the consolidation of political power, particularly to fight the LDP faction of the NARC government. They were also raising funds to influence the delegates at the Constitutional Conference because the elites around Kibaki were opposed to some of the provisions that were popular with the delegates.

After going into exile, Githongo wrote a comprehensive report and forwarded it to the president mentioning specifically who was involved in what. The then Anti-Corruption Commission and the Attorney General promised to investigate the matter and even travelled to Europe to interview Githongo. After coming back to the country, the head of the Anti-Corruption Agency said he had lost some of the evidence he had recorded. In 2006, the Attorney General publicly said that he will not pursue any suspects in the Anglo-Leasing scandal. According to him, successful prosecution would not be possible because of a number of significant gaps.

Table 8: Campaign income of political parties in the 2007 elections

Issue	PNU	ODM	ODM-K	Small parties
Consolidated tracked party income (sources unknown)	611 000 000	1 300 000 000	50 000 000	
Consolidated tracked party fundraising dinners	646 000 000	388 000 000	65 000 000	
Consolidated parliamentary and civic aspirants application fees	108 000 000	300 000 000	58 000 000	340 000 000
Consolidated misuse of state and public resources for campaign (as income)	445 200 000			
Total resources mobilised	1 810 200 000	1 888 000 000	173 000 000	340 000 000
Consolidated tracked party expenditure	2 100 000 000	1 900 000 000	157 000 000	NIL

Overall, campaign expenditure for the 2007 elections amounted to approximately KSh 5. 6 billion, more than the KSh 4. 8 billion the various political parties raised. Many parliamentary candidates funded their own campaigns, with most of their money coming from personal resources. It cost approximately KSh 8 million for a candidate to run a parliamentary campaign, double the KSh 4 million in 2002. Women and youth candidates monitored could only afford between KSh 1 million and KSh 2 million. They were thus clearly disadvantaged when compared to their comparatively well-endowed (older) male counterparts. The Political Parties Act seeks to regulate political party finances. It seeks to set up a partially state-funded Political Parties Fund to be managed and administered by the Registrar of Political Parties. Up to 95% of the fund shall be distributed proportionately to the total number of votes each party's parliamentary candidates secured in the preceding general election, with 5% retained for administration. However, if a party does not secure at least 5% of the votes cast in that election or the office bearers exceed the two-thirds gender rule, that party does not qualify to get the funds. The funds are allocated to assist in the promotion of democracy and public participation, where the activities to be funded include: promoting the representation in Parliament and in the county assemblies of women, persons with disabilities, youth, marginalised ethnic groups and other minorities; promoting active participation by individual citizens in political life; covering the election expenses of the political party and the broadcasting of the policies of the political party; and the organisation by the political party of civic education in democracy and other electoral processes, among others. The capping of administrative and staff expenses is restricted to not more than 30% of the moneys allocated to the political party.

The law provides that these funds shall not constitute more than 0. 3 % of the revenue collected by the national government. Political parties shall also retain the right to receive other funds from membership fees, voluntary contributions from lawful sources, donations, bequests and grants from any other lawful source. It is prohibited for parties to receive funds from non-citizens, foreign governments, inter-governmental or non-governmental organisations. Foreign political parties, or other foreign agencies, that share an ideology with a Kenyan political party may give technical assistance, but this shall not include assets or funds. The Act also limits the level of contribution by citizens or organisations: 'that no person or organisation shall, in any one year, contribute to a political party an amount, whether in cash or in kind exceeding 5% of the total expenditure of the political party'. Every financial year, a political party shall publish (in at least two newspapers of national circulation) the sources of all funds, liabilities and assets. Further, political parties are also required to make declarations of members, assets and liabilities 90 days before an election. Failure to do so or publishing false statements will result either in a party being deregistered by the Registrar and not receiving any more funds, notwithstanding other offences, or penalties envisaged in the Act. The Auditor General shall audit all these funds within three months after each financial year.

The law however has some major shortcomings, which include failing to detail how to curb and penalise the abuse/misuse of state resources by the party in power. The only attempt to check this is provided for in the ban on public servants from engaging in political party activities. While such provisions find expression in other acts like the Public Officers Ethics Act and the Electoral Code of Conduct, they are yet to be enforced. But there are new institutions established under the 2010 constitution which are mandated to check the abuse of public office. These include the Ethics and Anti-Corruption Commission (EACC) and the Commission on Administration Justice (CAJ). The

CAJ is mandated to investigate the abuse of power and maladministration in the public service but implementation of its findings remain a major challenge.

There are also other important issues that the law fails to address: there is no governance framework for political parties or individual candidates' campaign finances. Sources of donations to individual candidates and parties are neither regulated nor controlled; with no requirement to disclose information about campaign income and expenditure. It is left to the discretion of parties and candidates to use the means within their reach to generate campaign finances and thus creating fertile grounds for corruption.

There is also no ceiling on expenditure for electoral purposes, both on the political party and individual candidates. However, there is downward accountability to members and the citizenry, where the Act provides that 'any person shall be entitled, to inspect the audited accounts filed by a political party and, upon payment of a fee prescribed by the Registrar, be issued copies of the audited accounts'.

Ethnicity and political parties

Kenya comprises many ethnic groups, whose actual number is difficult to obtain given the fluid nature of these identities. Some groups also desire to have distinct identities because they can demand benefits such as single member constituency seats in the National Assembly and appointments in public sector bodies. Estimates from various sources, including the census, show that the country has about 40 groups. Some of these are further sub-divided while others have only developed a common name and ethnic identity in the past few decades. Other estimates place the number higher depending on how the identities are characterised and the major divisions acknowledged.

Nonetheless, on the basis of census results, the major groups whose individual share of the national population exceeds 10% are the Kikuyu (17. 15%); Luhya (13. 82); Kalenjin (12. 86%); Luo 10. 47%); and the Kamba 10. 07%). Their total share of the population is 64. 4%. The second largest groups constitute 21. 21% of the population. These groups are the Kenyan Somali (6. 17%), the Kisii (5. 71%), Mijikenda (5. 07%) and the Meru (4. 29%). The 2009 figures on the Kenyan Somali, however, remain controversial. In the 1989 and 1999 census, the number of Kenyan Somali was about 1% of the national population. Their share of the population rose to 6. 17% in the 2009 census. This sharp and rapid increase in the population of a border community raised concern within the government. The government called for a repeat of the enumeration exercise in Somali areas of northern Kenya arguing that households inflated the number of residents during the earlier count. There were also concerns that the census included citizens from the neighbouring Somalia, who may have crossed into Kenya in the past two decades of that country's instability and registered as Kenya citizens.

There are two other groups whose individual share of the population is about 2%. These are the Turkana (2. 56%) and the Maasai (2. 18%). In line with the continuing formation of identities, a new category, Kenyans (so stated, perhaps in reference to individuals from cross-ethnic backgrounds), was recorded during the 2009 census as constituting 1. 58% of the population. These three groups comprise about 6. 32% of the national population.

The rest comprise over 35 groups. Their share of the population is only 8%. They include people of other races, Kenyan Europeans and Asians, and minority and marginalised groups. These groups are poorly represented in elective bodies and public service. They cannot have representatives in Parliament because they have insufficient numbers to enable them to compete in ethnicised politics through the use of a majoritarian electoral system. This ethnic structure implies that about five ethnic groups are dominant in the country, but none of them is numerically large enough to have hegemonic control over the others. It also means that there are over 30 smaller groups whose numbers are miniscule compared to the larger ones. Some of these groups live in remote areas of the country and are poorly represented in elective and appointed bodies, both in the public and private sector.

The absence of a single numerically large group, the relative equality of the five main groups, as well as the existence of many smaller groups whose combined share of the population is still a minority have meant increased politicisation of ethnicity in Kenya. Ethnic political elites tend to mobilise political support on an ethnic basis and by forming coalitions with the smaller groups. An incentive for coalition-building in this regard is the first-past-the-post electoral rule, which can see the presidency won by a small proportion of votes cast. Both the electoral rules and the relative equality of the five ethnic groups have meant that the competing elites form coalitions or get substantial support from any of the three other numerically significant groups or from a grouping of the 30-plus smaller groups. The ability to win the support of these smaller groups, or even a significant group among them, further intensifies competition among the elites from the main groups. Because of this, ethnicity has become a major political and social problem. But it is also symptomatic of another problem: centralised presidential powers which have invariably been associated with patronage. In turn, this has resulted in widespread corruption because the practice has little accountability and makes communities vulnerable. It weakens state institutions and all mechanisms by which people hold their leaders accountable. It is clear from the foregoing that ethnicity is the fulcrum around which politics revolve in Kenya. Political parties are as narrowly based on ethnic coalitions and organised under putative ethnic leaders as they were at independence. Electoral politics in Kenya thus consists of highly cohesive bloc-voting ethnic groups. Kenyans generally vote for the same party as their ethnic kin, and particularly so if the presidential candidate comes from their ethnic group. Consistently, parties have been formed at the behest of a single leader who provides financial patronage and who draws a core of founders linked more by personal ties forged in the ethnic arena than by ideology. This mode of mobilisation has shaped political party formation in Kenya and, subsequently since 1992, ethnicity has been the bane of Kenyan politics and the single most important reason for the rise and fall of parties.

In the run-up to the 1992 elections, most parties drew their support from a combination of ethnic communities. During this period, the politically significant parties included FORD-K, FORD-A, the DP and KANU. FORD-K initially accommodated the Luo, Kikuyu, Luhya, Meru and Somali within its leadership. The bulk of its membership was, however, from the Luo and Bukusu sub-tribe of the Luhya. Events between 1993 and 1997 saw the party reduced to a Bukusu party after the departure of leaders initially from the Kikuyu (Paul Muite), Meru (Gitobu Imanyara and Kiraitu Murungi), Somali (Farah Maalim) and later from the Luo (led by Raila Odinga) groups. In the 1992 elections, although it was the only party with at least an MP in each of the country's eight provinces, the bulk of its MPs were from Luo-dominated areas of Nyanza, and in the Bukusu-settled areas of Western and Rift Valley Provinces, where it won all the seats. At its inception in 1992, FORD-A drew its support from the Kikuyu of Murang'a and Kiambu as well as those in the Rift Valley, and the Luhya of Kakamega and Vihiga. This support was mainly as a result of the leadership of Matiba, a Kikuyu, and Shikuku, a Luhya. After the party failed to clinch the presidency in the 1992 elections, most Luhya MPs defected to KANU, reducing its following in the

Luhya-settled areas. The party suffered another setback when Kenneth Matiba disowned it, making it lose its electoral support among the Kikuyu. In 1992,

Mwai Kibaki's DP mainly drew its support from the Kikuyu of Nyeri, Kibaki's homeland and its environs, Meru, Embu and also parts of Kamba-settled areas of Eastern Province. KANU drew its support mainly from the Rift Valley, where its leader and then president, Daniel Arap Moi, came from. Moi's Kalenjin tribe, together with the Maasai, Samburu, Turkana and Pokot – who have settled in the Rift Valley – supported KANU. Because of its long stay in power, KANU was also able to mobilise other small tribes that included the Somali in North-Eastern Province, tribes in the Coast Province, parts of Eastern Province settled by the Kamba, as well as the Luhya in the Western Province. The 1992 election results thus clearly indicated systematic ethnic bloc-voting

for the major parties.

Table 9: Parliamentary seats won by individual parties in the 1992 general elections

Party	Province								Total
	NBI	Coast	NE	Eastern	Central	RV	Western	Nyanza	
KANU	1	17	8	21	–	36	10	7	100
FORD-K	1	2	1	1	1	2	3	20	31
FORD-A	6	–	–	–	14	4	7	–	31
DP	–	1	–	9	10	2	–	1	23
KSC	–	–	–	–	–	–	–	1	1
KNC	–	–	–	1	–	–	–	–	1
PICK	–	–	1	–	–	–	–	–	1
KENDA	–	–	–	–	–	–	–	–	–
Total	8	20	10	32	25	44	20	29	188

Just as in 1992, the results for the 1997 elections reflected ethnic support. During this election, a number of multi-ethnic parties were reduced to mono-ethnic status, and it was only KANU that retained a multi-ethnic following. The DP drew its support mainly from the Gikuyu, Embu and Meru Association (GEMA) communities. All the Kikuyu votes, in the absence of Kenneth Matiba, were rallied behind Mwai Kibaki. Most of its 39 seats were also drawn from the exclusively Kikuyu Central Province as well as the Kikuyu-settled areas in the Rift Valley. The DP, however, lost its Kamba following to Charity Ngilu, who was running for president on an SDP ticket. Although Ngilu's campaign handlers tried to rally the women voters as well, this did not materialise and she mainly garnered ethnic votes. Most of the party's 15 MPs also came from Kamba-settled areas. The NDP contested elections for the first time in 1997 and drew its support from Luo areas, mainly as a result of Raila Odinga's candidature on its ticket. It swept all the seats in Luo settled areas except two, one of which (GEM) it lost on a technicality. All its 21 MPs, except George Nyanja, were Luo. FORD-K fielded a Luhya presidential candidate, Kijana Wamalwa, and most of its support thus emanated from his community as did that of most of the party's 17 MPs elected.

Table 10: Parliamentary seats won by individuals in the 1997 elections

Party	Province								Total
	NBI	Coast	NE	Eastern	Central	RV	Western	Nyanza	
KANU	1	18	9	17	–	39	15	8	107
FORD-K	–	–	–	1	–	3	9	4	17
FORD-A	–	–	–	1	–	–	–	–	1
DP	5	2	–	8	17	7	–	–	39
NDP	1	–	–	–	1	–	–	19	21
SDP	1	–	–	9	5	–	–	–	15
Safi	–	–	2	–	3	–	–	–	5
Others	–	1	–	–	3	–	–	1	5

| Total | 8 | 21 | 11 | 36 | 29 | 49 | 24 | 32 | 210 |

The ethnic orientation of political parties has persisted even in the era of coalition politics. The party coalitions that have been formed since 2002 have not been based on the similarity or semblance of ideologies, policies or programmes, but rather on ethnic calculations.

In 2002, mono-ethnic opposition parties came together under an umbrella political party. The first such party was NAK, which brought together the DP – with its GEMA following, FORD-K with its Luhya base and the NPK with its Kamba support – as a framework within which ethnic-based parties could unite. NAK was later transformed into NARC after renegade KANU legislators decamped to the LDP and later merged with NAK. Although the LDP was multi-ethnic, it also had an inbuilt ethnic arithmetic in its quest for power. It thus had within its ranks politicians who commanded support from their respective ethnic communities. They were Raila Odinga for the Luo, Kalonzo Musyoka for the Kamba, Moody Awori who took over from Musalia Mudavadi, who had decamped back to KANU for the Luhya, William Ole Ntimama for the Maasai and Najib Balala for communities from the Coast Province.

Consequently, opposition leaders were able to unite their ethnic blocs under the NARC umbrella, which saw Mwai Kibaki bring on board the Kikuyus, Ngilu and Kalonzo the Kambas, Wamalwa and Moody Awori the Luhyas, and Odinga the Luos. The other significant parties during this election included KANU and FORD-P. KANU's following among the Kalenjin was buttressed by support from the smaller communities while at the same time getting a share of its support from some of the big communities, especially the Kikuyu since its presidential candidate was from that community. Ethnicity was also evident in FORD-P as it delivered all the Kisii MPs since one of their own, Simeon Nyachae, was a presidential candidate. Although he performed dismally in the presidential race, Nyachae wrapped up the Kisii vote.

Table 11: Parliamentary seats won by individual parties in the 2002 elections

Party	Province								Total
	NBI	Coast	NE	Eastern	Central	RV	Western	Nyanza	
NARC	8	11	1	22	21	18	22	22	125
KANU	–	7	10	9	6	30	2	–	64
FORD-P	–	2	–	1	–	1	–	10	14
Safi	–	–	–	1	1	–	–	–	2
Sisi	–	–	–	1	1	–	–	–	2
FORD-A	–	–	–	2	–	–	–	–	2
Safi	–	–	–	1	1	–	–	–	2
Shirikisho	–	1	–	–	–	–	–	–	1
Total	8	21	11	36	29	49	24	32	210

The central role that ethnicity has played in political parties was likewise evident in the 2007 elections. In 2007, the main parties that contested the elections were completely new outfits with varying ethnic formulae.

The ODM opted for a broad leadership structure and had at its apex the Pentagon, which comprised all those who had sought to run for the presidency on the party's ticket. The Pentagon initially consisted of Raila Odinga, Musalia Mudavadi, William Ruto, Najib Balala and Joseph Nyaga. They were later joined by Charity Ngilu of NARC. The Pentagon, for all intents and purposes, was meant to present the face of Kenya both regionally and ethnically. Under this strategy, Raila was to deliver the Luo vote, Mudavadi the Luhya, Ruto the Kalenjin, Balala that of the coastal communities while Nyaga symbolically represented the GEMA region. Ngilu, after being incorporated, was the face of the Kamba while Ntimama, though not a

Pentagon member, was expected to rally the Maasai vote. It is instructive that the ODM did not have a key Kikuyu personality within the Pentagon as well as within its ranks. This was mainly informed by the fact that the incumbent, Mwai Kibaki, was expected to easily mop up the Kikuyu vote. Thus, although the ODM eventually metamorphosed into a single party, it was for all purposes a coming together of ethnic groups under the various regional representatives.

The ODM-K on the other hand, styled itself as a coalition of parties but ended up with only one constituent party – the LPK – after its hope of attracting Uhuru Kenyatta's wing of KANU collapsed when he allied with the PNU. The ODM-K was, however, a creation of rebel LDP legislators and followers of Kalonzo Musyoka. Apart from Kalonzo, who was primed to deliver the Kamba vote, the other key members lacked gravitas in their regions, with most unable to command support even within their constituencies. The officials included Julia Ojiambo, Samuel Poghisio, Lucas Maitha and Joe Khamisi. Apart from Poghisio, the other three all lost their parliamentary seats. In any case, Poghisio's ethnic community, the Pokot, are limited in numbers and are thus not significant in national political arithmetic. The ODM-K, therefore, entered the race shorthanded insofar as ethnic arithmetic goes

The PNU was more adept at ethnic calculations. Not only were its constituent parties region-specific, but its potential point men were also from all over the country. Although some of these point persons' influence had waned, as the results attested, they were part of the ethnic arithmetic all the same. NARC-K and the DP were to deliver in Eastern and Central Provinces and the Kikuyu in the Rift Valley, FORD-P the Kisii, FORD-K and New FORD-K the Luhya, Shirikisho the coastal tribes, and KANU the Kalenjin in the Rift Valley. Kibaki was to deliver Central

Province, Kiraitu Murungi Meru, Simeon Nyachae Kisii, Musikari Kombo, Moody Awori; and Dr Mukhisa Kituyi Western Province, Chirau Mwakwere and Danson Mungatana Coast Province, Gideon Moi Rift Valley Province, Raphael Tuju Nyanza, Kivutha Kibwana lower Eastern Province, and Yusuf Haji North Eastern Province. Thus, just like the ODM, the PNU expected its luminaries to mobilise their respective ethnic communities.

Voting patterns in the 2007 elections suggest that Kibaki's supporters were mainly the Kikuyu, Embu and Meru communities of Central and Eastern Provinces, while Odinga's were the Luo, Kalenjin and the Luhya. Kibaki (PNU) received 97% of the total presidential votes cast in Central Province, his ethnic community's home province. The only other areas where he scored above 50% were the North Eastern (50. 3%) and Eastern Provinces (50. 4%). Raila Odinga (ODM) received most of his votes from the Nyanza (82. 4%), Western (65. 9%), Rift Valley (64. 6%) and Coast (59. 4%) Provinces. Similarly, Kalonzo Musyoka (ODM-K) received his highest votes (43. 8%) from Eastern Province. Kalonzi could not obtain a majority presidential vote in this province because, apart from the Kamba, Eastern Province is also home to the equally populous Embu and Meru communities, which are historically allied to the Kikuyu under the GEMA grouping.

Table 12: Parliamentary seats won by individual parties in the 2002 elections

Party	Province								Total
	NBI	Coast	NE	Eastern	Central	RV	Western	Nyanza	
ODM	5	12	5	2	–	32	18	25	99
PNu	2	3	–	7	18	11	2	–	43
ODM-K	–	1	1	14	–	1	–	–	16
KANU	–	1	4	4	2	1	–	2	14
Safi	–	–	–	1	3	–	–	–	5
NARC-K	–	2	–	1	–	1	–	–	4

FORD-P	–	1	–	–	1	–	–	1	3
NARC	–	–	–	2	–	–	–	1	3
Others	–	1	–	5	5	2	4	3	20
Total		7*	21	10*	36	29	48*	24	32	207

As Table 12 shows, at the parliamentary level, just as at the presidential level, the ODM received the highest number of parliamentary seats in the Western (18 out of 24), Nyanza (25 out of 32), and Rift Valley (32 out of 48) Provinces, while the PNU won the highest numbers in Central Province (18 seats while the remaining eleven were parties affiliated to it) and the ODM-K in Eastern Province settled by the Kamba where it got 14 of its 16 seats. In the Coast Province, the ODM won 12 seats while the PNU and its affiliates won seven, with the ODM-K and KADU-Asili each bagging one seat. The results show a broad ethnic trend in the voting patterns.

Women's representation in political parties

Most party constitutions and policy documents provide for women representation in their structures. However, these remain cosmetic as party activities have for the most part remained in the tight grip of men. For instance, a look at women representation in top party organs in the 2007 elections presents a disturbing picture. In the ODM's Pentagon, there was only one woman, Charity Ngilu, out of a total of six persons. She was, in any case, still a member of NARC and only allied her party with the ODM for the 2007 elections. In the Summit of the ODM-K, there was also one woman, Professor Julia Ojiambo, out of nine people. The situation was even worse in the PNU, where there was no woman in its Presidential Advisory Board of seven members. More importantly, women's representation in the three parties' respective campaign secretariats was insignificant. Women were also poorly represented in their respective parties' election boards. The ODM had two women, Josephine Kuluo and Sarah Shee, in an election board of eight while the PNU had two, Mary Michieka and Amina Abdalla, in a board of 13 persons after Njoki Ndung'u, who was Secretary, resigned. The ODM-K's election board did not have any women.

The bottom line is that parties are only enthusiastic in courting the female vote for their presidential and parliamentary candidates, but are generally reluctant to place them in significant positions. Likewise, women have not benefited from affirmative action from their respective political parties and they are mostly to be found leading women's departments. The result is that women have remained relegated on the side-lines of party decisions and activities. They are, thus, not key players in the country's electoral process.

Some of the parties lowered the nomination fees for women candidates but the women faced many other hurdles. For instance, during the party nominations, the playing field was uneven for women right from the beginning. First, they were underrepresented in the organs charged with running the nominations. Secondly, owing to historical and social disadvantages, they were financially incapacitated and could not match the huge sums of money men utilised in the nominations. Thirdly, they were unable to put in place the kind of militia that their male counterparts had resorted to in order to intimidate their rivals.

The 2007 candidate nominations attest to this. Of the 46 and 50 candidates directly nominated by the PNU and ODM respectively, none was a woman even though the two party manifestos contained specific clauses about party commitment to women's concerns. Therefore, most women were locked out of the electoral process at the nomination stage. None of the political parties met the rule requiring them to ensure that no more than two thirds of the candidates represented shall be of the same gender. only 58 contested from the main parties. In the

PNU, only 9. 6% (13 out of 135) of the contestants were women, in the ODM-K 6. 7% (20 out of 300) and the ODM 4. 7% (nine out of 190). In the civic elections, only 9. 6% (1 475 out of 15 332) of the contestants were women. Overall, the ODM's women candidates performed fairly well as they were competing in the party's strongholds. Six out of the nine candidates were elected while in the PNU only four of the 13 contestants won elections. The ODM-K, on its part, failed to deliver even a single woman MP.

In an attempt to address the foregoing, the new political parties law has a provision that bars a party from receiving money from the fund if its registered national office bearers do not include at least a third of either gender. It is projected that with more women in the top party organs, they can impact positively on party and electoral matters to the advantage of women.

Party competition and the role of the opposition

The capacity of the opposition to check the government in power since the re-introduction of multi-party politics in 1991 has been generally weak. This has been attributed to a weak political system, which has been characterised by the massive presence of parties that lack any ideology, party discipline and loyalty – all prerequisites for an effective opposition. The main difference between the parties lies in their leadership, and not so much in their political ideology. The personalities, not the programmes, make the difference between them. The resultant similar approaches to issues have made it difficult for voters to differentiate what the various parties stand for, as the manifestos end up being mainly different only in language and in the details rather than substance. Moreover, personalities and ethnicity, rather than the manifestos, form the backbone of the parties' campaign strategies.

The opposition has also been derailed by lack of a level playing field. However, it is partly to blame for its inability to play its role effectively. In articulating their demands for multi-party politics, the opposition elements in Kenya were too quick in allowing themselves to be hurried by the KANU regime into elections without first insisting on the implementation of far-reaching constitutional changes that were necessary for governing post-electoral political activities. The opposition appeared content with multi-party electoral contest in the hope of unseating the incumbent party. As it turned out transitional politiIbid, article 102(1). ore complex and not only dependent on multi-partyism and electoral contest.

In addition, factionalism took root and the prospects of success for opposition parties dimmed. Arising from the internal wrangles, prominent opposition figures moved from one party to another, with the majority retracing their steps to the ruling party from where they had defected in the first place. This demoralised the opposition and undermined popular interest in democratic politics. Opposition political activity also came to depend on donor funding for sustenance. On the whole, this aspect fed into the elitism that was a defining feature of the parties. Few retained the mass appeal they had elicited when they were first formed. To this end, opposition parties were very effective in the urban areas, but not so much in the rural areas. The then ruling party, KANU, had a more formidable grassroots structure and used its long stay in power as the only known political party to maximum advantage. It thus sought to justify the assertion that multi-party politics in the way in which it had unfolded meant little for the practice of governance and for the ordinary Kenyan.

Although Kenya's opposition parties have faced great frustrations at the hands of the state, some of their problems are internal. This is mainly because most of them have attracted the bulk of their support from the cleavages of tribe, kinship and, to a lesser extent, religion. Unable to win power in the first two multi-party elections, many of the opposition parties splintered into factions or faded into irrelevance; others became victims of the short-term goals of their founders.

Parties have also been formed with the sole purpose of speculation. Not all parties have been formed to organise around specific political agendas. Entrepreneurial party founders have known that every election year will be good for business since people will want to give their political careers a fresh outfit. Small opposition parties have, from time to time, been offered for sale to the highest bidder, especially when splits occur in major parties in an election year.

After losing the elections twice to the ruling party, the opposition finally accepted the reality that their only chance of securing victory over the KANU regime was the unity of the myriad parties. But KANU, true to its machinations, was the first off the block to counter any such opposition strategy. Immediately after the 1997 elections, the ruling party realised that the country had a hung Parliament and that it was, therefore, prudent to reach out to some opposition parties without necessarily entering a formal coalition government. To this end, KANU reached out to the now defunct NDP and FORD-K. The former stayed put, with the relationship being transformed from 'cooperation' to 'partnership' and finally the NDP was dissolved and its members incorporated into KANU. FORD-K back-pedalled on the relationship after a few months of warming up to KANU. The merger between KANU and the NDP stung the Ibid, article 97(1)(c). The 12 nominated members represent special interests, including the youth, persons with disabilitiesK as the umbrella body for the three parties. NAK was later transformed into.

The Commission created 80 new Constituencies as provided for in the constitution but members disagreed on the formulaethat made it possible for the opposition to win Ibid, article 99. ted at the time were the People's Coalition for Change, fronted by FORD-P and Safina. These developments signified that the age of coalitions had arrived in Kenya. After NARC got into power and KANU became the opposition, not only did roles change but so too did behaviour. NARC substantially behaved, to a large extent, in a similar manner as the tyrannical KANU that it had kicked out of power. In a liberal democracy, the government of the day is constantly supervised and made accountable to the people by both the opposition parties and civil society. A vibrant opposition and civil society are, thus, essential pre-requisites for democratic governance. The aftermath of the 2002 elections which was supposed to herald the collapse of an autocratic state, saw a mass flow into government of key civil society organisations and individuals who had been part of the second liberalisation. This, it can be argued, inadvertently set fertile ground for the germination of a new seed of autocracy. Hence, it was not surprising that the coalition government under NARC restored the KANU culture of intrigue and manipulation.

The co-option of KANU and FORD-P legislators into the Cabinet on 30 June 2004 left many in doubt about the continued existence of opposition parties as the act was seen as an attempt to cripple the opposition. The justification given by the NAK wing of NARC was that the persistent wrangles with its partner, the LDP, demanded that the country should have government of national unity if its stability and credibility was to be restored. However, the constitutional and parliamentary conditions that would warrant the formation of a government of national unity did not exist. This explained why many, including members of the then so-called government of national unity, were deeply divided as to the nature of the government in place. The reasonable explanation was the need by the NAK faction of NARC to stem growing internal opposition and marshal enough

MPs to ensure the passage of crucial government bills, especially in the wake of numerous defeats in Parliament. There was a concerted effort by the NAK faction of government to cripple opposition by co-opting KANU and FORD-P legislators into government.

These moves were not unique to the NARC regime; indeed the previous KANU regime used similar tactics and strategies to stem opposition. KANU argued that those who were co-opted by uals and the party was not consulted as would be expected in the formation of a government of national unity. It consequently filed a case in court challenging the inclusion of its members in government without the approval of its leader as required by the party constitution. However, in an environment with no democratic culture and a lack of proper party disciplinary machinery for dealing with errant members, NARC had the advantage of being able to immobilise the opposition parties and get away with it, just as its predecessor did. The judiciary never got round to adjudicating on the matter.

One unique aspect of opposition politics in the post-2002 elections was the increasing salience of opposition from within the ruling party. This emanated from the bad blood between the two NARC factions, NAK and the LDP, over disagreements around the memorandum of understanding that brought the two together in 2002. Indeed, at one point observers started wondering whether KANU was really the opposition, as the LDP seemed to have usurped its role. In the post-2007 elections, backbenchers in the grand coalition government of the PNU and ODM pushed for the formation of a grand opposition. The grand opposition proponents had also attracted legislators from the fringe parties in Parliament that did not get Cabinet appointments. President Kibaki and Prime Minister Odinga had both condemned this effort, saying it would undermine the coalition.

Conclusion and recommendations

There are many registered political parties in Kenya. The main ones have ethnic-based support. Not many of the main parties go beyond one general election as they fragment immediately after elections or have their leaders moving on to form new parties. Generally, political parties are yet to institutionalise; they are vehicles for campaigning during general elections. They lack ideological orientation and tend to operate on the basis of the founder leaders. Although there have been laws regulating their operations, with the current Political Parties Act (2011) being the second in a series, the Act has not been effective. A case in point is an instance in April 2012 when about 100 MPs defected from the parties that sponsored them to Parliament.

The following recommendations are made:

- The Registrar should prepare amendments to the Political Parties Act to prevent members of a political party from changing party membership at least six months before a general election.

- Resources allocated to the IEBC and the Registrar of Political Parties should be increased to enable them to implement the Political Parties Act so as to a create a new political party culture in the country. All those in violation of the law, especially party leaders, should be held accountable in accordance with the Political Parties Act.

- The IEBC should strengthen the laws regulating the use of public resources and consolidate them into a single law for ease of execution and reference. The law should

- impose heavy penalties upon leaders who use public resources in elections.

Thelegislature

Parliament is a critical institution for democracy and citizens' participation in political processes through its three pronged mandate of law-making, oversight of the executive arm of government, and representation. An eff and properly functioning legislature promotes and safeguards good governance and the values of accountability, transparency and participation. The manner in which members of Parliament (MPs) are elected, the composition of Parliament, and how it actually functions all have a bearing on the quality of democracy a country enjoys. Each democracy answers these questions diff and also deals with their attendant issues depending on historical, political, social and other contexts. Kenya's legislature is a combination of these contexts as seen below.

The legislature in pre-independent Kenya

The history of the legislature in Kenya starts with the country's colonial era, which dates back to 1885. Initially, legislation was passed in the United Kingdom and conveyed to the new colony in the form of 'royal instructions'. In 1906, an executive council was established, chaired by the Governor General to assist in the administration of Kenya. Provision was also made for the setting up of a legislative council, which first sat on 17 August 1907. It comprised the Governor as chair, and nominator of the other seven members: four ex-officio members and three officials. It was an all-white council and, therefore, excluded the other races such as the Africans, Asians and Arabs.

As the white settlers grew in number, they formed colonist associations in the various parts of the protectorate. It was not until 1910 that the various branches of these associations formed a nation-wide convention of associations. The convention meeting in July 1911 passed a resolution providing for the election of un-official members of the legislative council. This was the first time that such a strategy was being mooted. However, it was not until 1919 when the Legislative Council Elections Ordinance was enacted. This provided for the election of eleven Europeans to the Legislative Council. Following the Legislative Council (Amendment) Ordinance of 1924, representation of other races was considered. Thus, five Indians and one Arab were elected to represent their respective communities. At the same time, a white clergyman was nominated to represent African interests on the council. By 1934, the legislative council was composed of both elected and nominated Europeans, Indians, Arabs and two white clergymen representing the Africans.

The first time an African directly represented African interests in the legislative council was in October 1944. Following the royal instructions implemented in 1952, the legislative council was increased from 16 to 26 members. European elected members were increased from eleven to 14; Asian elected members from five to six, and African nominated members' representatives from four to six. The first contested elections for African members to the legislative council were held in March 1957. While the African representation in the council remained at 22 from 1958, the combined non-African membership rose from 55 in 1958, to 63 in 1959, peaking at 65 in 1960.

The legislature in post-independence Kenya

The first post-independence legislature in Kenya was bi-cameral and comprised the house of representatives and the Senate as provided for in the Independence Constitution agreed upon in London, following the Lancaster Conference on Kenya's constitution. Each senator represented one of the 41 districts in the country at the time. The Senate was, however, dissolved following an amendment to the constitution in 1966. In order to absorb the senators into the single-chamber National Assembly, one constituency was created in each district. After decades of struggles over a constitutional dispensation, Kenya once more adopted a two-chamber legislature to comprise a National Assembly and the Senate.

In post-independent Kenya, the legislature has played a significant role in national governance. The legislature is involved in:

- Law-making which requires members to consider, refine and pass legislative bills to improve the lives of Kenyans;

- Budgetary allocations where members consider, debate and pass the financial statements including taxation measures for the smooth running of government operations; Oversight where members scrutinise the financial, administrative and management practices of public officers and other public institutions. The goal is to promote transparency and accountability in public office and resources;

- Representation of constituents, through which members are a bridge between the

- electorate and the government, relaying issues facing the voters to the government

- for consideration and pressing for action. On the other hand, an MP is expected to communicate to the public about the ongoing government plans and policies to address their concerns; and

- Making and unmaking of the executive where members have the power to remove the executive from office through a vote of no-confidence.

Under the constitution, these roles are shared between the National Assembly and the Senate. Specify the Senate:

- Represents the counties, and serves to protect the interests of the counties and their governments;

- Participates in law-making functions of Parliament by considering, debating and approving bills concerning counties as provided for in the constitution;

- Determines the allocation of national resources among counties, as provided for in the constitution, and exercises oversight over national revenue allocated to the county governments; and

- Provides oversight on state officers by considering and determining any resolution to remove the president or deputy president from office in accordance with the constitution

The passage of a constitution heralded a new dawn for the legislature. Under the former constitution, Parliament ran for a five-year term, starting from the date when the National Assembly would first sit after dissolution. The term could be shortened or extended. The life of a Parliament would begin with the president proclaiming the start of the first session, which would be held within three months after a general election, and end with the president proroguing it (sending members on recess). A session would be held each year but without parameters on how long or short it could be. In the fifth year, or earlier, the prorogation would end in a final dissolution. Also, Parliament could extend its term for a year in the event of a state of emergency or war. The constitution guaranteed Parliament autonomy over its calendar. In the 2010 constitution, however, it is envisaged that the life of the National Assembly and the Senate shall be five years, and the president no longer has the power to dissolve Parliament. Under the constitution, 'the sitting of either House [of Parliament] may ... commence at any time that [it] appoints'. Further, the term of Parliament is pre-determined, which expires on the date of the next general election

The 2010 constitution has altered the structure of legislative power as well the composition of Parliament. Parliament now derives its legislative authority 'from the people and, at the national level, is vested and exercised by Parliament'. There are two chambers of Parliament: the National Assembly and the Senate, which share the Republic's legislative power. While the National Assembly represents the people of the constituencies and special interests, the Senate represents the counties and serves to protect the interests of the counties and their governments. The 2010 constitution provides for up to 290 members of the National Assembly, an additional 47 women each representing a county, 12 nominated membersand the Speaker. The Senate shall comprise of 47 members, each representing a county, 16 nominated women senators, two nominated members representing the youth,two nominated members representing persons with disabilitiesand the Speaker. Further, a third tier of representation has been introduced at the county level, where there are elected assemblies which legislate for their regions. There are currently 1 450 wards in the country, spread over the 290 constituencies.

Table 13 (overleaf) illustrates the progression in the number of electoral constituencies in Kenya since 1963 through to 1997. The columns show the number of constituencies created in the respective provinces. At intervals of between eight and ten years, or whenever directed by Parliament, the Electoral Commission of Kenya (ECK) was required to review the number, the boundaries and the names of the constituencies into which Kenya was divided to make desirable adjustments. Just before the 2007 elections, Parliament rejected the changes proposed by the ECK, because they had been brought as an omnibus constitutional amendment with contentious changes. Thus, Kenya went to the 2007 elections with boundaries that had not been reviewed for eleven years. After the dissolution of the ECK in 2008, the task of reviewing boundaries was given to the Interim Independent Boundaries Review Commission (IIBRC), whose term ended in controversy before the results of its review could be published. The constitution sets the number of constituencies for electing members of the National Assembly at 290. Although the basic minimum qualifications for contesting the election of an MP in Kenya are spelt out in the constitution (including the former constitution), it is not easy to ascertain the education and professional background of the MPs. Details on the education background of the legislators are scanty. In addition, a significant number of legislators are likely beneficiaries of ethno-party politics and not necessarily due to their education status. Others simply get elected on account of their relationship with leaders Daily Nation, Saturday 9 December 2006. Daily Nation, Monday 28 February 2008. Daily Nation, Friday 25 February 2005. Daily Nation, Friday 15 April 2005. of the dominant political parties. The law prescribes that for one to get elected as an MP, one has to demonstrate the basic minimum education qualification required of such an office.

Table 13: Evolution of electoral constituencies, 1963-2007

Province	1963	1966	1988	1997	2007
Nairobi	7	8	8	8	8
Central	15	21	25	29	29
Coast	12	18	20	21	21
Eastern	21	27	32	36	36
North Eastern	5	8	10	11	11
Nyanza	20	23	28	32	32
Rift Valley	24	37	44	49	49
Western	13	16	21	24	24
Kenya	117	158	188	210	210

Before the 1992 elections, the Kenyan legislature was synonymous with the Kenya African National Union (KANU) since it was the only political party in the country. In the ninth Parliament (2002-2007), the dominance of the independence party (KANU) in running the affairs of the country was ended by the National Rainbow Coalition (NARC). KANU retained only 63 seats in the National Assembly while NARC had an overwhelming majority of 106 seats. The other party that had significant representation was the Forum for the Restoration of Democracy-People (FORD-People), with 14 MPs. One remarkable feature about the tenth Parliament (2007–2012) was the number of political parties represented, which was over 20. The Orange Democratic Movement (ODM) had the highest number of seats with 100 MPs followed by the Party of National Unity with 47 MPs. Other parties which had significant representation in the National Assembly included the Wiper Democratic Movement–Kenya (WDM-K) (17) and KANU (14).

Although women constitute slightly over half of the population of Kenya and are enthusiastic at election time as campaigners and voters, few of them ating in politics, bias against women and campaigns, including insults against women, financial constraints as well as the inability to attract the political support of other women are some of the factors responsible for this. Ignorance and illiteracy, lack of adequate material and financial resources, violence before and during the election and the nature of the electoral system are yet others. A possible remedy to the low number of women in politics may be establishing a constitutional and legal system that is more supportive of women. In contrast, women in Rwanda, Uganda and Tanzania have made greater strides in political participation and their presence in Parliament is greater. Although women have made huge contributions to the socio-economic and cultural development of the country, their peripheral position in political and decision-making positions is very much influenced by the culture of patriarchy, which assumes that men represent women. Since independence, there has only been a modest increase in the number of women elected to Parliament. With the re-introduction of multi-party politics in 1992, more women began to take part in political activity. They were 5. 7% of the candidates that contested the 1997 elections, compared to 2. 2% in 1992. Unfortunately, only 1. 9% of the candidates in 1997 made it to Parliament, compared to 3. 2% in 1992. In order to bridge the gap in the National Assembly, KANU and other political parties nominated 41. 7%, against 8. 3% in 1992.

Table 14: Women representation in Parliament.

Parliament	Total number of elected MPs	Number of elected women in Parliament	Number of women nominated in Parliament	Total number of women in Parliament
1963–1969	117	0	0	0
1969–1974	158	1	1	2
1974–1979	158	4	2	6
1979–1983	158	5	1	6
1983–1988	158	2	1	3
1988–1992	188	6	1	7
1992–1997	188	6	1	7
1997–2002	210	4	5	9
2002–2007	210	11	7	18
2007–2012	210	15	6	???313

The adoption of the constitution heralded a new era for Kenya in terms of women's representation in the legislature. There are specific clauses that pro-actively seek to engage women in the country's two legislative bodies. In the National Assembly, there will be 47 women elected from the counties, regardless of how many are elected for the 290 single-member constituencies. In the Senate, the law provides for 16 women nominated by political parties, as well as two members representing the youth, with an additional two representing persons with disabilities. The law makes it clear that one of the youth and one of the persons with a disability must be female. This has fundamentally changed the landscape of Kenya's legislature.

Table 15: National Assembly membership, 1969–2007

Year of election	Number of candidates		Elected members		Nominated members	
	Total	% Women	Total	% Women	Total	% Women
1969	606	0.66	155	0.7	12	8.3
1974	739	1.49	157	3.2	12	16.7
1979	747	1.34	158	1.9	12	8.3
1983	727	0.96	158	0.6	12	16.7
1988	852	1.41	188	1.1	12	8.3
1992	854	2.23	188	3.2	12	8.3
1997	882	5.7	210	1.9	12	41.7
2002	1052	4.3	210	5.2	12	58.3
2007	2 600	10.3	210	8.5	12	50.0

Another way of promoting women's participation in political structures is by creating awareness and encouraging the active participation of women in political and decision-making processes at grassroots level. Such a strategy is likely to positively influence the perception at the grassroots regarding the role of women in decision-making and elective leadership positions. The National Policy on Gender and Development had proposed the creation of a Parliamentary Committee on Gender and Development to address issues of gender relations. The committee was to ensure gender-balanced approaches in the legislature, national and sectoral budgets, as well as on other issues as may be brought to the National Assembly for discussion and approval.

Kenya's electoral constituencies are largely demarcated along ethnic lines. This ethnic bundling has its locus in the colonial history of Kenya, where geographical boundaries tended to emphasise tribal conglomeration. The dominant ethnic entities in Kenya are represented in the National Assembly. However, there has been systematic under-representation of the minority groups in the country, whose numbers do not constitute a critical voting mass necessary to win a parliamentary seat. Such groups include Kenyan Asians, Kenyans of Caucasian origins and other marginalised communities such as the El-Molo. Additional special interest groups include the youth and persons with disabilities. Although the principle behind nominating MPs was to take care of such groups and other national interests in the National Assembly, these groups remain unrepresented. These seats have largely been used as a reward to loyal party members and other cronies of political leaders. The constitution addresses this anomaly by requiring Parliament to enact legislation to promote the representation in Parliament of women, persons with disabilities, youth, ethnic and other minorities and marginalised communities.

The turnover of legislators in Kenya has been quite high in some of the elections (see Table 16). For instance, out of the 158 MPs when it was dissolved in October 1969, only 57 were re-elected in the subsequent election. This particular election was driven by the fallout between President Jomo Kenyatta and Jaramogi Oginga Odinga. In 1974, only 99 legislators were re-elected while 74 were new. In 1979, only 98 legislators won re-election. The 1983 elections,

which were in part influenced by the then President Moi who was pointing fingers at some of his erstwhile political comrades led by Charles Njonjo, saw 114 legislators re-elected, with only 59 being new.

Table 16: Turnover of members of Parliament, 1963–2007

Parliament	Number of seats	Re-elected MPs	Voted out	% turn over
1963–1969	158			
1969–1974	158	57	101	64
1974–1979	158	99	59	37
1979–1983	158	98	60	38
1983–1988	158	114	44	28
1988–1992	188	101	87	46
1992–1997	188	115	73	39
1997–2002	210	97	113	54
2002–2007	210	110	100	48

In 1988, the KANU government introduced queue voting (Mlolongo in Kiswahili) in which voters would queue behind their candidates of choice or the agents of the candidate. The party argued that it was a transparent and Africanised method of voting and aimed at preventing cheating. Introduced at the height of political repression, voters feared to make choices that the government did not like. In the end, 101 MPs were elected. The number of re-elected MPs increased during the multi-party era (1992 elections) to 115. In the 1997 elections, however, only 95 MPs were re-elected. During the 2002 elections, 112 legislators were making their debut in Parliament. The 2007 elections witnessed a complete break from tradition as over 60% of the sitting MPs were voted out. This could be linked partly to the various public complaints on the newly introduced Constituency Development Fund (CDF), which sends money to communities under their elected leader's control. It could also be partly attributed to the fact that the improved terms of service for the legislators made politics more attractive, hence the increased competition. In addition, the ethno-party voting patterns may have also contributed to this scenario. This is the case where a very prominent and generally effective MP is voted out not on the basis of performance but for 'belonging to the wrong political party'. '.

Remuneration and support

Until the passage of the constitution, the salaries and allowances paid to all MPs – excluding the president – had been subject to the provisions of the National Assembly Remuneration Act and could only be varied by an amendment to this law. Since Kenya's independence, the remuneration of MPs has been reviewed several times. Two recent reviews warrant attention. The first followed the recommendations of a committee reviewing the terms of service for MPs

which was headed by former legislator Odongo Omamo in 1994. Its recommendations were implemented by amending the National Assembly Remuneration Act, in November 1994. The other major review followed the recommendations of a tribunal headed by retired Chief Justice Majid Cockar in September 2002. The recommendations of this tribunal were unanimously adopted during the first session of the ninth Parliament in 2003 (2003–2007). The tribunal further provided for the establishment of a Parliamentary Service Commission (PSC), whose mandate would be to champion better terms of service for the members of the National Assembly.

Two years later, following incessant public outcry about MPs not paying taxes on their allowances, the PSC of the National Assembly again instituted a tribunal on 23 January 2009, (vide the Kenya Gazette, Notice No. 699) to review the terms and conditions of service for MPs and staff of the National Assembly. Its report raised the taxable pay of legislators but cushioned them against the cost of living by increasing some of their allowances, again inviting widespread public protests. On 30 June 2010, Parliament adopted the report by the tribunal together with comments and recommendations of the PSC. However, upon the adoption of the 2010 constitution, all benefits and remuneration of all state officers are currently handled by the Salaries and Remuneration Commission (SRC). The remuneration of MPs has two components: the salary and the allowances. The salary is standard and without annual increments. It is also the only element of the remuneration package that is taxed. A closer look at the perks enjoyed by MPs in Kenya shows that they are adequately remunerated. However, compared to similar positions in the public sector, they are way better off, and can only be compared to the perks received by the chief executive officers of some of the most profitable blue-chip companies in the country. Other benefits accorded to legislators include car grants and financed mortgages.

However, these benefits did not come without a fight. In some instances, the MPs resorted to arm-twisting the executive to get their perks, especially the car grants. In 2003, the media reported the then Finance Minister, David Mwiraria, as presenting the proposals for the legislators' perks reluctantly. According to Treasury reports, he was effectively held to ransom by MPs in a committee considering his mini-budget proposals. The MPs had threatened to block the minister's budgetary measures – including money for free primary education and subsidised health care – unless the government included their car grants in the package.

The increased perks for the legislators provoked a public outcry. It was not inspiring that the first business that the members transacted after being sworn in was to increase their salaries and remuneration. The timing may also have been wrong considering that at the time, there were more pressing national issues such as the teachers' pay crisis. An opinion poll carried out by a local daily on the ensuing debate to increase salaries and allowances for legislators showed that 84. 9% of the respondents disapproved of the timing. In the same study, only 10. 8% thought that the increase in salaries and allowances for the legislators was justified. Since that time, the media have been awash with public fulminations against the perceived greed of MPs. Some publicly expressed views have termed the increments as selfish and myopic. Perhaps what drew more fury from the public was the winding up allowance MPs chose to award themselves at the end of their term, as well as the fact that their allowances are not taxed, even though they impose taxes on the rest of the country by passing tax proposals. Reacting to the winding up allowance, the church organisations described the proposals as 'scandalous' while the Institute of Certified Public Accountants of Kenya, Central Organisation of Trade Unions, Federation of Kenyan Employers and the Kenya National Union of Teachers protested. MPs appeared to determine their salaries and allowances on the recommendations of a tribunal, without oversight from any other body. Perhaps this anomaly is what the constitutional dispensation sought to correct by recommending the establishment of an organ to determine perks for MPs, the president, ministers and judges. Both the rejected draft constitution of 2005 and the contentious Bomas draft constitution were in agreement on this fact.

Currently, each MP is allocated an office in a building adjacent to the National Assembly in Nairobi. Each office is fully furnished with essential accessories (computer, fax machine, telephone, internet connection, stationery) and has support staff. Each legislator has a personal assistant and every two MPs share a research assistant. All this support is aimed at ensuring that each prepares adequately for debate in Parliament. The legislators can also use these offices for researching proposals, bills and parliamentary questions. The Nairobi offices also make it easier and more convenient for legislators to meet their constituents who travel to the capital. If an MP doesn't want to meet a voter, he/she can decline. In each of the constituencies, there is a constituency office constructed and financed by the exchequer. The idea of constructing constituency offices was developed during the early years of the NARC administration to make it easier for the public to access their representatives. The offices also served as coordinating points for the Constituencies' Development Fund (CDF) kitty. However, despite this kind of support, parliamentarians lack adequate research and secretarial support, a problem that the current administration has promised to solve pending the completion of the new building to accommodate the Senate. There is inadequate office space in the current buildings to accommodate the required staff and secretarial staff.

Peoples' representation, pre-election promises and the failure to deliver

Kamukunji is one of the 17 constituencies in Nairobi County. This constituency resonates very well with Kenya's second liberation struggle. This is because the constituency formed a key battleground with the KANU regime given the strategic location of the Kamukunji Grounds where most of the rallies to campaign for pluralism were held. Prior to the 2007 elections, it had become clear that all was not well with the use of Nairobi's CDF. The then sitting MP, Norman Nyaga, ran into trouble with an angry electorate that accused him of not releasing money from the CDF kitty. cation facilities.

In 2007, Nyaga opted to initiate the rapid implementation of CDF projects in Kamukunji, justifying his actions as having been geared towards building up the capital base for meaningful projects. However, his explanations were not well received. There were several incidents when he was publicly humiliated by angry, shouting, booing and placard-waving constituents. The reason for this show of displeasure by his employers – constituents – was premised on the feeling that he had failed to show what the CDF kitty had done. Some constituents branded him 'an absentee leader'. Thus, it was not surprising that he was not re-elected during the 2007 elections. A similar fate befell numerous other legislators across the country because of the poor management of the CDF.

Law-making and debate

Legislative power in Kenya was vested in the National Assembly under the former constitution. Parliament could discuss and pass bills, alter the constitution by a vote of not less than 65%, pass a vote of no-confidence in the government, and extend the life of Parliament beyond five years when Kenya is at war or during other emergencies. The National Assembly would pass bills and the president's assent would make them law.

Parliament could only make laws by passing bills. The standing orders of Parliament break this down and provide for both private members' bills and government-sponsored ones. Although Parliament gives priority to the government agenda in discussing proposed laws, private members also brought their proposals. There have been very few private members' bills in the history of Parliament in Kenya, implying the limited ability of private members to fill the gaps in government's legislative capacity. This could be linked to a lack of technical, financial and research capacity on the part of the members. In turn, Parliament does not have a functioning committee that could help members in this area.

During the ninth Parliament (2003–2007), the Sexual Offences Bill (2006) stands out as a private members' bill that eventually became law (Sexual Offences Act [2006]). This bill was introduced by a nominated MP, Njoki Ndung'u. The bill consolidated laws on sexual offences scattered all over the statute books and recognised certain sex-based offences such as sexual harassment, which were not in the include: the National Assembly Remuneration (Amendment) Act (2003), the Constituency Development Fund Act (2003); the Anti-Corruption and Economic Crimes Act (2003), the Public Officers Ethics Act (2003); the Forest Act (2005), and the Privatisation Act (2005). The ninth Parliament was unique because, unlike the previous Parliaments, it did not pass a single amendment to the former constitution. The only bill that sought to enable Parliament control its own calendar, which had been pending since 2003, known as 'the Katter Bill' after its creator, Charles Katter, was never slotted for debate. During that time, the president declined to assent to the National Hospital Insurance Fund Bill, which had proposed sweeping changes on financing access to health care in the country. During the life of the ninth Parliament, over 50 laws were enacted. 2006 was the busiest year with a total of 30 bills tabled for debate.

Government-sponsored bills dominated every year of the ninth Parliament. Records reveal that both 2006 and 2007 topped with the highest number of privately sponsored bills introduced in Parliament. The dominance by the government in the legislative agenda of the House could be partly linked to numerous procedural motions (e. g. finance-related bills) that account for a significant portion of debate in every financial year. Besides, the government has a lead role in promoting legislation aimed at realising the ideals of each ministry. The low number of private members' bills could also be linked to the resources involved in putting a bill in place.

Many new bills were introduced and very few amendments to the existing legislation proposed during the ninth Parliament. This could be linked to the change of government after the 2002 general elections. In addition, most of the bills introduced and passed during the period 2003–2007 were of a substantive nature and have had a great impact on governance, popular participation and the general socio-economic development of the country. One such bill is the Constituency Development Fund Act, which made it possible to devolve 2. 5% of the government's ordinary revenue to develop all the constituencies in the country. Most of the development projects in all the constituencies in the country from 2003 can be linked to this law. Other bills have dwelt on how to improve various sectors of the economy, such as agriculture, finance, health, as well as labour.

In the early years of the ninth Parliament, the president vetoed at least three bills that Parliament had passed. One of these was the National Health Social Insurance Fund Bill (2004), which had sought to provide universal health insurance to Kenyans. The private sector, especially health management organisations, heavily criticised the Bill since it was seen to be in direct conflict with their business interests. Poor drafting was also cited as one of the reasons for the president declining to assent to it.

Law-making and debate in the tenth Parliament have been informed by events of the aftermath of the violence that gripped Kenya following the disputed 2007 presidential election. The tenth Parliament was interesting in that all parties represented, save for one, were part of the ruling coalition government. The standing orders governing how business runs in Parliament have also been revised. Parliament had also amended the constitution to give provision for a coalition government, as well as the position of a prime minister and two deputy prime ministers. Parliament also enacted the National Accord and Reconciliation Act (2008) to give effect to the power sharing arrangement between the ODM and the Party of National Unity (PNU). This grand coalition government comprIbid. Ibid. tical parties forming the PNU and ODM-Kenya. This way, the tenth Parliament changed the structure of government for the period 2008 to 2012.

During the early years of the tenth Parliament, there was an increase in the number of bills presented for debate. For instance, in 2008 alone, there were 24 bills debated, three of them from private members. In the same year, 16 bills were passed but none was from a private

member. The three private members' bills included:

- The National Assembly (Parliamentary Opposition) Bill (2008), which sought to create an official opposition in the tenth Parliament;
- The Offices of Ministers Bill (2008), which sought to regulate the size of the Cabinet by defining maximum and minimum numbers allowed as well as requirements for the office of a Cabinet minister; and

- The Fiscal Management Bill (2008).).

In 2009, a total of 18 bills were tabled and debated in the house. Surprisingly, almost half of those bills (at least eight) were from private members.

Oversight role

Oversight and supervision of governance remain the most critical functions of Parliament. Parliament plays its accountability and oversight roles through a number of ways, for example, through proposals for action and through the actions of the various departmental committees. The legislature is mandated to ensure that public policy is administered in accordance with legislative intent. The National Assembly plays a role in budget approval. The formulation and presentation of the budget is essentially the function of the executive, but the legislature is the public forum in which the government seeks approval for expenditure through the budget debate. The legislature is an institution of accountability, not financial management.

Departmental committees scrutinise proposed government policy before it is debated in Parliament and the parliamentary watchdog committees scrutinise the national financial accounts provided by the Controller of Budget and Auditor General to ensure accountability to the taxpayer. In turn, a close working relationship between the Controller of Budget and Auditor General and Parliament enhances public confidence that resources are used efficiently.

During the ninth and tenth Parliaments, the Public Accounts Committee and the Public Investments Committee were at the forefront of investigations into the alleged misuse of public funds by government officials. Examples include the investigation into the Anglo-Leasing and Finance Company scandal, in which the government allegedly lost billions of shillings in suspicious dealings with questionable local and foreign firms on security-related contracts. Parliament put pressure on the government, which led to the temporary departure from office of the Minister of Finance, David Mwilaria. This pressure further created momentum for the temporary departure from office of the two other ministers and several other top government officials in 2005.

Earlier, in 2001, the Parliamentary Select Committee on Corruption had tabled the details of senior government officials who had misappropriated public funds or had had suspicious dealings with the state. This list was popularly known as the 'List of Shame'. Relevant departmental committees under the tenth Parliament also investigated the abuse of public office under the tenth Parliament, such as was the case with the oil and maize scandals. All in all, Parliament has been a leader in raising the red flag in instances where there is a perception of an abuse of public office or resources. The oversight role of the legislature has greatly been enhanced during the tenth Parliament. In the aftermath of the post-election crisis, Parliament played a critical role in ratifying the provisions in the National Accord that paved the way for a coalition government, as well as the creation of the office of the prime minister. According to the revised standing orders of Kenya's National Assembly, the prime minister was allocated 45 minutes every week, when Parliament was in session, to address the National Assembly on any pertinent issues affecting the country's development agenda. This provided the MPs with an additional opportunity to engage the executive arm and bring the government to account.

Parliament had increasingly become autonomous in this period. It vetted public officials who required parliamentary approval more rigorously, with some of the appointments put forward by the executive being rejected. A glaring example was the ruling by the Speaker on the position of the leader of government business in Parliament. While the president had nominated the vice president to the position, it emerged that the prime minister had also put his name forward for the same position. In his interpretation of the National Accord, the Speaker declined to accept either of the names and instead offered to occupy the position temporarily until the two principals in the coalition agreed on the matter. That ruling endeared Parliament to the Kenyan citizenry because of its ability to find a seemingly easy solution to an intractable stalemate that threatened to destabilise the country's politics.

The increasing autonomy of the tenth Parliament also became evident during the standoff over the reappointment of the Kenya Anti-Corruption Commission director, Justice Aaron Ringera. The president had bypassed Parliament as well as the Kenya Anti-Corruption Authority (KACA) advisory board by reappointing the director and the PNU side of the coalition was determined to maintain the status quo. The ODM would hear none of that. The Speaker ruled that Parliament could debate whether or not the president had followed the law in reappointing Ringera. Most parliamentarians saw the reappointment as irregular and therefore null and void. After weeks of public exchanges, the director was forced to resign.

Rejecting presidential appointments

Creating the office of the prime minister strengthened the independence of Parliament. Being the leader of the largest party in Parliament, the prime minister derived his power from that institution. Marshalling the ODM MPs and allies provided a counter to the president, who remained in charge of the executive arm of the government. That had, to a great extent, worked to the advantage of the citizenry. In fact, the experience of the two years after the signing of the National Accord suggested that perhaps a hybrid of a parliamentary and a presidential system could be used to govern Kenya.

In other instances, Parliament toned down the excesses of the executive, such as rejecting

regulations to rein in the media and frustrating the passage of constitutional amendments to The reappointment of Justice Aaron Ringera as the director of the Kenya Anti-Corruption Commission (KACC) for a second five-year term in 2009 elicited fierce criticism from the public, civil society organisations (CSOs), as well as Parliament. MPs questioned the procedure through which Justice Ringera was reappointed. Ideally, Justice Ringera should have undergone a fresh interview before the KACC advisory board and his name should have been presented to Parliament for vetting. Only then could the president reappoint him. However, the president reappointed Justice Ringera without following that process. Those who supported the president's action argued that Justice Ringera had already been vetted by Parliament and hence saw no need of subjecting him to that process again.

With Parliament divided along party lines, the majority of members seemed determined to overturn the reappointment. In the event that they failed, MPs explored the possibility of swiftly amending the Appropriations Bill to withhold funds from the KACC. In the worst case scenario, members toyed with the option of repealing the law that had created the KACC.

Legislators argued that the KACC needed to be independent and that its director needed to have the blessing not only of the advisory board but that of Parliament as well. The process for appointing the director of the KACC is laid out clearly under the Kenya Anti-Corruption and Economic Crimes Act. The KACC advisory board oversees the recruitment and presents names of nominees to Parliament for vetting before the president can make the appointment. In the event of a reappointment of a serving director, it became clear that the procedure is never without controversy. The Parliamentary Departmental Committee on Legal Affairs and the Administration of Justice opined that the president had acted unprocedurally. The chairman of the KACC advisory board also faulted the president. Following fierce public debate on the merits of the president's action, the Speaker of the National Assembly allowed debate on the matter. The debate in Parliament resulted in legislators annulling the controversial Gazette notice containing Justice Ringera's reappointment, which they deemed inconsistent with the law. This eventually forced Justice Ringera to resign and paved the way for a new search for a KACC director establish a local tribunal to try the suspects of the post-election violence. The bill for the local tribunal was brought to Parliament twice, both times without success.

The second issue dealt with the evolution and adoption of new standing orders – the rules that govern how business is run in Parliament. The National Assembly adopted these rules on 10 December 2008, making it possible for Parliament to carry out its work with fewer fetters. The situation is unlike what prevailed during the KANU era when Parliament did the executive's bidding. Many MPs aver that few of them would have openly tried to oppose a bill or motion supported by the government. Although the parliamentary committees deliver on their core mandate of keeping a check on the executive, the implementation of their recommendations – as well as those of Parliament generally – has always been the weakest link in the chain. For instance, after thorough scrutiny of the annual reports from the Controller and Auditor General, it has never been quite clear whether the recommendations of the Public Accounts Committee (PAC) or the Public Investments Committee (PIC) have ever been implemented. Thus one thing is clear: Parliament has its say but the executive has its way. In executing their oversight roles the parliamentary committees face several hurdles. These include the asymmetrical flow of information. The executive enjoys superior access to information and often has incentives not to share that knowledge, especially if it reflects badly on the executive. The professional competence of the composition of the members in the technical committees (e.g. PIC and PAC) remains in doubt. Membership should be based on technical competencies so that the committees are able to function effectively.

In order to improve Parliament's oversight capacity, there is a need to train and support MPs to ensure they acquire knowledge on budgets and budgetary processes. In addition, the legislature should be more open to the media and civil society to ensure effective parliamentary oversight. In pursuing its oversight role, Parliament's latest stride is the establishment of the Budget Committee and the Office of Fiscal Analysis, which could assist legislators to understand the budget. The proposed committee was supposed to be composed of high calibre fiscal analysis, budgetary and economic policy experts to strengthen budget scrutiny and the overall budget process in Kenya.

In addition, parliamentary committees should have adequate resources to deliver on their mandate. A strong and independent media is necessary to support committees in their oversight work on executive actions. In addition, a strong civil society can also ensure that weaknesses are identified and pressure brought to bear on the government to implement recommendations. The leadership of the crucial parliamentary committees should possess the relevant competence that enables them to understand complex matters. They should be supported by well-trained staff, including researchers.

Public Investments Committee report on the accounts of state corporations (1)

In an assessment of the accounts of state corporations, the PIC considered the matter of grain handling by the port of Mombasa by M/s Grain Bulk Handlers Limited (GBHL). On examining the licence granted to GBHL, the committee was concerned that it was lopsided and gave the firm undue monopoly in grain handling at the port of Mombasa. The committee observed that it would have been prudent for the Kenya Ports Authority (KPA) to negotiate for equity in the firm on the strength of the value of land on which the facility is built.

The committee was also informed that the firm had applied for a renewal of the licence, which was due to expire on 17 February 2008, for a period of 20 years. Following this assessment, the PIC recommended that the KPA ensures that its grain handling policy allows for fair competition and that while considering the application by GBHL for renewal of the licence, KPA ensures that the prohibitive clauses are reviewed to safeguard the interest of the authority and fair competition in handling all commodities at the port. The PIC also recommended that the KPA ensure that the tariff payable by GBHL and other handlers reflect the prevailing competitive market realities.

Parliamentary reform

The National Assembly has over the years fought for autonomy (control of its budget, calendar, etc.) so as not to be held hostage to the whims of the executive. The former constitution gave the president power to summon, prorogue and dissolve Parliament. Each session of Parliament would be held at a place within Kenya and commence at such time as the president appointed. These provisions tended to undermine the autonomy of the legislature. The constitution made sweeping changes to secure the autonomy of Parliament by allowing it to control its timetable and calendar. With better facilities, it should be more effective in its legislative and oversight roles. Above all, Parliament should have a mechanism for getting its decisions implemented.

The role of parliamentary committees

Departmental parliamentary committees perform functions for which the National Assembly, in its corporate form, is not well suited, for example, fi out the facts of a case, examining witnesses, sifting information and drawing up conclusions. These committees ensure eff surveillance over the executive arm of the government. For instance, committees enable the public to participate in the legislative and governance process by either appearing before them, sending memoranda or making suggestions on how government operations could be improved. Hence, parliamentary committees are important organs for the scrutiny of public policy and activities. In a way, parliamentary committees take Parliament to the people and allow direct contact with members of the public by a section of it, especially when on study visits or inspection tours.

Parliament can establish committees and make standing orders to regulate its procedures and operations. Parliament can form four kinds of committees: committees of the whole House; standing committees; ad-hoc committees; and departmental committees. n. The composition of the committees is critical to understanding how they work. Committees are divided between the ruling party and the opposition, depending on their strength in Parliament. The ruling party has one member more than the rest. In the tenth Parliament all members are officially in government, except one. This is because all other MPs belonged to political parties represented in the coalition government. The back benchers, thus, assumed the role of the official opposition. However, efforts to get Parliament to pass a bill to establish an official opposition did not succeeded. During the entire period of the tenth Parliament, loose caucuses of legislators teamed up to constitute the opposition from issue to issue.

Unless otherwise specified in law, the leaders of the various committees are elected by MPs. The chair of the watchdog Public Accounts and Public Investment Committees must come from the official opposition. However, in the tenth Parliament, the chair of each of these committees came from the coalition government since there was no official opposition. The chair was elected by the members of that committee. These committees are empowered to summon ministers and other officials when there is a need.

Committee meetings are now open to the public and some of the committees advertise their public hearings in the press. The committee sets its own agenda and decisions are made only by its members. Any legislator can participate in the meetings of these committees, but voting is restricted to committee members alone. Every committee develops its own strategic plan.

The various committees can order any person to give evidence before them on matters of public interest. Unless specified to the contrary in the law, the executive is required to send high level officials to attend the hearings of parliamentary committees when required to do so. They can also visit ministries and departments to inspect or inquire into any matter of public concern. In the tenth Parliament, the committees were very strong as they were bolstered by the new standing orders.

Most decisions in the committees are made on the basis of consensus. However, there are times when the members disagree even with their own committees' reports. This was the case with the Departmental Committee on Legal Affairs and the Administration of Justice during the tenth Parliament, where some members withdrew support for the report on the appointment of the proposed head of the Interim Independent Electoral Commission (IIEC), forcing the individual to withdraw his candidacy. However, on the whole, consensus is encouraged. Like in most decisions in Parliament, democracy prevails: the majority carries the day whileFor more information see www. marsgroupkenya. org. For more details see www. mzalendo. com. For more details visit www. peoples-parliament. org. For more information visit www. kengonet. org. the minority has its say, so to speak. Government is required to implement the recommendations of the parliamentary committees. In the past, it was difficult for Parliament to monitor implementation, but there is now an implementation committee, whose mandate is to ensure that any recommendations made in Parliament are effected. The committees have the power to provide effective oversight of the executive. Any report that they bring to Parliament is adopted and becomes a public document which guides how the government ought to act on particular public issues. In the tenth Parliament, the Budget Committee detected a discrepancy involving KSh 10 billion in the supplementary budget, with a massive loophole through which the public would have lost money. This was detected and deleted from the supplementary budget. The budget error was initially raised by a local lobby, The Mars Group. The government is required by law to adhere to any report passed and adopted in Parliament. However, in most cases, the executive procrastinates on many of the items it is required to act on.

The new standing orders allow the Budget Committee to play a more prominent role in the budgeting, planning, passing and tabling of the budget. However, the revised standing orders have to be re-examined in view of the constitutional order. In the past, the Minister for Finance used to ambush Parliament with budgetary estimates. All this has changed. Each committee is allocated a budget expert who scrutinises the budget for ministries under its watch. Committees can alter or verify the details of the estimates to their satisfaction. They can even reduce the budget allocation for specific ministries. This was the case when the Attorney General's (AG's) travel budget was slashed by KSh 1 million when he refused to cooperate with the Committee on Justice and Legal Affairs. The AG was reportedly on a travel mission whenever he was required by the committee. It was felt that 'the AG works in Kenya but lives abroad', given his numerous travel escapades. Hence, by reducing his travel allowance, the committee offered him an 'incentive' to spend more time in Kenya and be available to answer questions raised by parliamentary committees.

Several factors constrain the work of the parliamentary committees. First, financial resources tend to disrupt their work. Second, the sessional nature of the committees results in a high turnover of members and the need to induct new ones every year. Third, numerous bureaucratic bottlenecks stand in the way of the adoption of the committees' reports. For example, the Speaker's approval is required before a report is taken to the plenary. A committee report becomes a public document only after it has been tabled. There are also rules restricting the extent to which the committee of the whole (Parliament) can change such reports. Public participation in the committees' work used to be limited because the sessions were behind closed doors. This rule has since been changed, and the constitution requires all of Parliament's work to be conducted in the open, except in specified special circumstances.

Brief history of the Parliamentary Budget Committee

Also referred to as the Office of Fiscal Analysis, the Parliamentary Budget Committee was created in May 2007 to enhance Parliament's oversight role and capacity to scrutinise the national budget and the economy. Its primary function is to provide timely and objective information and analysis concerning the budget and the economy. It provides technical support to all legislators and relevant committees.

under the new standing orders, the finance minister must prepare a budget policy statement and lay it before Parliament every year, not later than 21 March. The budget policy statement contains: (i) targets for the overall revenues, including domestic and external borrowing and aggregate expenditures; (ii) the total resources to be allocated to individual programmes and projects within a sector or ministry for the period identified and also specify the criteria used in allocating the available public resources, among other things. upon receiving the budget policy statement, the budget committee consults each departmental committee and prepares a report not later than 15 April of each year.

Public Investments Committee report on the accounts of state corporations (2)

Finally, the executive sometimes takes inordinately long to implement the recommendations of parliamentary committees. It is projected that the implementation committee will fast- track action on the recommendations by the committees. Most of the scrutiny of government expenditure by these committees always concentrates on dated events because of a huge backlog at the Controller and Auditor General's office. For instance, the Public Accounts Committee Report for 2007 examined government expenditure dating back to 1999. This does not help much in the prevention of the possible misappropriation of public funds. In mitigation, committees have adopted a style of working that aims at clearing the backlog of reports by the Controller of the Budget and Auditor General

In an assessment of the accounts of state corporations, the PIC considered the matter of the Kenya Reinsurance Corporation. The PIC found out that contrary to the terms of appointment,

M/s KPMG issued an audit report to the members of the Kenya Reinsurance Corporation Ltd, who published the company's accounts purporting them to have been duly audited and having received an unqualified opinion.

By that time, however, the accounts were still in draft form pending certification by the Controller and Auditor General. The committee was concerned that the private audit firm had ostensibly given an unqualified opinion on the financial statements of the Corporation for the year 2005 while the Corporation thereafter was found to have been grossly mismanaged, leading to the dismissal of its chief executive officer and finance manager in 2007.

The PIC also found out that the National Bank of Kenya and the Industrial Development Bank had also been reported as having acted contrary to the audit law by publishing uncertified accounts. In view of these concerns, the PIC recommended that:

- The chief executive of the Corporation ensures that the financial statements are audited in accordance with the Public Audit Act (2003).

- In future, private audit firms appointed by the Controller of the Budget and Auditor General, as stated in the law, must ensure that they present their results to him or her before presenting them to the client (the Corporation). Firms that deviate from this should be reported to the Accountants' Registration Board and be suspended from auditing parastatals or government departments.

- The chief executives of the National Bank of Kenya and Industrial Development Bank should ensure that their financial statements are prepared in accordance with the Public Audit Act (2003).

- The Minister for Finance should ensure that annual financial statements of all state corporations, including those in the banking sector, are prepared in accordance with the Public Audit Act (2003) and tabled before the House.

During the NARC regime (2003–2007) as well as the period under the coalition government, controversies erupted over the composition of some of the parliamentary committees. For example, nomination to the powerful House Business Committee has been mired in controversy. The jostling is premised on the fact that this committee determines the agenda of Parliament. Membership can increase one's bargaining power as this committee can influence the priority items for debate. The key factor guiding nomination to the various committees is a desire for party and/or national representation. There is a need to consider education and professional experience when nominating MPs to the various committees. It may thus be necessary for members to receive some training on the various issues they are expected to handle.

Representation of women in the various parliamentary committees replicates their small proportion in Parliament. Of concern in this respect is the fact that no woman has ever chaired any of the powerful parliamentary committees, such as the House Business Committee, the PIC or PAC. Increasing women's representation in the various parliamentary committees requires a supportive legislative framework that promotes women's representation in the National Assembly. The constitution has laid a framework for this by providing that representation in elected bodies should comprise not more than two-thirds of any gender.

Public participation in the legislature

The former constitution was silent on public involvement in the work of Parliament. However, citizens were allowed limited access into the public gallery to follow the proceedings. The MPs have, however, cultivated close links with their voters through meetings or visits to their constituencies. The regularity of such meetings depended on a number of factors, for example, the distance of the constituency from the of the National Assembly in Nairobi as well as the ambitions of a sitting elected member, that is, if the MP intends to stand again

The citizenry participates in the work of the legislature through various ways. First, this happens during the election of the members of the legislature when the electorate determines its leadership. Second, citizens participate by determining issues that are debated in the House. MPs go on recess three times a year as provided for in the parliamentary calendar. Such breaks provide opportunities for MPs to interact with the electorate. Such interaction is critical in that it enables MPs to inform their constituents on the various bills and other legislation debated and approved by Parliament. The recess further provides for an opportunity for the MPs to get some feedback from their electorate on issues of local and national importance. Additionally, MPs visit their constituencies even when Parliament is in session to meet their constituents. MPs have allowances to facilitate travel to their constituencies to enable interaction with their electorates.

The constituency office has also created a platform for citizens to interact with their MPs. Following the inauguration of the NARC administration at the end of 2002, each constituency received KSh 1 million to build an office space where MPs could regularly meet their constituents, a move that was motivated by the introduction of the Constituency Development Fund (CDF). The CDF offices have enabled MPs to maintain some level of visibility in their constituencies. Initially, constituents would seek out their elected leaders at their homes or travel to the capital.

A vibrant civil society in Kenya has also enhanced public participation in governance.

The Kenya Bribery Index by Transparency International, for instance, has offered the public an opportunity to evaluate the performance of the National Assembly. The legislature gained access to the Kenya Bribery Index reports partly because of the influence MPs have over resource allocation decisions, including the CDF and bursary funds. Access to these resources by legislators introduced increased bribery risks for the National Assembly. This is because most CDF-related projects require formal contracts, which are a principal conduit for bribery. MPs also started getting involved in directing development projects, which was by law a preserve of the executive arm of government. In past Kenya Bribery Index surveys before the introduction of the CDF, the National Assembly had never featured as a bribery-prone institution.

Another CSO that has been active in keeping track of how Parliament performs and raising public awareness on its operations is the Institute for Civic Awareness and Development. This institute has from 1998 been compiling detailed evaluation reports that document the performance of each legislator in Parliament with regard to: debating bills; participation in budget-making and budget-related debates; participation in motions; raising points of order; and raising questions. The quality of speech in these contributions is also rated. This project aims to achieve two objectives: (i) to enhance the participation of legislators in their core mandate of legislation; and (ii) to ensure a better understanding of the institution of Parliament by the people of Kenya. Through such documentation, people are able to scrutinise and gauge the performance of their elected leaders.

It is, however, important to note that public participation in the old order was hindered by the opaque nature of the legislature.

Save for the limited access through the public gallery and public opinion polling, the Kenyan legislature is by its nature 'elitist'. It is, thus, out of reach for the majority of Kenyans. To the ordinary citizen, Parliament is a mysterious ivory tower in many respects. For instance, physical

access to the National Assembly is severely curtailed by numerous security screening points in and around the premises. However, in tandem with the increasing democratic space that followed the re-introduction of competitive multi-party elections, information about the operatlso published in the Kenya Gazette and can be bought from the government bookshop. The reports of the PAC and PIC are also sold. There is an increased flow of information from Parliament, especially for the period 2003-2007, as well as the tenth Parliament.

Although the parliamentary agenda is currently posted on the National Assembly website, there are limited channels through which the public can influence debates on bills under consideration. One of the channels is through various CSOs that organise workshops on certain proposed laws that interest them. This way, the public has an opportunity to influence the direction of debate on a particular bill. Different CSOs have varying degrees of leverage in accessing Parliament as well as influencing debate. The influence of these CSOs is in the area of lobbying for the adoption of various laws, for example, CRADLE on the Sexual Offences Bill; and the International Commission of Jurists-Kenya Chapter in its campaign for the Freedom of Information Bill. In addition, reports of the hearings of various parliamentary committees are made public thus offering citizens another avenue for influencing debate in the National Assembly.

The wider public feels that Parliament has become more open and transparent due to the increased democratic space in the country. Perhaps this could further be linked to the rise of a better informed public, free media as well as the willingness of the leaders to change. However, the linkage between the National Assembly and the public still remains loose. People are not as engaged as they should be. The citizenry largely depends on the patronage of the legislator, leading to asymmetrical power relations.

The 2010 constitution has sought to correct these anomalies by making the National Assembly more accessible and accountable to the people. The constitution provides for public access and participation in Parliament, requiring that: 'Parliament shall conduct its business in an open manner and hold its sittings and those of its committees in public; facilitate public involvement in the legislative and other business of Parliament and its committees'. It further provides that: 'Parliament may not exclude the public, or any public or private media, from any sitting unless in exceptional circumstances as may be determined by the Speaker of the National Assembly. ' The constitution also makes provision for the right to petition Parliament to consider any matter within its authority. Live coverage of debates in the National Assembly is a milestone in this regard. This continues to demystify the legislature and increase public interest in its business.

The public has also a role in the recall of MPs. Article 104 of the constitution provides that the electorate has the 'the right to recall the member of Parliament representing their constituency before the end of the term of the relevant House of Parliament'. The Elections Act (2011) further elaborates on this principle by providing grounds for recalling a member of either house. The Act provides that a member of Parliament may be recalled where a member 'is found, after due process of the law, to have violated the provisions of chapter 6 of the constitution; is found, after due process of the law, to have mismanaged public resources; or, is convicted of an offence under this Act'. But this clause is rendered useless by a subsequent one that provides that such a re-call 'shall only be initiated twenty-four months after the election of the member of Parliament and not later than twelve months immediately preceding the next general election'. The two clauses are confusing when read together. There is no reason why the electorate has to wait for 24 months to initiate a petition if the MP has violated chapter 6 of the constitution. There is a strong case for amending this provision. The latter clause was sneaked in at the late stages in the development of the legislation by MPs who were trying to limit the exercise of this power by the electorate. Initially nearly all MPs had been opposed to such a clause.

Finally, the internet has emerged as an effective platform through which the public hold MPs accountable. Various blogs by individual public members as well as organised blog pages share ideas on issues related to the performance of the Kenyan Parliament. Social media in general has fed into public discourse on matters of governance. Some of the most useful sites include:

1. The Mars Group, a local lobby on good governance in Kenya. The Mars Group was

2. able to rally the public and Parliament on a discrepancy in the supplementary budget estimates in 2009. This revelation forced Parliament to have a fresh look in order to correct the error.

3. Mzalendo (Patriot), which helps keep an eye on the Kenyan Parliament. This site helps the public to actively infl the performance of the Parliament through web-based dialogues on various issues. The site contains useful information including: the Hansard, bills, committees, motions, legislators and their contacts. People can directly post a question or comment on any issue directly related to their MP.

4. Bunge La Mwananchi, (The People's Parliament). Besides the website, this lobby group holds regular 'people's parliamentary sessions' at the Jevanjee Gardens (a public park) in Nairobi.
5. Kenya Network of Grassroots Organisations (KENGO), whose website has a section on Kenya's Parliament.

Control and audit of National Assembly fi

All public funds appropriated by Parliament and disbursed for a purpose shall be applied for that purpose alone, and the expenditure must conform to the authority governing it. Since the budget of the National Assembly is financed fSNV (2004) Strengthening Local Governance: Finding Quality Advisory Approaches. Nairobi: SNV. The estimates provided are meant to cater for the salaries and expenses of the National Assembly.

Table 17: Estimates of National Assembly recurrent and development expenditure

Fiscal year	Budgetary allocation (KSh)
2002–2003	3 356 970 710
2004–2005	5 400 000 000
2007–2008	6 588 572 070
2008–2009	7 245 304 550

Perhaps one of the most conspicuous cases of the misappropriation of public funds allocated to Parliament was the payment of excess and unwarranted mileage claims by its members. An examination of mileage claims by MPs for travelling between their respective constituencies and Parliament buildings shows that some distances recorded were far in excess of the official schedule provided by the Ministry of Roads and Public Works.

This weakness notwithstanding, it is notable that one of the peculiarities of the Kenyan legislature is its role in controlling a popular and critical devolved fund: the Constituency Development Fund. All the 210 constituencies in the ninth and tenth Parliaments received cash allocations for development purposes that was funded from this fund. The CDF kitty accounts for 2.5% of the revenue collected in the country to meet local development needs at grassroots level. The management of the CDF accounts is clearly spelt out in the law that established it in 2003 and in the revision of 2007. It allows the legislators to be patrons of the CDF committees and to nominate the chairpersons and some of the committee members. Some government officers, by virtue of their positions in the constituencies, are automatically members of these committees. One of the contradictions of the CDF Act is that apart from giving the area legislator the mandate to supervise how the funds are used by being the patron, it also expects MPs to provide oversight on the management of the fund.

Questions have been raised about why the legislature wants to control funds for development, a role that should be played by the executive. It is a legitimate question that will need to be addressed sooner rather than later. The principle of the separation of powers requires that the duty of building roads, schools, bridges, hospitals, dispensaries, airstrips and other amenities should be left to the executive. The role of Parliament in any democracy is to make laws and formulate policies, besides keeping the executive in check. Policy implementation is the duty of the executive, through an impartial civil service. Initially, the idea behind the establishment of the CDF was to eliminate the skewed allocation of budgetary resources on the basis of patronage and the Harambee system, through which senior public officials (including legislators) were expected to contribute huge sums of money for development in numerous fund-raising exercises in their constituencies, which fuelled corruption and patronage.

Although there are positive indications that the CDF is transforming communities, for example, through the construction of essential social amenities such as schools, health facilities and access to roads as well as providing bursary funds, there are equally worrying trends. MPs have been accused of cronyism, partisanship and other parochial considerations in the constitution of the management committees for this fund, the allocation of its resources, as well as tendering for various development projects drawing from the fund account. The distribution of projects undertaken using money from the fund is sometimes skewed geographically to serve the legislator's political interests. The danger of having CDF money managed and controlled by legislators is that in the absence of a highly informed public, most voters could wrongfully perceive these funds as the benevolence of their leaders. This may serve to entrench even very unpopular leaders and to deny citizens opportunities to experience good leadership. Kenyan citizens, therefore, need to transform themselves into strong lobbies to check how the funds are

used in their constituencies and, whenever things go awry, blow the whistle and seek redress.

Conclusion and recommendations

Kenya's legislature has developed towards becoming an autonomous governance institution. Although the executive has dominated it for years, there has been a good attempt to regain independence and to effectively play an oversight role. To enable the legislature to fulfil its mandate and play its oversight role, the following recommendations apply:

- The House Speakers should facilitate the improvement of the technical capacity of members of the Senate and the

National Assembly. It is important that members are well-oriented towards their duties, and that essential skills and key competencies necessary for the execution of their engagements are enhanced. The Speaker should also develop a framework for the improvement of the capacity of county assembly representatives.

- Since there are no institutions overseeing the work of Parliament, there is a need to build the capacity of civil society to play a watchdog role on the bi-cameral legislature and, the county assemblies.

- The Ministry of Finance should develop regulations for the management of the CDF. The Ministry should also seek to amend the law that provides for an MP to be the patron of the CDF in order to promote accountability on the use of public development funds.

- Civic education on the role of various elected leaders should be provided in order to equip citizens with the skills to hold them accountable.

Provincial and local governments

As mentioned in an earlier chapter, the Independence Constitution created a dualist system of governance where there was a central government and eight regional governments, which had power over regional affairs. The constitution reflected the compromise reached between the hard-line positions of the dominant political parties: the Kenya African Democratic Union (KADU), which sought a federal state, and members of the Kenya African National Union (KANU), who preferred a unitary state. With regard to devolution, thLocal Government System in Kenya, Op Cit. respects. For instance, while the edifice of regionalism was specially entrenched, Schedule One, which dealt with the exclusive authority of the regions' executive and legislative powers, was not entrenched. Thus, it was possible to take power away from the regions.

Immediately after independence, Kenya embarked on amending its constitution. A series of amendments were done in less than three years to dismantle Majimbo. The first amendment deleted nearly all-non-entrenched provisions relating to the regions, such as their taxation powers, the formation of regional police units and the establishment of local authorities. The second amendment of 1964 eliminated the titles of regional presidents, who were later renamed chairmen. Only one person was to be called president, and that was Mzee Jomo Kenyatta! Indeed, KANU stalwarts argued that the regional assemblies were not governments per se but conduits for propagating the central government's policies and programmes at the regional level. This amendment transferred the power to alter regional boundaries to Parliament. The provisions for sourcing regional revenue independently were deleted. Consequently, the regions were made dependent on grants from the central government.

The third amendment of 1965 altered the percentages of MPs that were needed to amend the constitution from 75% to 65% in both houses. By amending the 'percentage rule', entrenched provisions such as fundamental human rights, the structure of regions, the Senate, judiciary and the amendment process itself were tampered with, and they could be amended by a 65% majority. As a result of these amendments, it became easier to amend the entire constitution.

The seventh amendment of 1967 provided for the merger of the Senate and the House of Representatives to establish a unicameral legislature. With the Senate abolished, the role of protecting regional governments' interests at national level was quashed. Finally, the ninth amendment of 1968 – which abolished the provincial councils and deleted from the constitution all references to the provincial and district boundaries – and an alteration thereof dissolved the financial powers of the regional assemblies. This marked the end of regional governments, which were replaced with the Provincial Administration.

The Provincial Administration

The Provincial Administration traces its origin to the colonial era. Colonial authorities introduced this institution not only to represent the formal mechanisms of national government decision- making but also as a means of political influence. During this period, its main functions were to collect taxes, maintain law and order and pacify the natives in the colony. It also provided judicial services (lay services) and participated in legislative matters in the local authorities. Until the Constitution of Kenya 2010 was promulgated, the couve that, a location headed by a chief. Several locations constitute a division, headed by a district officer and then a district, headed by a district commissioner. Several districts are grouped together to form a province, headed by a provincial commissioner.

None of the officials in this hierarchy is elected, but appointed by the president, and enjoy a wide range of quasi-judicial and administrative powers, derived from the colonial period, which can significantly constrain and circumscribe the enjoyment of rights and public participation in civic affairs. The way this system operates varies. For example, in 1983, the president re-introduced a semblance of decentralised governance based on districts by implementing the District-Focus for Rural Development structure. Under this system, the district became the focal point for resource distribution. The district commissioner became a critical player in designing and implementing development programmes.

The NARC government did not make any radical changes in the structure of the Provincial Administration. The Constitution of Kenya 2010 provides for restructuring rather than

'abolishing' (as seen in previous Bomas and Wako Drafts) of the Provincial Administration

in line with the prihe Provincial Administration has been revolving around what 'restructuring' means.

The new constitution provides that each county recruits its own staff based on respective needs. However, some staff, for example teachers, are recruited at the national level and dispatched to counties. Each county has a public service body to recruit its own staff. Further, the constitution creates and rationalises devolved government, which exists for the management of all 47 counties. The counties as constituted in the constitution are the equivalent of the 1992 districts.

Local government institutions

After the abolition of the Majimbo structure of government, the former constitution decentralised power into local authority units, which were restructured by the Local Government Act (Cap. 265) and placed under the Ministry of Local Government. The law gave rural county councils and urban municipalities, town and urban councils the power to manage and run these local authorities.

Kenya had 175 local authorities comprising three city councils (Nairobi, Kisumu and Mombasa), 42 municipalities, 63 town councils and 67 county councils. Most functions related to the provision of public services, promotion of good governance and the stimulation of economic growth. Table 18 depicts these structures.

Table 18: Local government structures

CENTRAL GOVERNANCE			
President Government Parliament: National Assembly			
7 x PROVINCES & NAIROBI AREA Provincial Commissioner 69 x DISTRICTS Governance is divided into levels of division, location and sub-location.			
LOCAL GOVERNANCE			
urban areas			Rural areas
3 x city council Nairobi, Kisumu, Mombasa (circa 1 043 395 inhabitants)	43 x municipal council (c. 94 000 inhabitants)	62 x town council (c. 46 000 inhabitants)	67 x county council (c. 295 000 inhabitants)

A local council was also empowered to make by-laws relating to the provision of services by itself or by private bodies, which are enforceable under national law. Each council has diff roles, shown in Table 19.

Table 19: Nature and authority of councils

Type	Description	Authority structure
County council	A rural local authority whose area of jurisdiction overlapped with that of an administrative district.	Since the abolition of regional governments in 1965, no local councils corresponding to the provincial boundaries have been created. The law provided that no local authority shall extend outside a single province.
urban council	An urban council was regarded as part of a rural government, providing services that enabled the surrounding rural community to market their products and obtain their supplies and government services conveniently. It was a county division overlapping with the administrative divisions.	The urban council operated under the supervision of the county council within which it fell.
Township councils	They had the same status and powers as county councils and operated under the supervision of no other local authority. This status was given to large urban centres within county councils, whether or not they were district or provincial administrative headquarters, for example, Voi, Karatina, Kajiado townships.	County, town and urban councils were presided over by a chairperson/or deputy chair.
City and	Although the minister could create	City and municipal councils had

municipal councils	municipalities at will, most of them were in provincial headquarters and other large towns. Only Nairobi, Mombasa and Kisumu were designated as city councils while Eldoret, Nakuru, Kabarnet, Thika, Nyeri, Embu and Machakos were municipalities.	a policy-making body comprising the mayor and councillors, and the executive composed of the town clerk and chief offi

Membership of councils consisted of elected and nominated councillors (the number is determined by the minister). Nominated councillors represented the central government, or any special interest, and their number did not exceed a third of the total. They served the political practice as well as ensured that the party in power was represented in every local government council. As such, nominated councillors articulated the interests of the government in all important issues under consideration by the council. Political parties that took part in an election were supposed to be represented in each

local authority committee. Upon formal election, the elected councillor's term of office was equivalent to the electoral cycle of five years while that of nominated and appointed councilors could be fewer, depending on the discretion of the nominating party or the Minister for Local Government. A mayor (or chairperson) and deputy were elected by councillors according to the rules set by the Electoral Commission of Kenya (ECK). Mayors and chairpersons held office for

two years before going back to elections.

Relationship between central and local governments

The local government system was supposed to decentralise power through the delegation of authority for planning, management, and resource mobilisation and allocation at local levels. In Kenya, local authorities exercised 'permissive' and mandatory powers, depending on the discretion of the Minister for Local Government. Permissive powers enabled councils to carry out certain tasks or activities subject to the minister's approval. Mandatory powers are those laid out in the law, such as the prohibition of the sale and movement of livestock with the object of preventing theft, control of the felling of timber, and the prohibition of the wasteful destruction of trees. Lack of autonomy at times caused conflict between the town clerks, who were the accounting officers appointed by the Minister for Local Government, and the councillors and mayors. The conflict between the central government and civic authorities repeatedly manifested as the Minister for Local Government dissolved or threatened to dissolve non-performing councils. The Nairobi city council had borne the brunt of these turf wars several times. Local authorities in Kenya had a national forum to lobby for the promotion of strong local government inership to ALGAK was automatic upon the creation of a local authority. A study on the association's financial sustainability recommended that membership be only upon application and the payment of registration fees and annual subscriptions. After 1999, membership was on the basis of choice and meeting the set criteria.

Local authorities in Kenya did not operate independently of the central government. The law gave the central government overweening powers over local authorities. The Minister for Local Government could elevate any area into a municipality, county or township, with or without proposals. The minister was also consulted on virtually every activity of the local authority – be it on budget approval or confirmation of any other decision for implementation. The minister had the power to hire and fire, and even to dissolve local authorities. The Provincial Administration, under the Office of the President (which was separate from the Ministry of Local Government), also exercised power over local authorities. The district commissioner, for instance, wielded influence in the councils' decisions and the manner in which they were carried out. For example, 'Every municipal and county council submitted to the Provincial Commissioner copies of the estimates submitted to the minister and the Provincial Commissioner would thereupon make any recommendations to the Minister of Local Government with respect to such estimates' (Cap. 265:212). District Commissioners assisted in mobilising communities to attain local authority-based development objectives

In addition, when the minister nominated the councillors to represent the central government, or any special interest groups, he/she included the provincial commissioner in the case of Nairobi, and the district commissioner in the case of councils. In other instances, the district officers were nominated as councillors in urban councils to represent the interests of the central government. Other government departments also affected the conduct of local authority functions. For example, the Ministers of Housing, Education, Health and Transport were stakeholders in the manner in which standards in their respective fields were upheld. Thus, although the local authorities disliked the central government controls, their desirability to ensure that a uniform minimum standard of efficiency was obtained in the interest of taxpayers compelled them to put up with it. The Ministry of Local Government was represented by the provincial local government officer (PLGO), whose tasks included supervising the activities of the councils within his or her area of jurisdiction. In supervising and controlling the councils, these officers liaised with the council clerks to guide the activities. They also investigated activities falling short of expectations, and filed reports to the minister.

The town clerk was the administrative authority in each council, appointed by the Public Service Commission (PSC) and seconded to the Ministry of Local Government. The mayor was the political head of the council and was elected by the councillors. Executive decisions at the council were made by the town clerk to facilitate the implementation of policies. The relationship between the mayor and clerk was often characterised by battles for supremacy. The mayor and councillors at times lobbied for the dismissal of a town clerk because the power configuration in council politics tended to see the elected mayor, rather than the town clerk, as the executive officer.

Local government elections

The urban-based council was headed by a mayor, elected by councillors at the first full council meeting following a general election. The chair or mayor was the political head of the local authority, and presided over all council meetings. Councillors were responsible for individual wards and were accountable to their electorates. Policy-making powers rested with the councillors, who made decisions that guided development, planning, priority setting, the allocation and management of resources, and the selection, implouncil members proportional to the number of seats they won in the elections. The councillors then elected their mayors, chairpersons and their deputies. The grid below shows a sample of how the composition and sizes of councils varied

Council	Elected	Nominated	Public offi
Ol Kejuado county council	30	15	1
Mavoko municipal council	9	3	1
Machakos municipal council	11	3	1
Kiambu municipal council	6	3	1
Nairobi city council	75	25	

The Local Government Act governed the establishment, functions and elections of local authorities in Kenya. The government had extensive powers to establish, alter, amalgamate or divide local authorities, in consultation with the electoral body. The law mandated the minister to dissolve all local authorities upon the dissolution of Parliament to allow their elections to happen simultaneously with the general election. Councillors were elected every five years and had to be members of a political party. In the December 2007 elections, 118 parties endorsed 15 332 candidates for civic elections, out of which 1 478 were women. A councillor represented an electoral district called a civic ward. The defunct ECK was allowed to divide local authorities into various electoral areas and prescribe their boundaries and names. A local authority may make any representation for the alteration of the boundaries of an electoral area.

Some of the powers vested in the minister appeared to conflict with the defunct ECK's mandate. The election of a councillor could be challenged in a magistrate's court. Magistrates' courts are subordinate to the High Court and are more accessible to the population. The high turnover of councillors at elections posed a challenge to continuity in local authorities.

Local authorities also struggled with capacity. A survey conducted by the Netherlands Development Organisation (SNV) on internal factors affecting service delivery in Keiyo county council listed the lack of skilled staff, staff suspicion about the way the council works, poor distribution of duties, duplication of duties, poor flow of information, poor performance attributed to lack of facilities and the high expectation of financial aid as critical challenges. Some local authorities lack harmonisation in their service delivery due to underperforming councillors; although measures to curb such problems had not been instituted by the time the study was being conducted.

Financing of provincial and local governments

Prior to the 2010 constitution, the Provincial Administration was financed principally by the exchequer or Treasury, and by additional funding from the international donor community or development partners through bilateral and multilateral 'aid'. The central government derived its revenue mainly from taxation. Under the devolved system of government, counties are expected to raise revenue through taxes, duties, surcharges, fees, levies and charges, partly from the functions set out in the Fourth Schedule. Counties can also get funding from donors but it is not clear how international donor funds will be channelled to them. What is clear, however, is that enabling the counties to control the generation and allocation of development funds will increase not only equity but also public participation in development because people will be keen to contribute to decisions on

development projects.

Access to information

Local authorities in Kenya faced challenges relating to public access to information. Most councils used the manual information storage system, which is cumbersome and often out-of- date. In isolated cases where these authorities had begun embracing information communication technology, it was limited to financial management and secretarial services. There were also concerns that most of the information for public use was too detailed and complex for public consumption. The accuracy of the information available to the public, especially the kind relating to the budget, was also an issue of concern. There were instances when macroeconomic forecasts were inaccurate. Access to information was not explicitly provided for in the former constitution. The Official Secrets Act limited this right and prevented public officials from releasing confidential information – even where corruption was suspected. In the interests of transparency and accountability, this legislation needs to be repealed. Government regulations also prohibited public officials from speaking to the media and disclosing information on activities undertaken under their authority. Responses to requests for access to information remained bureaucratic and slow. Officials routinely invoked phrases such as 'contrary to public policy', and 'in the interest of the security of the state' to limit public access to information. This stifled public debate on governance and the formulation and adoption of policies since there were no clear benchmarks to distinguish circumstances where disclosure would be denied. Citizens were, however, able to participate in governance through the elected councillors in their respective wards where they had adequate and relevant information. The law required local councils to publish any important information and make it accessible to citizens. To facilitate the flow of information, most councils (e. g. the Machakos municipal council) produced service charters, communicated to citizens through the media, public notices, and open forums through the Local Au 6(3). Article 189(a). ld for between KSh 200 and KSh 1 000. The budget estimates for Kiambu municipal council, for instance, were available to the public at KSh 300. Citizens could also access information on the city council through the customer care desk and the council's departments. However, the public could not access any information regarding the salaries and allowances of the councillors

Local government and participatory democracy

Participation is a key element of democracy. In Kenya different mechanisms such as audits, an open door policy, the publishing of accounts, performance contracts and results-based

management are applied to encourage citizen participation in policy-making. Public hearings are also held to present policies. Budgetary elements of the local authorities were also prioritised according to the needs of citizens. In many countries, rigid conventional approaches to planning are being discarded and laws are being put in place to facilitate community participation in local governance. The promulgation of new laws was given a boost in 1996 by the launching of the UN-HABITAT Global Campaign on Good Governance whose theme and vision is 'Inclusive Cities'. An inclusive city is a place where everyone, regardless of wealth, gender, age, race or religion, is enabled to participate productively and positively in the opportunities that the city has to offer. It is a place where those who are traditionally marginalised break out of the cycle of exclusion.

The outputs of participatory governance processes are given different names. These include: strategic plans (SPs), city development strategies (CDSs), integrated development plans (IDPs), corporate strategies, multi-stakeholder policy and action plans (MPAPs), and citizens' charters. In Kenya, the Local Authorities Transfer Fund (LATF) sought to strengthen participatory development by involving stakeholder participation in local authority activities. The LATF drew 5% of the total income tax collected by the government and disbursed it to all 175 local authorities. In the financial year 2008–2009, the LATF was allocated KSh 9. 25 billion, approximately 46% of all local authority revenues. The release of these funds was conditional, pegged on improved budgeting, financial reporting, revenue enhancement and participatory planning by the respective local authorities.

Reducing debts through participatory budgeting

Before the 1999/2000 financial year, when the Local Authorities Transfer Fund (LATF) was introduced in Kenya, the municipal budget used to be a closed-door affair involving the administration and a small role for civic leaders. Most of the civic leaders were not competent enough to understand the budget because of the short exposure time. The heads of departments would compile their financial estimates and present them to a budget committee chaired by the municipal treasurer. The committee would scrutinise the estimates for rationalisation before coming up with expenditure and revenue budgets. The committee would then scrutinise the revenue budget and adjust it to capitalise the expenditure budget. Because the Ministry of Local Government would not approve any budget with a deficit, the budget committees would include only those revenues they were sure would not be realised to obtain approval. This, coupled with ineffective financial management, resulted in all local governments carrying over huge debts – KSh 13 billion by 30 June 2000 (uS$ 185. 7 million). This debt was reduced to KSh 728. 8 million (uS$ 10. 4 million) by 30 June 2004 because of the implementation of the LATF Act and the introduction of its participatory budget component, the Local Authority Service Delivery Action Plan, in the financial year 1999/2000.

LASDAP, which aimed at matching local authority expenditure to the needs of the respective local authority areas, was characteristic of good governance as set out by the UN-HABITAT Global Campaign. The process of planning under LASDAP involved all the stakeholders (the municipal government, civil leaders, private sector, civil society organisations, development partners and the citizens/communities) in identifying and prioritising their development needs by drawing up a list of their preferred projects. Such projects included health facilities, markets, community sanitation, waste disposal and education. Although this was a noble move towards participatory democracy, the local authorities were constrained by human resource and financial management deficits. In essence, the success of LASDAP and the other funds was predicated on management reforms within the local authorities. The challenges local authorities faced in responding to citizens' needs (e. g. lack of autonomy, lack of resources, poor civic leadership, low transparency and accountability) gave rise to the formation of neighbourhood or residential associations which articulated grievances and lobbied for change. According to a survey carried out by the Institute of Economic Affairs, there were approximately 200 registered residents associations in Nairobi that were engaged in improving security, roads and clearing waste. These included the Karen-Lang'ata Residents Association (commonly referred to as Karengata), which engages the Nairobi city council delivery. Residents associations in Nairobi formed an umbrella association: 'We Can Do It'. There is also a countrywide umbrella: Kenya Alliance of Residential Associations (KARA). These groupings lobby for improved services, facilitate the formation of new associations and provide technical assistance to potential associations.

The contribution of the private sector to local politics and decision-making is realised through the Local Government Sector Working Group, which brings together the private sector, civil society, the universities and local authorities to jointly address issues of governance and service delivery. Following the introduction of the single business permit (SBP) in 1999, a consultative forum was initiated by key players in the commercial sector. This forum brings together the Ministry of Local Government, the Kenya Association of Manufacturers and the Kenya National Chamber of Commerce and Industry. It deals with operational issues surrounding the implementation of the SBP as well as creating awareness within the business community.

Public participation in the budget process is limited by inadequate information, as well as a lack of capacity and mobilisation on the part of civil society. Though public engagement with the budget process remained limited and fragmented, the Medium Term Economic Framework began to provide a basis for more meaningful interaction between civil society organisations and the legislature. Additionally, the media played an important role in disseminating discretionary budget information. There is great scope for the media to undertake more critical and analytical reporting on the budget. Participatory democracy is addressed in different ways by the local authorities, as indicated in the foregoing. However, the Local Government Act was silent on citizen participation in decision-making processes at local authority level. Although the law provided for public access to council budget information, it did not guarantee access. Local authorities were only required to publish a summary of their approved budgets in the newspapers. The fact that copies could only be made available to interested citizens upon payment restricted access to information to only the few who could afford it. The law did not provide for clear procedures and guidelines on how local authorities could involve communities in monitoring the quality of service provision. Though elected councillors sat on LASDAP committees, they could not effectively represent citizens as they were not independent and could, thus, be manipulated.

LASDAP in Korogocho

Other examples of the success of public participation include the role of citizen initiatives in responding to inadequate services from local authorities, such as the Nairobi Central Business District Association (NCBDA). The NCBDA's mission is to work in partnership with government, donors, the city council of Nairobi, the private sector, civil society and other community partners to identify needs, develop strategies, share public policy and implement programmes to strengthen and market the economic vitality of Nairobi and its regional role. The NCBDA is dedicated to making Nairobi an attractive investment and tourist destination, and a pleasant place to live and work in. Its objectives are increased private sector involvement, community participation and a capital injection by government into the development of Nairobi

A case study of the Korogocho Ward, Kasarani Constituency, shows how corruption prevents initiatives such as LASDAP from meeting their objectives. LASDAP approved more than KSh 15 million between 2002 and 2006 for a health dispensary, allocating KSh 6. 5 million to the building, KSh 2 million to solid waste, garbage conservancy facilities construction/enhancement and electricity supply for street lighting, another KSh 2. 5 million to road grading and gravelling, and KSh 1. 5 million to toilets, water and sanitation infrastructure rehabilitation, among other priorities identified by the stakeholders.

Four years later, the electricity project had not started. The public toilets were never constructed and the plots set aside for them had been put to other uses. None of the other projects identified had been implemented apart from the rehabilitation of a road, which was 80% complete. Further, only three students had got bursaries yet records showed that 64 needy students had benefited.

Attempts by Korogocho residents to get help from the city procurement office failed as the office was not keen to assist them in finding out what had happened to the funds. The residents finally found out that some councillors were involved in corrupt practices; they had influenced the drafting of the proposals, and influenced the awarding of contracts to their own companies. Self-interest and corruption by councillors, who were elected by these residents, undermined the potential of LASDAP to provide basic services

Public participation, however, remains low. A study by the Kenya Institute of Public Policy Research and Analysis revealed that household participation in decision-making processes on devolved funds was very low. Respondents said that while 32. 8% of them were involved to the extent of receiving information or attending barazas (public meetings), less than 10% attended meetings to discuss specific issues and less than 5% felt that they were involved in decision-making. Over 90% of respondents indicated that they were not involved in setting the development agenda for their areas. This underlines the necessity for increased efforts to

enhance public participation.

Oversight of provincial and local executives

The central government exercised considerable regulation over local authorities. Council resolutions related to policy-making were always subject to ministerial approval. The local authority committees, the ministry and the public provided checks and balances on the authority of the mayor, town clerk and the council at large. The Nairobi city council, for instance, had 15 ad-hoc committees. Local authorities started organising public budget hearings to increase community involvement. Revenue, expenditure, and financing were reported on a gross and net basis, and transactions classified by economic and administrative categories, not by function. The local authorities were also audited by the Kenya National Audit Office (KENAO), which is independent of the executive and legislature. KENAO is mandated to audit all central government ministries and departments, local authorities, semi-autonomous government agencies, special funds, extra budgetary funds and state corporations.

The constitution and devolved government

After several failures of decentralisation, including delegation and fiscal decentralisation, Kenyans agreed to have a two-tier government. The constitution establishes a devolved system of government aimed at expanding the democratic space and allowing greater public participation in governance. The sharing and devolution of power is a key national value and principle of governance.

The two-tier devolved structure comprises the national and the county governments. There are 47 counties, similar to the old rural county councils whose boundaries were coterminous with the old administrative districts. The objectives of this devolved government are:

- Ensuring the democratic and accountable exercise of power;
- Fostering national unity by recognising diversity;
- Giving powers of self-governance to the people and enhancing the participation of the people in the exercise of the powers of the state and in making decisions that affect them;
- Recognising the right of communities to manage their own affair and to form networks and associations to assist in that management and to further their development;
- Recognising the right of communities to manage their own affair and to further their development;
- Promoting social and economic development and the provision of proximate, easily accessed services throughout Kenya;
- Ensuring the equitable sharing of national and local resources throughout Kenya;
- Facilitating the decentralisation of state organs, their functions or services from Nairobi;

- Promoting the participation of the people in the making of decisions affecting them; and

- Enhancing checks and balances and the separation of powers.

Devolved governments, under the new structure, revolve around three core values: democratic principles and the separation of powers; reliable sources of revenue and autonomy to govern and provide effective service delivery; and the inclusion of not more than two-thirds of the members of representative organs from the same gender. A county government comprises a county assembly and a county executive committee. The executive authority of a county is exercised by a county executive committee, comprising a governor and deputy county governor, together with an executive committee appointed by the governor from non-county assembly people. In other words, members of the executive committee do make county laws; they are outside the county assembly just like the Cabinet, whose members are not among those elected. Voters directly elect the county governor, deputy governor and members of the assembly. There are special seats for women and persons with disabilities as well as youth. The county governor serves for two terms ooperations of the counties, while they are also allowed to raise their own revenue by collecting levies. The constitution has also established an equalisation fund which will be used to provide basic services for marginalised areas. These provisions will prevent the political mischief that frustrated operations of the devolved system of government after independence.

With regard to the relationship between the national and the county government, the constitution provides for a two-chamber legislature. The Senate – or what one may call the 'House of Counties' – to protect the interests of the counties in the national Parliament. Each county elects one representative to the Senate and there are 16 special seats for women and an additional four seats for the youth and persons with disabilities – two men and two women in each category. The constitution, however, does not spell out the relationship between the Senate and the county assemblies.

Already some laws relating to devolution have been passed. These are: first, the Transition to Devolved Government Act (No. 1 of 2012), which provides a framework for the transition to devolved government pursuant to section 15 of the Sixth Schedule to the constitution, including the formation of an authority to oversee the transition. The second law is the Intergovernmental Relations Act (No. 2 of 2012), which establishes a framework for consultation and cooperation between the national and county governments and amongst county governments, and it also establishes mechanisms for the resolution of intergovernmental disputes pursuant to articles 6 and 189 of the constitution among other things. A third law, the Devolved Government Bill (2011), was rejected by the president in February 2012, citing that county government would usurp the role of national government by having governors preside over county security committees under the arm of the county governments. The reaction, as discussed above, was to 'appoint' county commissioners even before the devolved units are formed. One critic corrected the president by stating:

Parliament has not in any way transferred any function of national government to counties. There is no reference to any security function being deployed to counties. Instead, the Bill allows the governor to chair a County Security Council subject to the structure set out in Police Service Act and other security legislation to be enacted. Already vide section 41, the National Police Service Act, creates a County Policing Authority which is chaired by the governor or a member of the county executive committee appointed by the governor. In that committee we have two elected members nominated by the county assembly. It is, therefore, baffling for the President to now reject the Bill on grounds which he already accepted in the National Police Service Act. In fact in the Act, Provincial Administration is already deprived of any security function.

The governments at the national and county levels are distinct and interdependent; none is subordinate to the other. The constitution provides that they conduct their mutual relations on the basis of consultation and cooperation. This implies the independence to make decisions in the functional areas without interfering with each other. However, the constitution requires the national government to ensure access to its services in all parts of the country 'as far as it is appropriate to do so'. This needs to be done with mutual respect because article 189(1) requires either of the governments to perform 'functions, and exercise its powers, in a manner that respects the functional and institutional integrity of governments at the other level, and respect the constitutional status and institutions of government at the other level and, in the case of county government, within the county government'.

To promote interdependence and cooperation between the two levels of government and even among the county governments, the Inter-governmental Relations Act (2012), establishes several organs. These include the National and County Government Coordinating Summit. This is the apex body and comprises the president and the 47 county governors. It is established with the aim of promoting national cohesion, unity and national interest. It also has the responsibility of facilitating and co-ordinating the transfer of functions, power and competencies to either level of government but in line with the constitution. The Inter-government Technical Committee serves as the secretariat of this body.

The second body is the Council of County Governors. This is established for consultation among county governors on matters of common interest. The Council also facilitates the sharing of information, dispute resolution, and builds the capacity of governors. It receives reports and monitors the implementation of inter-county agreements especially those concerning inter-county projects. The council has the mandate to establish other inter-governmental forums and sectoral working groups.

Although the structure to support devolution is very much in place, there have been tensions between those who want a centralised government and the supporters of devolution. What took place in the formative years of Kenya's independence is being repeated. The national government and the executive would prefer to be in control rather than let local institutions operate as independent units. Although the government has introduced legislation to support county government, there must be vigilance against those who want the centre to maintain control over the devolved units. Although tSet up under the Land Consolidation Act (Cap. 283). Set up under the District Disputes Tribunal Act. Land Adjudication Act (Cap. 284:20). he institution that is helping in the transition to county government, should be provided with sufficient resources to secure the process of establishing county governments.

Conclusion and recommendations

Local governments have been in Kenya since independence. The Independence Constitution specifically provided for devolution with semi-autonomous units, Majimbo, but these were dismantled shortly after independence. The local government units were then integrated into central government and have remained under the central government without any autonomy. The central government has stifled their operations and therefore constrained the space for participatory democracy at this level. Thus instead of promoting democratic governance, local authorities have largely existed as appendages of central government's channels for collecting revenue rather than delivering services.

The constitution provides for autonomous devolved governments. It contains several provisions that will prevent the national government from stifling the counties. Secondly, the constitution provides a legal basis for people's participation in the affairs of their governments. They will be electing representatives to the county assemblies where key decisions will be made. However, there are tensions between centralists and supporters of devolution. This was the case in the formative years of Kenya's independence. Nothing much has changed. Experience has shown that the central government and the executive would prefer to be in control rather than let local institutions operate as independent units. The two laws above have addressed some of the concerns raised by Kenyans relating to intergovernmental relations and also to oversee the complete transition to devolved governments.

It is recommended therefore that:

- Legislation is developed to further sketch out the relationships between the Senate and the county governments: both the legislative arm led by the Speaker and the executive arm led by the governor.

- The responsibilities of the Senate must be anchored on a sound law to prevent the possibility of stifling the operations of the county. The county governments are not administrative units for service delivery. They are institutions through which people will be making critical decisions on what affect them.

- A law must also be introduced to establish mechanisms for the relationship between the various county institutions and the people at the county level.

Traditional authorities

Pre-colonization

The pre-colonial traditional institutions of governance in Kenya were of two types: decentralized and centralized governance systems. Most parts of Kenya, however, had the decentralized system. In this system, decisions were made through consensus among the group members responsible for making such decisions. In some communities, village elders or councils of elders played that role while, in others, it was the responsibility of an age group or a lineage group. The group would make decisions through consensus and through extensive consultations. They had the responsibility of making laws, controlling social affairs and allocating resources.

Communities with centralized systems were generally few. These relied on the system of chieftaincy, where the chief was the central fi of authority and was responsible for making key decisions affecting the community. In Kenya, the Wanga Kingdom among the Luhya of Western Kenya stands out as an example of a community that thrived on chieftaincy. As already mentioned, many other groups had decentralized systems of government, and decision-making was consensual.

Traditional authority was generally imbued with reverence, both in decentralised and centralised political systems. In the decentralised systems, or large parts of Kenya generally, the authority of elders came from the prestige of being perceived as people with wisdom to guide the society and promote its cause. Collective prestige gave their words weight and that was why their word on matters such as law, social control and allocation of resources was fi and binding. In centralised systems such as those of the Wanga, the King made such decisions but also through consulting his own council of elders. Nonetheless, the authority rested in the chief.

The colonial era

Colonialism undermined these traditional systems of governance in varying ways. Because of the need to introduce a central fi to lead in tax collection, the colonial administration introduced 'chiefs' even in the decentralised systems where the council of elders made decisions. The chief sometimes would be picked from among the elders. This led to new forms of power and hierarchy and, therefore, the destabilisation of the existing governance system. It also meant that the traditional leadership was not formally recognised; the colonial government did not incorporate the elders or the age-set system of governance into the new administration. Instead, it grossly undermined them in order to create a new system through which the administration would eff reach the base of the society and collect taxes.

The post-colonial era

At independence, the new government adopted the colonial administrative structure intact. That meant the continued neglect of the traditional governance system; the council of elders, the age-set system and the lineage, where they existed, were not incorporated into the new administration. But that did not mean that the government did not find them useful in some respects. The government, for example, allowed them to continue playing certain roles relating to the practice of customary law.

In general, the role of traditional leaders today is pervasive even though the traditional leaders are not formally entrenched in the administrative structures of governance. These roles range from those done in conjunction with the state to roles regarding the application of customary law. The roles include adjudication of land disputes, arbitration of community disputes or conflict resolution in general. In recent years, however, traditional leaders are increasingly assuming political responsibilities; some of them act as political gate keepers for their communities – politicians use them as entry or access points to their communities. There are also instances where traditional leaders play the ceremonial role of anointing or blessing certain individuals to run for elective posts. They also play the role of interceding with the state, especially the head of state, on behalf of their communities. In addition, they preside over matters of a personal nature such as marriages, inheritance and divorce. They arbitrate familial disputes and even advise the youth and facilitate initiation rites of passage.

Given the nature of these roles, traditional authority and leadership is more resilient in some areas of the country than in others. In areas where land individualisation and titling was completed in the early 1960s, traditional authority is rarely visible because private life is highly individualised. Matters of communal interests that require mediation by elders or other traditional institutions are few. However, where land privatisation is ongoing, the traditional authority is quite resilient; elders are called upon to identify boundaries, resolve familial disputes and arbitrate disputes over boundaries between communities. But as argued later, even though the traditional authority is not resilient in all areas, there has been a tendency to 'invent' traditional leaders and authority for the purpose of servicing the political interests of politicians. Thus, even in areas where a traditional council of elders ceased to operate a long while back, there is now a tendency to re-activate the elders to help the community speak with one voice on political matters. In some parts of the country, the elders have also been recruiting younger generations of leaders, arguing that traditions and customs will die if there are no custodians of community values. The elders play both traditional and modern community roles because these roles often lead to factionalism, especially if there is disagreement on how to perform them. All the same, the growing importance of the council of elders in community aff has attracted politicians; they align with some of the elders to promote their political ambitions. Where this has happened, the traditional authority becomes politicised and factionalised along local political lines.

Development of traditional authority

The traditional leadership in Kenya is mainly organised around councils of elders. The institution of the council of elders exists in two forms. In some communities, such as the Ameru and the Njuri Ncheke, the council of elders is an institution rooted in the culture of these societies. It is well established and there are clear traditional procedures of acceding to the council of elders. Decisions coming from their deliberations are binding to all members of the community. Communities rely upon them for socio-political direction and to resolve disputes. Those involved in solving matters such as land disputes are formally recognised as agents of customary law and practice. The government office at the local level collaborate with them in addressing disputes, especially about land.

In some other communities, where traditional leadership did not centre on organised structures, the council of elders is a recent phenomenon. Councils have come in place of clan and lineage modes of traditional authority. The new set up comprises senior citizens who informally get together to play some roles in the communities as and when the need arises. Their decisions are not binding to the members of the society. Their roles are confined to the social sphere, such as resolving familial disputes or intra-community disputes.

The roles that traditional authorities play have evolved in tandem with certain important challenges. Assisting state officials to solve land problems, for instance, has had its own challenges. Lack of funds to support the elders' role has led to community members being required to fi support some of these roles. This is giving ground to cynics who argue that these traditional institutions are becoming increasingly commercialised because the ability to pay for their services determines the pace at which they address the individual's land problem. In communities where the elders are a recent phenomenon, members include retired public servants. Because of such composition, cynics argue that these institutions are not expressly about the steadfast promotion of adherence to the customary law, norms and values of that particular community, but for other auxiliary reasons, such as fi 'something to do' or making easy money.

In some communities, traditional leaders are the notables. Seniority and respectability is not earned the same way it was before the advent of colonialism and the money economy. Seniority can be acquired by being a senior government office wealthy or even a senior academic. To this extent, the traditional nature of this leadership is limited and tempered by modernity. These leaders can play in the world of ancient traditions as well as in the realities of modern day Kenya. As such, in some situations, they have been accused of taking decisions based on African customs when it suits them and ditching them when they do not.

In addition, these leaders are also influenced by actors outside their communities, such as human rights institutions that seek to change some of the cultural norms that, in diff times, legitimated their leadership. In modern-day Kenya, traditional leadership doesn't seem to have autonomous space. In most cases, it works in strategic alliances with the government, such as in the case of land dispute tribunals or with non-governmental organisations and human rights institutions. One such example is the collaboration between the Kenya National Commission on Human Rights (KNCHR) and the Luo council of elders to protect the property of women widowed by HIV/Aids. The KNCHR has been collaborating on a similar project with the Njuri Njeke of the Meru community. Such engagement is introducing modern and progressive ideas on good governance and human rights.

The government and civil society have pragmatic and strategic engagements with these structures because they occupy important public space and influence communities. They are, therefore, important actors that the government and civil society need to cultivate partnerships with in order to carry out development work, especially in rural communities.

Traditional authorities and the constitution

Except for recognition in customary law and Kadhi's courts on matters to do with marriage, divorce and social order, traditional authorities seem to have lost their formal authority. The constitution starts by affirming 'ethnic, cultural and religious diversity' in the preamble. Further, article 11 recognises the role of culture by providing that it is 'the foundation of the nation and is the cumulative civilisation of the Kenyan people and nation'. The state is obligated to promote all forms of national and cultural expression through literature, the arts, traditional celebrations, science, communication, information, mass media, publications, libraries and other cultural heritage; recognise the role of science and indigenous technologies in the development of the nation; and, promote the intellectual property rights of the people of Kenya.

Parliament is required to enact legislation that ensures communities receive compensation or royalties for the use of their cultures and cultural heritage; and to ensure the protection and ownership of indigenous seeds and plant varieties, their genetic and diverse characteristics and their use by the communities of Kenya. The constitution further protects cultural rights in article 44, by providing that every person has the right to use the language and to participate in the cultural life of the person's choice. Further it is provided that any person belonging to a particular cultural community has the right to enjoy the culture of the community and use the language as well as establish, join and maintain cultural and linguistic associations and other organs of civil society. Finally, the constitution asserts that a person shall not compel another person to perform, observe or undergo any cultural practice or rite.

These provisions attest to the recognition of traditions and cultural organisations and, therefore, the recognition of traditional authorities in the society. Indeed, in furtherance of culture, courts and tribunals have been obligated to respect and promote the principle of 'alternative forms of dispute resolution including reconciliation, mediation, arbitration and traditional dispute resolution mechanisms'. Again this is a role that traditional authorities are already playing in diff communities. In eff this role, the judiciary, through the Chief Justice in April 2012, cautioned that these traditional dispute resolution mechanisms should not be used in a way that contravenes the Bill of Rights. The Chief Justice warned that they should not be used in a manner that is repugnant to justice and morality or results in outcomes that are repugnant to justice or morality or that are inconsistent with the constitution or other laws.

The constitution recognises various aspects of culture, including envisaging the settlement of disputes through traditional justice systems. However, the role of traditional structures of governance, and in particular traditional authorities, has been downplayed. Where the existence and operation of traditional authorities in Kenya were likely to remain concealed rather than explicit, the 2010 constitution appears to give them a lease of life.

The role of traditional leaders in public life

Traditional leadership, politics and public administration

In communities where clan identity is strong, traditional leadership in the form of elders is the key to determining political leadership. This is so in the former North Eastern Province (among the Somali community), in former Eastern Province (among the Borana, Samburu and Rendile communities) and among the Maasai in the south Rift Valley, where clans negotiate and agree on who to support for public offi This practice reinforces the informal nature of Kenyan politics, which in turn undermines or diminishes accountability. Diff elders have different levels of influence. For example, the Luo council of elders has limited influence on who becomes an MP in the Luo areas of Nyanza but could symbolically bless the presidential candidate, who may indicate his favoured candidates. Some of the traditional leadership also seems to be sustained or be propped up by political leaders and, therefore, instrumental to the construction of Kenyan politics. As such, these traditional leaders at times seem malleable to the desires of political leaders from their communities. The leaders are also co-opted by the government in dealing with issues such as the restoration of peace, as well as resolving land and family disputes. In addition, the lower levels of the Provincial Administration were, for a long time, occupied by persons who fi the profi (the village headman, the sub-chief and at times the chief). The profi of the administrative chief and his assistants, who are all civil servants, is changing, with some job-holders having university education. So has the profile of the traditional leaders, with some university professors serving in these capacities. As such, accountability acrues more to the government and the political leaders of the area than to the community.

Traditional leadership, land administration
There are many conflicts that relate to land in Kenya because there is a serious conflict between some of the customary law norms in relation to land tenure and ownership on the one hand, and state law on the other. At times, the difficulties arise out of the way the formal judicial forums interpret and enforce customary land law norms. There is a history of injustice resulting from a formal and legalistic application of such norms. The government finds it useful to work with traditional leadership in order to provide justice to people in rural areas, whose approach to land tenure and ownership is heavily influenced by customary law.

Traditional leadership participates in the resolution of land disputes through the Land Control Boards, Land Adjudication Committeesand Land Dispute Tribunals. Under the Land Adjudication Act (Cap. 284), the land adjudication committee has the power to arbitrate any question referred to it by the demarcation officer or the recording officer using recognised customary law. The adjudicating officer has the power to appoint the committee, in consultation with the district commissioner. The decisions of the committee are appealed to the arbitration board, which is appointed by the provincial commissioner.

The law doesn't declare that persons who serve in these committees must be elders. But practice has it that elders and senior or retired civil servants constitute such committees. The inference could be that the moment the law says customary law, elders in the reference to senior citizens from any area are the most suited to serve in such committees. Again, the people have little to do with the selection of these commInterview with a programme officer at the Institute of Economic Affairs on 15 October 2008. not paid but receive honoraria for sitting in meetings and get some funds for their transport. This monetary gain exposes them to the risk of being compromised by wealthy parties to some of the conflicts. As mentioned above, there are instances where those with the ability to pay for such services have their cases determined faster than those that are not able. However, the law bars the elders from participating in issues that affect them so as to avoid conflicts of interest. In practice it is not clear if this is enforced.

The Land Disputes Tribunal is more explicit. The Minister for Lands constitutes a panel of elders for each registration district, who serve at the discretion of the minister. The minister also determines the terms and conditions of service. Affected persons can appeal to the appeals board of the High Court. This law defines 'elders' as persons in the community or communities to which the parties by whom the issue is raised belong, and who are recognised by custom in the community or communities as being, by virtue of age or experience or otherwise, competent to resolve the issues between the parties.

This law explicitly talks about elders in the traditional sense. It also carries a definition of who an elder is. The law uses a gender neutral reference of 'persons', but it doesn't require that the minister should appoint women to such panels. However, according to the administrative guidelines, it is a requirement that one third of the members of the Land Disputes Tribunal be women. This is in tandem with the provisions of the new constitution regarding gender balance.

Some of the problems of engaging elders at this level arise from the fact that issues relating to land are becoming very complicated as a result of rising populations and urbanisation.

Traditional leadership, dispute resolution and peace-building

In the area of dispute resolution and peace-building, there are forms of traditional leaders that operate invisibly and far away from the state, who are far less accountable, and the justice they dispense sometimes conflict with Kenya's international human rights commitments, especially with regard to women. Second, there are those that are state-sanctioned, such as those involved in peace-building in northern Kenya. These traditional leaders are more likely to account to the state than to the people they serve. However, the emerging trend of strategic partnerships with human rights institutions, including the state human rights watchdog, the KNCHR, might be a starting point in making these actors more accountable and in seeking to meet acceptable standards in a democracy, such as inclusiveness and gender justice.

Traditional leadership and administration of justice in general

Earlier, this chapter discussed the role of traditional leaders in resolving disputes that specifically relate to land. In this section, the role of traditional leadership in the administration of justice in general is examined. The role of traditional leaders in informal justice delivery systems has been part of public life for as long as Kenya has existed. There are two types of dispute resolution that involve traditional leaders. The fi is state-sanctioned, where traditional leaders work as adjuncts to the Provincial Administration in resolving disputes in their areas of administration. The other role of traditional leaders is relatively invisible in comparison with the judicial system and operates away from the eye of the state. These systems mostly deal with personal law matters that relate to inheritance and other family disputes.

Some of the government-endorsed informal justice systems help the state to extend its arm to potentially ungovernable areas such as the banditry-prone pastoralist areas of northern Kenya. Disputes in these areas relate to cattle rustling and, in some instances, extend to rape and disgracing family honour. This dispute resolution is done under the watchful eye of the Provincial Administration. It is important to note that the judiciary does not cover some of these areas – the best that the people get are seasonal mobile courts. This is not adequate for dealing with the many disputes that arise. Generally, judicial coverage in Kenya is still very limited.

It is very difficult to enforce accountability for these systems because of their informality and relative invisibility in comparison to the formal judicial structures. The structures for decision-making in these forums are not defined in some cases. These forums also suffer from a significant gender and youth deficit – in terms of composition and the gender justice of the rules they apply. Most of the rules applied are African customary law norms (deeply steeped in patriarchy), some of which are perverted and commercialised. In some situations, corruption has pervaded these systems. There are also questions of due process and some of the punishments meted out are considered inhuman and degrading. Some of the procedures may silence certain participants, such as women and youth.

There is a weak linkage between the informal justice forums and the judiciary. Their decisions are not, therefore, subject to any review that would ensure compliance with say, international human rights standards. Civil society organisations have tried to intervene by targeting the actors in these informal justice delivery systems for paralegal training to make human rights and the rights of women part of the rules that are considered in the resolution of the disputes in these forums.

Traditional governance and competitive politics

The Meru community, on the eastern slopes of Mount Kenya, comprises six sub-tribes.

The Ameru people exercise community leadership through two institutions that are also the custodians of the customs, traditions and ways of life: the clans and the Njuri Ncheke – the council of elders. The Njuri Ncheke is a cultural institution and is also a traditional Parliament of the Ameru. With origins dating back to around 1733 the council of elders serves as the custodian of Ameru cultural heritage. Njuri Ncheke was traditionally made up of 'political' representatives or traditional leaders (mugwe), who were drawn from the six sub-groups of the Meru ethnic group. Leaders from these six sub-groups formed a 'federal grouping' (Akiama ba Njuri). The leaders of the six sub-tribes exercised a combination of political and religious powers. Njuri Ncheke membership is open to 'any mature Meru man' but it is confirmed through an initiation process. However, with regard to leadership of the Njuri Ncheke, only those appointed by clan elders – on the basis of their seniority in the community – can become Njuri Ncheke representatives at the local or clan level. The clan level representatives are entitled to attend meetings of representatives at Nchiru (the Njuri Ncheke Parliament) where they can participate in the election of their leaders. Only men are considered for membership – and therefore leadership of the Njuri Ncheke. At Njiru, the headquarters where Parliament convenes, members discuss policy decisions under the overall chairmanship of the elders.

Further, the Njuri Ncheke makes 'laws' (rules to be adhered to by the Ameru) during their meetings. The 'laws' are executed by a kiama (committee), which comprises Njuri Ncheke leaders selected for particular functions.

Today, however, the institution has been restructured and transformed. It is headed by a chairman and a secretary-general, with the support of 'chairmen' from each of the sub-groups. Its leadership structure is well devolved to the local level; every administrative unit in Meru has its council of elders, who are then represented at the apex body (Parliament) by their chairmen.

The transformation of Njuri Ncheke and the manner in which the leadership of the council is elected has meant new challenges. It has evolved divisions along sub-ethnic group lines because politicians in each of the Meru sub-groups prefer one of their own to chair the council. The government has been profiling the role of the council of elders as an institution to include resolving land disputes. This has led to an increased role of the elders on local matters.

The increased importance of Njuri Ncheke at the level of the government is also a recent phenomenon. It followed the appointment of several Meru elites to senior and influential government positions in early 2003. These new leaders began to mobilise the solidarity of the Meru community to consolidate their local bases of political support. This was also required to leverage the community at the national level. From early 2003, political leaders established a relationship with the Njuri Ncheke council of elders. In this relationship, the Njuri Ncheke plays the role of providing ethnic defence to the elites during elections or even when the tenure security of the elites at the national level is under threat. Because of this relationship, political elites have been influencing the elders to make decisions and political pronouncements that favour them. Elders support the political factions of those who pay them the most. Some of those interviewed gave an example of two senior politicians from the community who sought the intervention of the Njuri Ncheke to appeal to the president to reinstate two politicians who had been suspended from Cabinet on allegations of corruption. The council of elders sought audience with the president. Even though the two were not immediately reinstated, their engagement in this highly politicised space was sufficient demonstration of the council's influence

Conclusion and recommendations

Traditional leaders have been useful in Kenya's public life in various ways. They are involved at varying levels with the comm framework to promote the role of traditional leaders in public affairs. Further, although the state collaborates with traditional leaders or councils of elders to resolve disputes, such as those on land and boundaries, there are no rules to enforce accountability on them.

Traditional authorities are becoming politicised. The association of their leaders with influential and powerful individuals has led to instances where the elders make statements in favour of such leaders. This has in turn led to their roles in the society being questioned with regard to their neutrality as arbitrators of social disputes. Increased use of money in land disputes and in getting the elders to make interventions is lending credence to the argument that the elders cannot be trusted to make socio-political decisions objectively. Furthermore, politicians have also begun to join the ranks of some of these institutions, which the elders are happy about because they get an opportunity to mingle with influential individuals. This new development has enforced the cooperation of formal and traditional authority.

In view of the role that traditional leaders are playing in the governance of society, it is

recommended that:

- Government introduces to Parliament legislation to promote the role of traditional institutions and leadership in public affairs. The legislation should seek to strengthen their roles in dispute resolution, mediation and reconciliation. The legislation should be developed in line with article 159 of the constitution on judicial authority, which requires the judiciary to recognise the principles of promoting alternative forms of dispute resolution, including traditional dispute resolution mechanisms.

- Resources be allocated to the KNCHR, the Equality and Gender Commission, and the Commission for the Administration of Justice (ombudsperson) to enrich traditional authorities and prevent them from being abused and exploited to further the interests of politicians, to educate the established traditional leadership institutions on the values and principles of governance under the new constitution and to further these values at the local level. Educating traditional leaders on matters of governance is also critical so that they can have a better understanding of issues such as gender equity and the

- importance of women's rights with regard to property rights

Development assistance and democratisation

The role of development assistance and Kenya's democratisation process has taken different forms, depending on the needs of the time. During the Cold War years, Western donors provided development assistance to the Kenyan government because it acted as a bulwark against communism in the region. During that period, development assistance did not have the objective of building governance institutions or even supporting governance-related activities. Donors shied away from supporting governance reforms because the government would have interpreted this to mean support to critics and the opposition in general. Those who made efforts to support governance reforms provided assistance only for the technical capacity-building of public sector institutions. The process through which development assistance was provided did not involve public participation. The executive, notably the Ministry of Finance and other relevant ministries, negotiated the agreements without debate, even in Parliament. Development assistance was thus depoliticised. This prevented the development of broad consensus on economic reforms and even on the terms of development assistance; it was not possible to initiate public debates on the type of projects that any development assistance would support. This stifled public debate on issues that related to international aid and on Kenya's foreign policy itself.

With the end of the Cold War, Western donors began to impose conditions on development assistance. These included embracing political pluralism, good governance, fighting corruption and promoting economic reforms (liberalisation). During the 1990s, Kenya seemed to meet some of the donor conditionalities, but was a reluctant reformer and left many providers of development assistance frustrated. Stop-go-stop was the characteristic feature of donors' engagement with government officials and President Moi in particular. He would agree to some reforms under pressure from the World Bank and the IMF, but renege on their implementation once funds had been disbursed. Again, negotiations for the funds did not involve public debate. Only the Ministry of Finance would be involved. The government did not involve the relevant parliamentary committees; Parliament was under the control of the executive. The executive would hold talks with the donors without involving any other agency. The general public would also not be involved because the information on some of these negotiations was unavailable. Sometimes the opposition political parties would raise issues in Parliament but the executive would proceed with negotiations irrespective of the discussion because the government always managed to mobilise support in Parliament against the opposition.

In 2003, the NARC government came to power on a reformist platform, promising to promote people's participation in development decision-making. In line with the new space for participation in policy-making, ministparliamentary committees.

With regard to foThe Kenyan parliament passed the Constituency Development Fund Act in 2003. The Act provides for the transfer of initially activitiesrk. The new government offered an opportunity to develop a comprehensive policy.

The Ministry of Foreign Affairs originated the first draft through a team of consultants and in-house specialists. The process itself did not involve extensive consultations with the public. The team consulted those knowledgeable about foreign affairs but 'there were no elaborate arrangements to involve the people or through which citizens would engage in making the policy'. The draft emphasised economic diplomacy and trade as the new areas to inform

Kenyan foreign relations. After the draft was completed for review by Parliament, the ministry passed the draft to the Parliamentary Committee on Defence and Foreign Relations. The Committee reviewed the document with support from a team of consultants that the Committee hired to help. However, the Committee did not have the opportunity to present their findings to the House for debate. Parliament was dissolved in December 2007 before discussing the draft.

In summary, Kenya's foreign policy and development assistance have not been the subjects of popular political debate. The executive tends to dominate the processes around foreign policy and any negotiations with donors. Where efforts are made to involve the public, it is usually through the Parliamentary Committee on Defence and Foreign Affairs. Civil society's voice is generally absent in these negotiations and processes. Some of those interviewed argue that civil society's involvement in foreign policy issues is generally weak. Some groups are involved in specialised issues but they are yet to evolve a strong coalition for articulating their concerns on foreign policy

Access to information on development assistance

Under the old constitution, Kenya's Parliament rarely discussed aid. MPs interviewed appeared to have little knowledge of the aid process. Also, Kenyans do not normally get information on external assistance. There are no public documents that they can refer to. The Department of External Relations in the Ministry of Finance is the custodian of most of the documents, but accessing data is not easy; the website which should provide most information is devoid of data. Similarly, MPs ded through budget sector public hearings. That was the one condition that the donors imposed in the late 1990s to ensure the budgeting process was open and accountable.

The role of Parliament in discussing development assistance is now provided for in the 2010 constitution. Article 211 provides for Parliament to develop legislation to prescribe the terms on which the national government may borrow, and also provides for Parliament to impose borrowing requirements. The constitution also requires the Cabinet Secretary for Finance to provide information concerning any particular loan or guarantee, and its usage. These provisions have enabled Parliament to have an increased oversight role on development assistance, and international aid in general. Public participation in these hearings is generally low. Issues around donor aid and development assistance rarely come up for discussion during such forums. One of the key problems with accessing government information in Kenya is the Official Secrets Act. The law was meant to protect the country from the disclosure of information that was prejudicial to state security, and is yet to be repealed. Without the law providing easy access to information, the public will continue experiencing challenges in accessing government information, including on development assistance. The discussion that follows is based on Organisation for Economic Co-operation and Development (OECD) data; the Ministry of Finance did not have data that could be accessed with ease to facilitate this analysis.

Trends in development assistance

Data by the Organisation for Economic Co-operation and Development – Development Assistance Committee (OECD-DAC) shows a growing increase in development assistance to Kenya from 2004. Country programmable aid (CPA) or aid meant for development programming and which excludes emergency and food aid, debt forgiveness, administrative costs, support to NGOs and technical cooperation, increased from US$ 701 million in 2004 to US$ 1 564 million in 2010, representing an increase of 123%. Total official development assistance (ODA) increased by 103%, from US$ 931 million in 2004 to US$ 1 890 million in 2010. Table 20 shows the trends in aid disbursements between 2004 and 2011.

Table 20: Trends in development assistance, 2004–2011

Year	Country Programmable Aid (CPA)	Aid
2004	746.3	990.2
2005	883.9	1094.6
2006	895.4	1294.4
2007	1315.9	1697.8
2008	1234.6	1669.1
2009	1663.5	2186.6
2010	1619.8	2025.7
2011	2193.2	2831.2

In terms of sector composition, population services and reproductive health constitute close to one third of total programmable aid. The second significant sector is economic infrastructure, which was about 17% in 2008 and 16% in 2010. Budget support appeared only in 2009 where disbursements totalled about US$ 212 million representing 14.38%. This composition is shown in both tables 21(a) and 21(b).).

Table 21(a): Country programmable aid (CPA) by sector in US$ million and per cent share, 2008-2011

Sector	2008 US$ million	2009 US$ million	2010 US$ million	2011 US$ million
Population policies and reproductive health	354.9	433.6	444.6	494.1
Water Supply & Sanitation	102.2	102.2		160.2
Agriculture	107.6	116.0	130.8	158.6
Economic infrastructure	197.7	252.7	249.0	370.7
Education	96.7	92.6	36.4	55.2
Environment	26.5	33.5	59.1	43.8
Government and civil society	89.0	113.2	128.3	123.7
Health	112.4	131.5	128.3	123.7
Multi-sector	29.9	56.0	55.9	77.1
Other productive sectors	14.0	12.2	39.2	24.6
Other social sectors	28.8	51.2	59.7	73.6
General budget support	3.4	252.7		317.1

Table 21(b): Country programmable aid (CPA) by sector in per cent share, 2008-2010

Sector	% share of disbursement		
	2008	2009	2010
Population policies and reproductive health	31.2	27.82	29.0
Water supply and sanitation	8.8	6.35	9.7
Agriculture	9.0	5.53	7.0
Economic infrastructure	17.0	15.35	15.6
Education	8.3	5.78	2.3
Environment	2.3	2.09	3.9

Government and civil society	7.4	6.99	8.0
Health	9.6	8.31	15.0
Multi-sector	2.6	3.4	3.5
Other productive sectors	1.2	0.78	2.5
Other social sectors	2.4	3.23	3.7
General budget support		14.38	
Total	**100.0**	**100.00**	**100.0**

Among Kenya's top ten donors are the United States of America, International Development Association (IDA), the concessional lending arm of the World Bank Group, France and the United Kingdom. Table 22 shows the top ten donors between 2008 and 2010.

Table 22: Top donors, 2008-2011 (constant 2011 US$ million)

Country	2008 US$ million	2009 US$ million	2010 US$ million	2011 US$ million
united States	328.42	439.47	441.34	528.82
IMF		225.33		317.08
IDA	197.34	177.25	235.23	267.71
AfDB	42.42	66.47	107.69	166.93
Japan	63.84	82.35	92.81	102.59
united Kingdom	64.21	99.11	111.73	101.24
France	64.63		139.50	100.38
Germany	69.55	68.10	65.75	83.96
Eu institutions	47.60			71.90
Global Fund			69.92	
Bill and Melinda Foundation		53.71		65.23
Denmark	49.73	57.06	55.11	
Sweden	60.43	65.93	44.53	

The United States' share of the ten donors is about one third. This makes the US the most significant donor in the country, in terms of their share of development assistance. The IDA follows with a share of less than 20%: ranging between 19% in 2008 and 16% in 2010. France is the third most significant donor in terms of share among the top ten: in 2010 France had a share of 10% of the total aid by the top donors.

In terms of general composition, the share of CPA comprises three quarters of the total volume of aid to Kenya. Humanitarian and food aid is the second largest share – constituting about 20% in 2008 and about 13% in 2010. Funding to NGOs is about 2% during the same three year period.

Table 23: Composition of aid, 2008–2010 (disbursement in US$ millions)

Type of aid	2008		2009		2010	
	US$ million	%	US$ Million	%	US$ million	%
Country programmable aid (CPA)	1160.8	73.9	1519.7	75.58	1564.3	82.7
Administrative costs	4.1	0.3	3.9	0.19	4	0.2
NGO funding	28.9	1.8	20.8	1.03	34.6	1.8
Other un-allocated funds	41.3	2.6	43.8	2.18	33.1	1.8
Implied student costs	6.7	0.4	7.4	0.37	7.4	0.4
Humanitarian and food security	306.3	19.5	405.8	20.18	239.2	12.7
Debt relief	23.7	1.5	9.2	0.46	8.2	0.4

Donor fragmentation appears high. Although there are many donors in each sector, only a few contribute about 90% of assistance. This means that donors are generally spread thin in the sectors. This is a problem the government and the development partners themselves seem to be aware of. In June 2012, the Ministry of Finance identified overcrowding of development partners in some sectors and lack of harmonisation of development programme procedures as some of the problems facing 'aid effectiveness' in the country.

Table 24: Donor fragmentation

Sector	Number of donors	Donors in (top 90%)	CPA (US$ million)

Education	22	3	32.6
Health	19	2	222.0
Population policies and reproductive health	21	2	431.5
Water supply and sanitation	18	1	141.3
Other social infrastructure	17	2	53.7
Economic infrastructure	18	2	230.3
Agriculture	20	3	102.4
Other production sectors (Forestry, fi in dustry, mining, construction, trade policy and tourism)	13	0	36.6
Environment	16	2	55.7
Government and civil society	21	3	120.3
Multi-sector	22	4	52.3

Conditions for development assistance

Government support comes in two forms: budgetary support and project support. Many international development partners have not been keen on budgetary support. Budgetary support has been unreliable because of the history of conditionality and unpredictability of support, both of which were the key features of Kenya's development assistance in the 1990s. Freezing aid in the middle of implementing important programmes led to the government arguing that development assistance should not be factored in completely into the national budget. The recovery of the economy in the period between 2003 and 2007 also led to increased revenue collection. The government was able to finance about 95% of the annual budget. This emboldened the thinking to exclude donor support from the budget-making process. The ability to finance the budget has made the government less responsive to donor conditionality on governance; the government is not particularly responsive to donors' demands, especially demands about addressing governance.

The entry of China as an important aid partner is making the government even more reluctant to listen to Western donors' aid-conditions. Although Western donors imposed certain demands on the government, it was usually difficult for the government to comply because fulfilling them was dependent on the legislative and political processes outside the control of the executive. Kenya's frustration can be illustrated by the conditionality in relation to the disbursement of the Poverty Reduction and Growth Facility (PRGF). The government and the International Monetary Fund (IMF) agreed on this facility in 2003. When the new NARC government came to power in 2002, the IMF imposed pre-requisites to the disbursements relating to the facility. In relation to governance issues, the IMF demanded the strengthening of the governance architecture and the enforcement of anti-corruption laws and regulations, as well as the enhancement of the Kenya Anti-Corruption Commission's (KACC) capacity by giving it prosecutorial powers, and improving the capacity of the Director of Public Prosecutions to prosecute corruption-related cases. The government was required to show progress in developing systems for the annual declaration and verification of wealth, assets and liabilities of ministers and other senior public officials as provided for under the Public Officers Ethics Act (2003).

The conditions required the government to take a number of governance-related actions. These included providing access to the relevant officials' wealth/financial declaration forms and developing an aggressive asset recovery and restitution system, as well as having Parliament pass the Public Procurement and Disposal Bill (which was enacted in 2005). The conditions required the government to establish the Public Procurement Oversight Authority (PPOA); act on the findings of the Goldenberg Commission of Inquiry by prosecuting the key suspects; act on the Commission on Illegal and Irregular Allocations of Public Land by taking legal action against those who had grabbed public land; and set up the ombudsperson's office (Public Complaints Standing Committee).

The conditions also required the acceleration of parastatal reforms and the enactment of the Privatisation Bill (now enacted as Cap. 485C, Laws of Kenya). This included the privatisation of the National Bank of Kenya. The government was supposed to implement measures designed to strengthen the financial system, which included amendments to the Central Bank of Kenya Act and the Banking Act, as well as to review the financial position of the National Social Security Fund with a view to restructuring it. The government found it difficult to meet some of the conditions because it did not have control of the parliamentary legislation process. The IMF had to give waivers on 'non- observance', though the actual disbursements never took place until much later in 2005. For example, at the end of the second IMF review in 2007, after the IMF released US$ 56. 8 million, requisites for further IMF disbursements. This waiver prevented the IMF from giving new requirements. By the time the third and final review on the facility came up, the government had not yet met all of these conditions. In completing the review, waivers were approved for non-observance in a number of areas. Because the government could not entirely control or predict events in the political realm or the legislative process, these demands took very long to fulfil. For example, both the procurement and the privatisation laws were only passed in 2005, paving the way for the release of funds for which negotiations had begun in 2003.

The other problem with conditionalities that tie aid to legislation is that Parliament may not always pass the required laws and amendments to the satisfaction of international development partners. For example, the IMF demanded that the Anti-Corruption and Economic Crimes Act (2003) be amended to allow access to the wealth declaration forms of ministers, MPs and other top government officials. Parliament passed an amendment that fell short of this requirement because they pegged access to such forms on judicial approval – meaning that a judge had to authorise such access.

Since the post-2007 election violence, international development partners have been either concerned about the commitment of the government to undertake reforms identified by the National Accord as Agenda 4 reforms or on the longstanding issues that contributed to the crisis. These issues included undertaking institutional and constitutional reforms, land reforms, addressing youth unemployment, promoting accountability and transparency and ending impunity, undertaking measures to promote national unity and cohesion, and addressing regional imbalances in development. The government mobilised support for a new constitution under Agenda 4. The passing of the 2010 constitution provided an opportunity to comprehensively address the Agenda 4 reforms.

How development assistance is provided for in Kenya does not translate into increased citizen participation in public affairs or even in extensive and structured public debates about the assistance. When donors impose conditions, these are not publicly discussed or debated in any consistent manner. In any case, donor conditions have diminished in tandem with the increased financing of the national budget using national revenue. Some argue that the government has adopted a 'don't care' attitude to donor demands on governance issues for the same reason. But recent years have witnessed the increased involvement of civil society in the process, especially in demanding that the government be more open in budgeting and accounting. Civil society groups are now getting more involved in scrutinising government budgets and the budget- making processes. The Mars Group and the Institute for Economic Affairs (IEA) have taken leadership in budget analysis and tracking with a view to ensuring that the government is accountable. Development donors pick up the issues raised by civil society for discussion with government officials.

In the past, there was inconsistency in the conditionalities that tied aid to good governance, public accountability and democratic reforms. Brown demonstrates how, between 1990 and 2002, international aid providers were ambivalent on political reforms. Donors were easily satisfied with economic reforms even when the government reneged on political reforms or ignored their commitment to important governance issues. That ambivalent approach to reform led to some arguing that donors confuse recipients because they have no standard approach to development assistance. They behave differently. One informant noted that 'international aid providers confuse recipients. There has been a lack of uniformity on how multilateral and bilateral donors behaved in respect of conditionality lending. 'Some have also criticised the approach adopted by civil society and other pressure groups in demanding for reforms. With reference to the struggle for constitutional reforms in 1997, critics blamed donors for whipping the opposition and civil society to accept minimum Inter-Party Parliamentary Group (IPPG) reforms, yet Kenyans were generally supportive of comprehensive reforms. Brown makes similar observations and argues that international aid providers were risk averse and did not trust the radical change that many Kenyans led by the National Convention Executive Council and opposition leaders were advocating for; the donors prioritised concerns about political stability and security

International aid for democratic development

International aid for civil society is premised on the thinking that strong civil society organisations (CSOs), which are organised democratically, enhance the political space necessary for citizens to organise and participate effectively in public affairs. Donors in

Kenya have supported civil society to provide civic education and implement human rights programmes. The concept of social auditing has also found favour with international donors and other grant makers. Today, there are several initiatives being funded to monitor the use of public expenditure monies, projects under the Constituency Development Fund and other devolved funds. Critics of 'aid to civil society' argue that donors tend to be benefiting Nairobi-based organisations and therefore elite-led civil society groups based there. To such critics, this approach ignores the grassroots-based associations that are widely spread throughout the country. Nonetheless, funding to civil society is generally unstable. There are occasions when CSOs wait for a long time before funds are released. This is common where funding is through the basket funding model. Significantly, CSOs are funded on the basis of projects. This form of funding does not guarantee the sustainability of the projects after the end of donor support. In results in funds drying up before the culture of public engagement in demanding government accountability has been fully developed.

This notwithstanding, the support that Kenyan civil society receives for the governance, human rights and justice sectors illustrates the impact of international aid on democratisation in Kenya. Donor support to CSOs demanding democratic reforms in the early 1990s played a key role in enabling civil society to compel the government to repeal the constitution and permit multi-party politics. This opened the space for more reforms. For instance, in 1993, civil society mobilised other actors, especially opposition political parties in Parliament, to start demanding constitutional reform and democratic development in general. From then on, civil society became an active participant in the struggle for constitutional reform. Civil society groups are increasingly involved in national civic education programmes that encourage participation in public affairs. Donors offer them support to provide voter education, human rights training, and to undertake paralegal training and social audits, among others. Development assistance to CSOs in this respect, therefore, can be understood as promoting government accountability – CSOs promote the political empowerment of citizens by enhancing their capacity to demand greater accountability from their government.

CSOs' participation in struggles for democratic governance resulted in the consolidation of a movement for democratic reforms in the early 2000s. The opposition political parties also formed a coalition with the support of civil society groups. That enabled NARC to win the election. Donors began to provide support to governance initiatives in the public sector and to government programmes in particular. This new attention to public sector governance programmes occasioned delays in disbursing assistance to CSOs. In a sense, this muted a critical public voice that had been central to improving government accountability, with several consequences. Civil society's engagement in monitoring the governance record of the new government declined, while some organisations lost staff to the new government. These events underscored the risks associated with civil society's dependence on foreign assistance for democratic governance activities. After the post-election crisis that followed the December 2007 elections, disbursement of development assistance to CSOs regained consistency and became predictable. Even though development assistance to CSOs involved in democratic governance has been in place for some time, much of it is spent on the project model of funding. CSOs are not supported sufficiently to engage in long-term projects. Short-term projects are not adequate to nurture a culture of ownership among beneficiary communities. For this reason, CSOs claim that building a culture of accountability has not been easy. Still there are those who argue that donors have an ambivalent approach to disbursing assistance to CSOs. They point out that some donors have a preference for certain individuals and their organisations. This has partly been blamed for the perceptions that support to civil society only benefits the elites in Nairobi.

Harmonisation of fire sources

Aid conditionalities in the 1980s and 1990s resulted in Kenya having unpredictable development assistance, both in terms of volume and the honouring of commitments. That, in turn, occasioned a situation in which many donors provided uncoordinated development assistance. There was a proliferation of projects and donors, with many donors crowding a sector that they considered favourable to them. In 2003, the government held a consultative group meeting with development partners and requested the establishment of harmonisation, alignment and coordination (HAC) to improve on the effectiveness of development assistance in the country. And in 2007, 17 development partnersin Kenya agreed to commit to the Paris Declaration on Aid Effectiveness (2005), which required donors to, among other things, align behind a country's system, coordinate better to lower transaction costs, and to scale up for more effective aid. In committing themselves to adhere to the Paris principles, the development partners and the government developed the Kenya Joint Assistance Strategy (KJAS) 2007–2012.

The KJAS sought to guide donor engagement with the government. The three main principles of engagement are: improving the country strategy to advance social well-being and to achieve the millennium development goals; more effective collaboration among international aid providers and the government; and a focus on outcomes. The strategy commits the partners to work with the government to achieve the development priorities set out in its Vision 2030. It commits the partners to use government systems for the management of their programmes. The government, through the Ministry of Finance and the 17 partners, signed the partnership principles in September 2007. The partnership principles reiterate the commitment to coordination, ownership, capacity development, use of government systems, the strengthening of governance and improving financial management as well as mutual accountability.

In September 2009, the government and the development partners transformed the HAC Group into the Aid Effectiveness Group (AEG), located in the Ministry of Finance's External Resources Department. The AEG continues to deliver on the role of the HAC but with increased attention to the Paris Declaration and the Accra Agenda for Action (2008), and priorities of the government. The group also has the mandate to share information and analyse obstacles concerning the Paris Declaration.

These are positive steps towards the harmonisation of financial resources and streamlining the coordination of development assistance. To date, however, not all development partners have harmonised their programmes and projects with the priorities of government. Some sectors are also poorly aligned. The main challenges include: off-budget financing by some donors

lack of timely reporting on direct payments by development partners; lack of harmonisation of development partners' procedures; over-crowding of development partners in some sectors, with some development partners being virtually present in all sectors. Home government regulations also prevent some development partners such as USAID from providing budget support – that is, they cherry pick what to support.

Although all partners and the government signed up for the principle of mutual accountability, the instinct is still for some development partners to unilaterally suspend support when they feel the government is reneging on important governance ideals. For instance, some partners withdrew their support from the Governance, Justice, Law and Order Reform Programme in 2008 when government agents broke into a private media house and destroyed equipment on the allegation that the media house was planning to broadcast material that prejudiced security. In 2008, development partners threatened to cut aid unless the report of the Commission of Inquiry into the Post-Election Violence (CIPEV) and the Independent Review Commission (IREC) report on elections were implemented.

The GJLOS Reform Programme

In November 2003, the new NARC government launched the Governance, Justice, Law and Order (GJLOS) Reform Programme to support over 30 government institutions (ministries, departments and semi-autonomous agencies) and to coordinate efforts to promote governance and justice reforms. With support from 17 development partners, the programme adopted a sector-wide approach, but did not align financing with the government system. The development partners and the new government did not have confidence in the transparency, accountability and effectiveness of government institutions and systems. Both the partners and the government agreed to outsource finance disbursement and management to a private firm. They established the Financial and Management Agent (FMA) to manage the basket fund and develop the capacity of government departments in various areas, including the development of work plans and financial management. Donors outside the basket funds made direct disbursements to the departments, which amounted to limited harmonisation.

From the outset, the programme struggled to integrate into the mainstream government budgeting process, the medium-term expenditure framework (MTEF). The Ministry of Finance continued with the budgeting process; it did not align the GJLOS to the Public Safety, Law and Order (PSLO) Sector working group under the MTEF. The GJLOS programme and how it was implemented became a challenge for government planning systems. First, it aroused competing institutional interests, both among institutions within the GJLOS and between the GJLOS and other sectors, not least of which was the PSLO Programme, which was already anchored in government planning and resourcing systems. The programme did not align with the MTEF PSLO; sectors and departments in both the GJLOS and PSLO reflected some variance, including the double allocation of resources. It was evident that GJLOS and government planning were not harmonised. Those problems were not so much about ownership but more about turf control and the perception within government, especially the Ministry of Finance, that the GJLOS was a parallel programme. Though committed to coordination and harmonisation, it appeared not to have been able to use government systems at the outset. The use of an external agency to manage the resources brought more challenges, with some departments getting double allocations.

Conclusion and recommendations

There is limited public engagement on foreign policy and development assistance issues. Not many civil society groups are effectively engaged with development assistance issues because negotiations are usually between the Ministry of Finance and the relevant development partners. Agreements themselves are rarely made public or opened to public debate. The data on development assistance is also not accessible to the public. The Ministry of Finance does not publish figures on development assistance, which implies that people cannot engage in a meaningful debate on these issues.

It is recommended that:

- The Ministry of Foreign Affair presents the draft Foreign Policy to the public for debate before presenting the policy to Parliament. The Ministry should establish forums where citizens can review the policy and give input. The government should provide more resources to the Ministry and to the Parliamentary Committee on Defence and Foreign Relations to facilitate people's participation in Kenya's foreign policy.

- Development partners allocate resources to specialised civil society groups, in particular those with experience in budget tracking, to continuously monitor aid composition, budget support and the use to which aid is made. The near absence of the voice of civil society on this issue is a cause of worry and should be addressed by development partners and in particular the donor-leadership in the Aid Eff Group.

www.ingramcontent.com/pod-product-compliance
Lightning Source LLC
Chambersburg PA
CBHW031055080526
44587CB00011B/693